OCEANSIDE PUBLIC LIBRARY
330 N COAST HWY
OCEANSIDE, CA 92054

D0713115

Civic Center

WASHINGTON
& NAPOLEON

RELATED POTOMAC TITLES

Envoy to the Terror: Gouverneur Morris and the French Revolution,
by Melanie Randolph Miller

Napoleon's Troublesome Americans: Franco-American Relations, 1804–1815,
by Peter P. Hill

Wellington: The Iron Duke, by Philip J. Haythornthwaite

*The Revolutionary Years, 1775–1789: The Art of American Power
During the Early Republic*, by William Nester

*The Hamiltonian Vision, 1789–1800: The Art of American Power
During the Early Republic*, by William Nester

Joel Barlow, American Diplomat and Nation Builder, by Peter P. Hill

WASHINGTON & NAPOLEON

Leadership in the Age of Revolution

Matthew J. FLYNN *and* Stephen E. GRIFFIN

Potomac Books
Washington, D.C.

Copyright © 2012 by Potomac Books, Inc.

Published in the United States by Potomac Books, Inc. All rights reserved. No part of this book may be reproduced in any manner whatsoever without written permission from the publisher, except in the case of brief quotations embodied in critical articles and reviews.

Library of Congress Cataloging-in-Publication Data
Flynn, Matthew J.
    Washington & Napoleon : leadership in the age of revolution / Matthew J. Flynn and Stephen E. Griffin. — 1st ed.
        p. cm.
    Includes bibliographical references and index.
    ISBN 978-1-59797-278-9 (hardcover)
    ISBN 978-1-59797-583-4 (electronic edition)
    1. Washington, George, 1732–1799. 2. Washington, George, 1732–1799—Military leadership. 3. Napoleon I, Emperor of the French, 1769–1821 4. Napoleon I, Emperor of the French, 1769–1821—Military leadership. 5. Political leadership—United States—History—18th century. 6. Political leadership—France—History—18th century. 7. United States—History—Revolution, 1775–1783. 8. France—History—Revolution, 1789–1799. I. Griffin, Stephen E. II. Title. III. Title: Washington and Napoleon.
    E312.F558 2011
    973.4'10922—dc23
                        2011023382

Printed in the United States of America on acid-free paper that meets the American National Standards Institute Z39-48 Standard.

Potomac Books
22841 Quicksilver Drive
Dulles, Virginia 20166

First Edition

10 9 8 7 6 5 4 3 2 1

31232009170822

CONTENTS

PREFACE

O ver the course of writing this book, a number of new studies of George Washington have been published. They include Edward Lengel's very recent *Inventing George Washington: America's Founder, in Myth and Memory* (2011), Ron Chernow's biography *Washington: A Life* (2010), and John Ferling's *The Ascent of George Washington: The Hidden Political Genius of an American Icon* (2009). When added to Joseph Ellis and his fine biography *His Excellency: George Washington*, released in 2004, there has been no shortage of attention paid to Washington.

This is as it should be, given that man's importance to the American experience. All the authors above seek to illuminate the man, and all of them succeed in various ways, thereby emphasizing Washington's key role in the formation of the early Republic. Of course, even in the face of this rash of literature, the question remains, what is new about George Washington? Writers and scholars have been trying to better understand Washington, both his actions and his person, for many years, so this recent line of approach is not necessarily "new." Having said this, no one would deny the value of each generation putting a current stamp on important historical figures and in this way reinvigorating the discussion that surrounds them.

Understanding this need, we also seek a way to better gain insight into one of the most important figures in American history. George Washington as a near contemporary of Napoleon Bonaparte suggests that this comparison might be very fruitful in terms of developing new thinking about Washington and about Napoleon as well. The study of Napoleon faces its own quandary when asking what is new about this dynamic figure. Scholarship in the past decade has faced this question and answered it with a look at the Napoleonic Empire, rather than a look at the man. In a real sense, this approach is an admission that those writing on Napoleon believe that there is no need to focus on Napoleon at all, not because he is understood, but because his essential parts have been revealed. Mainly for this reason, there are no new substantial and scholarly studies of Napoleon to point to in contrast to the steady stream of literature on Washington.

This book is an attempt to offer a new look at both men by placing them alongside each other. It is meant as a place of departure, raising the question of what is new and then answering that this comparative analysis certainly is new and necessary. At a time when writers and scholars look to place events in the current of world history, a comparison of Washington and Napoleon is appropriate and invaluable. Never were two individuals more capable of providing insight into the change that grew out of the revolutions besetting both France and the burgeoning United States. These events helped further define an Atlantic World, a creation evolving and changing in many ways, politically, militarily, culturally. A recent study, an edited collection titled *Napoleon's Atlantic: the Impact of Napoleonic Empire in the Atlantic World* (2010), admits the need to make the comparison but passes over the Washington era to focus on Napoleon. We suggest an earlier starting point that includes Washington to better address how two revolutions shaped the Atlantic World.

In writing this book, we sought to inject some discomfort into a discussion of each man that has grown too familiar: Washington's admirers scorn anyone offering probing questions that might shake their veneration; Napoleon's attackers dismiss anyone not faulting the man personally for what befell Europe during his lifetime. Opposition to those defining the history of each man in this way is needed. In taking up this challenge, we indeed hope to initiate a step toward finding new ways of thinking about both of these important historical figures.

ACKNOWLEDGMENTS

I would like to thank Lindsay Griffin, my wife and a consummate historian herself, for reading several drafts. And special thanks to Matthew J. Flynn for his part in making this project possible.

—Stephen E. Griffin

I would like to thank many people for making this book possible, among them Kate Olson-Flynn, my wife and biggest supporter, and Oscar Rothenberg, a dedicated intellectual who read and shaped the manuscript on frequent occasions. As always, friends and family also aided me greatly with comments and suggestions. I appreciate all their efforts. Last, I would like to extend a special acknowledgment to Steve Griffin, my writing partner. Without him, there would have been no book comparing Washington and Napoleon.

—Matthew J. Flynn

INTRODUCTION

G eorge Washington became president of the United States just as the French Revolution burst open the conventions of European culture and society in 1789. It was a momentous time. As Americans consolidated the gains of 1776, the French embarked upon a more radical revolution of their own. While the two countries produced different results—representative government in America and absolute rule in France—their respective destinies were molded by generals. In the standard narratives, the virtuous Washington nurtured his new republic, while the ambitious Napoleon Bonaparte embraced authoritarianism and empire in France. The contrast raises several questions: Why did Washington not seize control as Napoleon had done? What crucial difference or differences separate the republican Washington from the despot Napoleon?

These questions are even more compelling given Washington's propensity to exhibit behavior often akin to that of his near contemporary across the Atlantic Ocean. Granted, the political ambitions of the Virginian seem to pale in comparison to that of the upstart Corsican. Indeed, one exhibit that today greets the visitor to Washington's home of Mount Vernon in Virginia calls attention to the strong-man regimes of Napoleon, Oliver Cromwell, and Julius Caesar while acknowledging Americans' gratitude that Washington had the strength of character to rise above tyranny and take the nation with him down the republican path.[1] The Mount Vernon Ladies' Association guards this heroic ode to Washington's legacy, and most Americans prefer this favorable view of the first president. The intended import of the exhibit is clear: Washington stands apart from the infamous tyrants of the past.

Both Washington and Napoleon faced many of the same opportunities, which each used to advance their own ambitions. Both were men of the Age of Enlightenment, which had spread to the wider Atlantic world. When Washington died in 1799, Napoleon had a eulogy performed in his honor, espousing the debt all republicans—including him—owed the great American leader.[2] Yet, if one pillar of the age had passed, the other was just rising: Napoleon's role as a standard-bearer of the Enlightenment was soon evident in his evolution from republican to emperor. This was seemingly a contradictory outcome, but the ideology he embraced was broad enough to fit republicanism and absolutism under the same banner. Napoleon served France, and as French power expanded, he thus served Europe as an enlightened leader, much as Washington had done for the United States. The French general addressed this similarity to Washington while in forced retirement on St. Helena, the island that served as his prison after June 1815. Napoleon told one of his biographers, Emmanuel, comte de Las Cases, that the age itself had defined the two men, that he would have been a Washington had he been in Washington's place, and that Washington himself would have been a Napoleon had he lived in France. As it was, Napoleon felt he had acted as a "crowned Washington."[3] An astute assessment, it underscored the emperor's tendency of minimizing his determination to shape his destiny via military force, but at the same time, it emphasized the bonds between the two men.

Washington was thus as ambitious as Napoleon. Likewise, Napoleon was as dedicated to serving France as Washington was to serving America. For this reason, prosaic labels of citizen-general or tyrant are simplistic and dismiss a more complex historical reality. Perhaps each man should be remembered today as both a great champion of the Enlightenment *and* as an ambitious general serving his own interest, for what was the Enlightenment but a blurring of rigid social stations? By placing the meaning of "life, liberty, and the pursuit of happiness" in flux, the Enlightenment remade society, allowing men of great talent to explore the full potential of these ideas. Both Washington and Napoleon did just that, and in the process they refashioned the meaning of service to one's country and to oneself.

What then accounted for the differences in the respective outcomes of the revolutions in which they participated? We believe that while both men possessed enormous ambition, they channeled this drive in directions that would produce forms of government most acceptable to their respective societies. American society, tempered by concepts of English rights, allowed republicanism as the ultimate expression of the Enlightenment. French society, born out of absolutism and scarred by revolutionary excesses, recognized Enlightenment principles in despotism. Both Washington and Napoleon understood this reality as it related to his respective country and adjusted his ambition accordingly for political power. How the Enlightenment resonated in America and Europe illustrated the differences between these two famous men, rather than any innate goodness in Washington or any depraved disposition in Napoleon. They were neither blessed nor corrupted. Rather, they shrewdly weighed the times, and each man looked to secure power within the confines of the Enlightenment that produced two different political realities. A comparison of these two giants of an age offers a superb opportunity to pursue a critical analysis of Washington and to offer a more balanced critique of Napoleon. By drawing the parallel, Napoleon humanizes Washington, revealing his more complex motives. In turn, Washington redeems Napoleon by making him a servant of the state. The two men very much complement each other, and together they present a different picture of their lives than is present in biographies focused only on one man or the other.

Certainly, there are differences that separate the two. Napoleon's Europe had long since ceased to be a frontier, and established states vied for power. In America, by contrast, the warring nations sought to establish spheres of influence. The scale of combat in Europe in terms of the size of armies dwarfed conflicts in the New World (and this is true even if one argues that the importance of battle is still present regardless of the size of the forces involved). When it came to their physiques, Washington towered over the much shorter Napoleon, lending credence to the modern belief that Napoleon craved power and jealously hoarded it to compensate for his diminutive stature. Washington, on the other hand, free of such insecurity, appeared to grudgingly assume positions of leadership from a sense of civic duty and looked to surrender these positions at the earliest opportunity.

A closer look reveals that despite their differences, Washington and Napoleon had much in common. Both came from modest homes of a relatively struggling lower aristocracy, which provided them with a subsistence living but little more. Both benefited from family connections that gave them entrée into the military, a career they used to fuel their ambitions. Both became generals who fought to protect their respective Enlightenment governments. Finally, both enjoyed a near god-like veneration that has persisted to this day. The six-foot three-inch Washington steadied his troops as much as the five-foot four-inch Napoleon rallied his. Parity in this respect would be a tremendous accomplishment on the part of Napoleon until one realizes that his height was just a bit below average for the time and therefore not the issue then as it is today. Washington, however, was not so lucky; his height indeed set him apart from his peers, a distinguishing quality he learned to capitalize on, but one that could not overcome his own fears of intellectual inferiority. It seems the "Napoleonic complex" rested with Washington rather than Napoleon after all.

Other contrasts reveal further similarities between the two leaders. Napoleon proved a master at winning decisive battles, while Washington skillfully clung to a strategy of attrition that purposely avoided the pitched battle. Even though he could rarely pursue it, Washington's goal during the Revolutionary War was to achieve a decisive victory to end the war in one action. The tool to achieve such an end was the Continental Army, whose chief attribute was the revolutionary zeal its citizen-soldiers brought to the battlefield, an impulse sustained by a small cadre of dedicated fighters. Like Washington some fifteen years before him, Napoleon sought decisive victory on the battlefields of Europe as he led a revolutionary force bolstered by an elite corps to achieve this end.

This military analysis can be pushed further. Washington's shaky performance during the colonial wars along the Virginia frontier suggests that he was not the professional soldier that Napoleon was. Of course, Napoleon's early military adventures in attempting the liberation of Corsica fail to show his later genius. Furthermore, Napoleon, in sharp contrast to Washington, received formal military training. But Washington's early military career fighting on behalf of England in the interior of the American continent would prove to be a valuable learning experience. The acquired knowledge left him short of the label of professional, but he was certainly well equipped to lead American forces during the Revolutionary War. In the end, both men were seasoned soldiers.

Military success cast an ominous shadow on the domestic front, however. As a military equal of Napoleon, Washington posed as great a threat to the life of the fledgling American republic that Napoleon did to representative government in France. Yet, when examining this stage of their lives, stark differences arise. First, the outright seizure of power by Napoleon during the coup of Brumaire in 1799 contrasts sharply with Washington's refusal to lead a similar coup during the Newburgh Conspiracy in 1783. Washington punctuated this difference by surrendering his sword once the Revolution - ary War was over and retiring to private life. Second, while Napoleon soon crowned himself emperor of France, Washington played a key role in ensuring the creation of the office of president by refusing to consider more authoritarian forms of government. He reinforced this stand by stepping away from the office after two terms, which became an enduring precedent. The contrast could not appear more complete.

An evaluation of these men as statesmen reveals this judgment to be premature. Both of them assumed their respective offices with a similar purpose in mind: transferring sovereignty from the people to a successful government dedicated entirely to the general good. In pursuit of the stability that would grow out of such an end, both men looked to achieve similar results in terms of economic reconstruction centered on furthering private enterprise, protecting private property, and establishing a solvent state revenue apparatus. In the short term, both societies buckled under the weight of such ambitions. In the United States, Washington marched at the head of an army to put down the Whiskey Rebellion and demonstrate once and for all the unity of the new nation. In Europe, Napoleon stretched the power of France to the limit to enforce his Continental System, designed to cripple England by denying that nation access to Europe's commercial markets. In both cases, in the name of protecting reform, the people bestowed sovereignty onto a man they perceived as dedicated to the general good. These men delivered in the long term, since both leaders could point to a lasting accomplishment as head of state: the U.S. Constitution and the Napoleonic Code.

Only by setting these two figures alongside one another can the story of both men be told in a way that examines their dynamic personalities but still brings to the foreground the important role of their respective societies in shaping the career of each man. Washington was constrained from accepting absolute rule because he heeded the will of the American populace and accepted the citizens' interpretation of the American version of the Enlightenment, which precluded authoritarianism. The French, conversely, readily accepted an "enlightened" despot and perhaps even encouraged it, helping produce Napoleon by allowing him to force himself upon them. It was the American citizenry's commitment to the ideals of the Enlightenment, in particular to the pursuit of "life, liberty, and property" espoused by followers of John Locke, that saved that nation from the route France would take a few years later. Still, France hardly believed that Napoleon had merely prevented its descent into the "state of war" so ominously predicted by Thomas Hobbes. Rather, that nation in the person of Napoleon had achieved the marvel of enlightened despotism that served as a calling card of the age, at least in Europe. Thus, today, to heap praise on Washington as the savior of democracy is to give credit where it is not due. In fact, to give this praise to Washington smacks of demagoguery that was antithetical to the American spirit at the time. And to castigate Napoleon for excessive ambition is to ignore the willing participation of French society in creating the Napoleonic Empire.

By making this point, this book calls attention to the restraining hand of the body politic on the admittedly dynamic figure of Washington, as well as its failure to take this step in France and contain the ambitious Napoleon. In late-eighteenth-century America, Enlightenment ideals ingrained in society combined with an inspired generation of leaders to produce the longest lasting modern republic the world has seen. But the credit for the American experience must ultimately lie with the American populace of that century, not with the acts of a few individuals such as Washington. The same measure can be taken today, but the conclusions are far less certain since the American suspicion and fear of militarism that helped to produce a republic have been eroded with the passage of time and with the brilliant successes of the American military. The loss of republican values suggests a troubling future for American democracy, particularly at a time when the PATRIOT Act generated little concern among the public that individual civil liberties had been traded for what was hoped to be security, when American citizens tolerated the abuse and torture of those deemed a threat to the United States by secretive government agencies reaching across political party affiliation and administrations, and when the state demands the almost exclusive right to use military force in its foreign policy. What is the mind-set of the American public now? Is it more like that of the Americans in 1776 or of the French in 1800? The answer speaks to the thin line between republicanism and autocracy—the thin line between Washington and Napoleon.

1

HUMBLE BEGINNINGS
The Makings of a Gentleman

I t is often said that childhood and life experience as a young adult have a remarkable effect on the outcome of an individual's life. Particular circumstances produce particular results. This is certainly true of George Washington and Napoleon Bonaparte. A close look at the early years of each man's life highlights the similarities between them and shows in Washington a feigned deference to power teamed with a hunger for social advancement. This same close look reveals Napoleon's unlikely ability to distinguish himself in a tumultuous age where his success in scheming to achieve power was remarkable. They were two men looking for and capitalizing on opportunities to secure their way in the world. Any benefit or bane to their countrymen would take a back seat to this goal.

WASHINGTON

George Washington was born on February 22, 1732, to a decidedly middle-class family, but one that enjoyed high-ranking social connections thanks to generations of family history in Virginia. The Washingtons had come to the Virginia colony in 1675 when adventurer John Washington, a colorful character in his own right, arrived on American shores. While he served in respectable positions, such as justice of the peace, and worked as a farmer, he is known today for his less than "Washingtonian" dealings: several marriages to women of low repute, questionable business ventures, and interactions with Indians that even his peers whispered amounted to murder. In spite of these indiscretions, as the generations of the Washington family progressed in Virginia, they became more and more prosperous. By the time of George's birth to Augustine Washington—the grandson of John—in 1732, the family had met with some success but not with the ultimate prize of financial independence and its accompanying elite social status. Nevertheless, as events soon proved, the Washington family was one from which an ambitious man could emerge and make something of himself.

George was Augustine Washington's third son but the first child of Augustine's second wife, Mary Ball. In the normal course of eighteenth-century Virginian society, this tertiary status would have meant some schooling in England and a life of modest comfort for George, first under the direction of his father and then, subsequently, his older brothers. However, George's life took a different tack. When he was eleven years old, his father died. With Augustine's death, the family's fortunes declined, and George's chance for formal schooling in England was gone. Therefore, most of his education, which was quite limited, came in the form of copybooks, such as *Rules of Civility & Decent Behaviour in Company and Conversation*, which he memorized when he was sixteen. The lack of formal education was something Washington always regretted, especially later on when dealing with the distinguished members of the Continental Congress. However, the copybooks, particularly those on social etiquette, may have done him more service than any formal education ever could have. These "rules" served as the basis of a gentleman's actions in society; Washington learned a code of deferential behavior that would help him advance his social standing in the future. One rule cautioned the reader to always keep the company of good men; another, to "Submit your Judgment to others with Modesty." Rule 1 was to always offer "some sign of respect to those that are present." Already the seeds of the actor, as Paul Longmore labeled him in *The Invention of George Washington*, were taking hold in the man destined to play such an important role in the future of America.[1]

Augustine's estate was divided among George's two older half-brothers and his second wife, Mary. Thereafter, at a very young age, George was left to his mother's bidding. Mary was a hard-driving woman who would live to see her son made commander in chief of American forces and later become president of a newly independent nation. Unfortunately for George, Mary Ball Washington never approved of the life he led away from her side, and in fact she would tell George from time to time that he was neglecting his duty to her. It was under her watchful eye at her property, Ferry Farm, that George first became not a father to his nation but a surrogate father to his four younger siblings. It was Mary's intention that George lead her branch of the family and manage her agricultural affairs. At the age of eleven, George Washington had his first taste of responsibility and command.[2]

Augustine's death and the weight of his mother's farm that was placed upon his shoulders created in Washington two personality traits. The first was a need to escape the grind of daily responsibility. The second was a consuming ambition to seek greater and greater tasks that necessitated wielding greater responsibility. These contradictory qualities could not last long, and the second soon eclipsed the first, as evidenced by his relationship with his older half-brother Lawrence, Augustine's second son. The elder Washington was on his way to becoming a powerful figure in Virginia society, and he furthered this goal by marrying into the most prominent family in the area. In 1743 Lawrence wed Anne Fairfax, a cousin to Lord Thomas Fairfax in England and a daughter of the head of the American branch of the Fairfax clan, William Fairfax. The Fairfax estate was but four miles away from Lawrence's home at Little Hunting Creek, the future Mount Vernon, so the proximity of the two families no doubt facilitated the union by allowing these two to meet often. But Lawrence's easy disposition and likable personality had much to do with the marriage as well. It was an advantageous turn of events for the Washingtons. A royal grant had established Lord Fairfax as the largest landholder in the Virginia colony, his property consisting of some five million acres in the immediate area and reaching west into the untamed wilderness. The Fairfaxes represented the pinnacle of success and power in Virginia, and the Washingtons were now, if only by marriage, a part of that family.

Through Lawrence, Washington was exposed to the upper-class lifestyle of colonial Virginia gentry. To young George Washington, the Fairfax family resembled the height of European elegance and nobility. Though few records exist recording Washington's impressions upon entering the Fairfax residence at Belvoir, his later actions suggest its inhabitants suitably enthralled him. His life at Mount Vernon in the years to come was an imitation on a smaller scale of what the Fairfaxes had demonstrated to him in his youth. In truth, Lawrence gave George a new chance at success by exposing him to the role of plantation owner in a much more glorious light than he had learned to endure at his mother's estate. George relished the opportunity to embrace such a future, but the question was how to achieve his new goal. As the third son of a Virginia planter family, George did not have a bright future as a gentleman farmer, and inheriting his mother's modest estate was not going to be enough to propel him into the upper reaches of society. At present, he could only play the part. The actor had arrived.

Since Washington did not share the good fortune of a wealthy family background, he looked for another way to advance himself. His connection to the Fairfax family through Lawrence served him well. Land speculation was big business in the eighteenth century, and the Fairfax family was deeply involved in it. While they enjoyed vast land holdings, the unsettled nature of the frontier raised some doubt as to the exact value of the land. Someone, a trusted friend, had to make this trip to underwrite the value. When the Fairfaxes asked George to assume this responsibility, he became a backwoods surveyor (a growing and respectable profession), first in the Shenandoah Valley in present-day western Virginia, more than one hundred miles from home.

Washington enjoyed his time in the backcountry immensely. It was an escape from his mother's farm, which, after Augustine's death, had become run-down and melancholy. At times, in the classic position of a poor third son, George had been forced to decline social engagements for want of feed for his horse. At age seventeen he became surveyor of Culpeper County. By the time he was eighteen, he had made his first land purchase when he bought 1,459 acres at Bullskin Creek in the Shenandoah Valley. George's vocation had given him some land and, as he had hoped, a start in the world.

Unfortunately, just as George had begun to establish himself, his brother Lawrence was stricken with tuberculosis. Despite a trip to Barbados that was supposed to ease his affliction (and would provide George with his only trip overseas), Lawrence Washington died in 1752.

His brother's death, while tremendously saddening to George, provided him with the greatest opportunity in his young life to date. Virginia, like other colonies, possessed a poorly trained volunteer militia that served primarily as a social club and only as a titular defense force. As a renowned veteran from the War of Jenkins' Ear earlier in the eighteenth century and an adjutant general of the force, Lawrence had been in charge of raising and drilling the volunteers. With Lawrence's death the post was broken into four concurrent commands. While lacking military experience, George sought appointment to one of these new posts with all the vigor he could muster. Thanks to his powerful connections, he became a major in the Virginia colonial militia at the age of twenty-one.

While Washington's military appointment was not unusual in the patronage system common in the eighteenth century, it came at an auspicious time. Britain and her colonies were involved in a global struggle for European dominance with longtime rival France. The two powers had clashed repeatedly on the American continent, and in 1753 this rivalry again spilled over into open conflict in a number of areas, including territory adjacent to Virginia. Both Britain and France claimed the enormous territory of the Ohio River valley. Virginia's lieutenant governor, Robert Dinwiddie, wanted this land for the Ohio Company, a group of speculators that included, among others, himself and Augustine and Lawrence Washington. French soldiers and traders stationed in the Ohio valley posed a problem for Dinwiddie in securing his aim. He resolved to remove these French agents, which he set out to do with London's blessing. The governor followed a two-pronged strategy. The first involved sending an envoy to inform the French that the British claimed the disputed land, and ordering them to leave. Second, if the French failed to depart, Dinwiddie planned to use military force.

To implement the first strategy, Dinwiddie faced the problem of whom to send. The trip would be physically demanding, requiring the individual to traverse more than five hundred miles of wilderness most likely during the harsh winter months. The envoy also had to have some standing in Virginia; a diplomatic mission was not undertaken by just any sort of lowly frontiersman. Washington seemed a perfect fit. While he had not been to the Ohio territory, he had grown accustomed to the outdoors during his time as a surveyor in the Shenandoah Valley. And he enjoyed the blessing of the Fairfaxes. Understanding the magnitude of the opportunity, Washington began his trek west in November 1753 with, in the words of historian James Flexner, the "air of one born to command."[3]

A diplomatic mission to a French military encampment on behalf of king and country was clearly beyond the experience and capabilities of this young albeit politically connected provincial officer. Washington said so candidly long after the event, acknowledging his surprise that "so young and inexperienced a person should have been employed on a negotiation with which subjects of the greatest importance were involved."[4] A few local officials complained to Dinwiddie, and their fears were soon realized. Though physically strong enough to make the difficult journey—at times he outpaced his companions—his inexperience in diplomacy plagued him repeatedly. When he and his few traveling companions met Half-King, a Mingo chief and Native American ally of Britain known to his adopted Seneca tribe as Tanacharison, Washington acted brashly enough to insult this crucial source of manpower for the mission. He reminded Half-King that the chief was allied to the English cause. Half-King responded by telling Washington that the alliance covered trade but said nothing of land concessions. He then asked the purpose of Washington's mission. Washington said nothing, realizing that he had boxed himself into a corner, since his purpose was land acquisition. To his relief the chief agreed to accompany the Virginian's party, although Half-King provided a military escort of but four Indians. When Washington pushed for an immediate departure, Half-King sought time to prepare and expressed his annoyance with the impetuous Washington. Washington acquiesced, and the party did not leave for three more days. When it did so, it was not completely clear to the Indians or to the Virginians who was in charge.

The tension that existed between Washington and Half-King remained in play for much of the journey. In fact, Washington exacerbated things to a great extent, again because of his inexperience. He failed to understand that the puny size of his expedition exposed its limited authority, a failing all the more pronounced in light of the mission's purpose. He once more insulted Half-King when he met the first group of Frenchmen and attempted to keep the chief out of contact with them by entering the camp while his

Indian escort remained outside. The Indians filed in anyway, amusing the French. The French also took note of the sparseness of Washington's delegation and cleared him to continue his journey.

Despite his difficulties, Washington eventually reached his destination of Fort Le Boeuf, located near modern Waterford, Pennsylvania. There he met a seasoned French commander, Jacques Le Gardeur, sieur de Saint-Pierre, who accepted his missive, penned a reply, and quickly sent him on his way back to Virginia. Washington and his entourage began their arduous return in the midst of winter. He again outstripped his companions in physical strength, pushing forward with one of them and a guide in a determined effort to deliver the French reply as soon as possible. Haste again nearly undid him. Against the advice of his traveling companion, Christopher Gist, he had chosen an Indian guide of suspect credibility who was likely a member of a tribe allied with the French and who, after a short time on the trail, turned and leveled his rifle at the two British envoys and fired. He hit neither of them, and both men lurched forward and disarmed him. Gist favored the execution of the Indian, but Washington stayed his hand. Instead, they sent the treacherous guide off into the wilderness and moved ahead in a different direction, although they remained in great fear of an ambush for the next several days. The last river to cross before reaching safety remained unfrozen. The two men elected to cross in a makeshift raft that immediately collided with large ice floes, knocking Washington into the freezing water. Unable to cross, Washington and Gist endured a night of acute discomfort. The river froze over the next day, allowing them to cross, and so it was with this last great effort that Washington returned to Virginia and reported his findings to Dinwiddie.

Dinwiddie could not have been too surprised by the results. Singularly unimpressed by Washington and his entourage, the French had decided not to acquiesce to the wishes of King George II and withdraw from the Ohio valley. Too small in number and led by such an inexperienced man, the English diplomatic effort had not cowed the French. In fact, Dinwiddie must have known that the brash and young Washington would not control Half-King. Without that chief providing a large Indian escort, there could be no hope of intimidating the French with the plausibility of an English-Indian alliance that would threaten their interests in the area. It is also possible that

Dinwiddie overestimated the ability of Half-King to rally Indians to the English cause, so in this sense he bore most of the responsibility for the failed diplomacy. More likely, however, Dinwiddie understood the very tenuous English-Indian relations in the area. Washington's inexperience ensured that there would be no miraculous change. That Washington would try and fail was almost assured. Dinwiddie must have shrewdly recognized that Washington had pursued this assignment that was far beyond his ability for the sake of hoping to win advancement in colonial society. This goal would have been hard to miss, as Washington had taken the very forward step of showing up at the governor's mansion pleading for the job.[5]

At the same time, Dinwiddie could be reasonably sure that the fit and young Washington would be able to return from this mission alive, overcoming the elements and with a little luck, any man-made dangers as well. With the diplomatic formality out of the way, Dinwiddie could take his next course of action, a military expedition to claim the Ohio valley for Virginia. An unforeseen bonus aided Dinwiddie's plans. Washington had kept a journal describing his travels, one that exposed French designs on the Ohio valley. Dinwiddie insisted that Washington publish his account of the trip, which he hoped would galvanize the Virginian populace into supporting his offensive west. The *Journal of Major George Washington* appeared in several colonial newspapers, with mixed impact. Much of the public recognized Washington's ties to the Ohio Company and understood that he and the governor stood to gain financially from any military action against the French. They would not go to war to benefit but a few. Others did heed the call to arms, fearing French advances into Virginia. Most significantly, the journal's publication underscored Washington's role as a pawn of the governor. In this rather ignominious fashion, Washington took a step forward onto the world stage.

After Washington's failure to dislodge the French through diplomatic means, Dinwiddie set in action his plan of a more forceful nature to challenge French control of the Ohio valley. For a time, Washington was mentioned as the military expedition's leader, but much to his credit, he insisted that he was not ready for such a daunting command. He did accept a promotion to lieutenant colonel, however, and agreed to serve as the executive officer of the force. This opportunity was momentous for Washington, since he now enjoyed a significant position of military authority. More importantly, it must have signaled to him that his plan to advance in society through a military career was succeeding. This new assignment would allow him to improve his reputation as an officer but risk very little of his still-burgeoning reputation as a gentleman. After all, this mission was mostly intended to be a saber-rattling exercise designed to demonstrate British resolve on the issue of the Ohio territory. But fate soon intervened to force an unpredicted outcome. Lieutenant Colonel Washington's superior officer never arrived to accept his position, so Washington would serve as the de facto commander from the start of the expedition to the end.

Dinwiddie issued clear orders to the expedition. Washington was to lead the men already assembled into the wilderness and, before engaging in battle, inform any Frenchmen he encountered of British willingness to attack. Hopefully the French would back down. Dinwiddie wanted the land in the Ohio River area, but he would secure it without a fight if he could. Some Virginian militiamen, teamed with an Indian contingent, might be enough to induce the French to surrender the contested area. Considering the known French strength in the region, it is difficult to see how such a modest-sized unit could have achieved more than this limited goal. Dinwiddie could not hope for much more from Washington. Then, after reinforcing Washington at some indefinite point in the future and superseding him with a more seasoned commander, Col. Joshua Fry of Oxford University, the army could act to expel the French if necessary.[6]

As events would prove, Washington, acting on his own, upset Dinwiddie's plans. Leaving in early April 1754, Washington led 186 men west with the first goal of meeting Half-King. A difficult march moved him toward the Monongahela River and into contact with Half-King at the head of only twelve warriors in western Virginia. With this small force, Washington continued to advance northward into the wilderness to find the French. However, contrary to orders, Washington ambushed the first group of French soldiers he came across on May 28, 1754, killing several of them and capturing the rest. What seemed at first to be both a crushing military and moral victory for the British quickly became obvious for what it really was. Washington had attacked and killed French diplomats engaged in a mission similar to that of Washington's own the year before when he had traveled safely through French lines. The wounded French commander, Joseph Coulon de Villiers, sieur de Jumonville, had tried to explain this fact after ordering his men to throw down their arms. But Half-King struck the Frenchman in the head and killed him instantly, even washing his hands in the blood spilling from the man's brain. This act sparked the massacre of nine other French soldiers by Washington's Indian escort. Washington did nothing to stop them, possibly amazed at this barbarity. Once again, Half-King had proved an agent impossible for the Virginian to control.[7]

Isolated in the backwoods but expecting reinforcement, Washington now prepared for the inevitable French counterattack. It was not long in coming. A month later, a French army 1,100 strong and led by Louis Coulon de Villiers, brother of the slain French commander, attacked the Virginians, who now numbered 400 and had dug in at the hastily raised and poorly situated Fort Necessity, just south of the previous contact and southeast of present-day Uniontown, Pennsylvania. Half-King and the few Indians under his command quickly abandoned the Virginians. Recognizing the exposed position of the fort, they had predicted the French would easily defeat the outnumbered militiamen. When the French arrived, they fired on the post with impunity from concealed positions in the woods. A sudden burst of rain offered a reprieve from enemy fire, but it also flooded the shallow trenches shielding Washington's men and soaked the powder stored in a magazine with a leaking roof. When the rain abated, the garrison of Fort Necessity was in more danger than before. By the end of a day's action, at least a hundred of Washington's men had been killed or wounded, and the Virginians faced imminent defeat. Despite the fact that he had been reinforced again, this time by two hundred men led by Capt. James McKay, Washington surrendered to the French.

Agreeing to terms, Washington evacuated the fort on July 4, 1754. To his surprise, the French allowed him to march his forces back to Virginia. Washington had not been so kind to the diplomatic party he had ambushed just days before. French leniency enabled Washington to claim a stalemate, and some recognized it as such back in Virginia. Others were not so sure. The agreement Washington had signed when he gave up Fort Necessity acknowledged that he had assassinated Joseph Coulon. Washington countered that he had signed the document because he had not understood the terms due to a poor translation.[8] Regardless of this explanation, the agreement allowed the French to saddle the English with the odious distinction of having commenced hostilities in what became known in the Americas as the French and Indian War, in Europe, the Seven Years' War. Spanning several continents, it would actually last almost nine years.

Washington's inadequacy, born of inexperience or not, had helped to foster war on the American continent. Ironically, it was in this period that Washington shed any suspicion that he was not qualified to hold a military command. His defeat merely reinforced his awareness of using a military career as a path to responsibility and fame and therefore social advancement. He had good reason to think so despite his debacle in the wilderness. Upon his return to Virginia, his fellow colonials hailed him as the hero of the Battle of Fort Necessity. That state's legislative body, the House of Burgesses, recognized him and several of his officers for "their late gallant and brave Behavior in the Defense of their Country."[9] If true in specifics—he was certainly brave—the honor ignored the consequences of the military action: outright hostilities with France. If his countrymen could overlook the results of his actions, so too could Washington. Clearly, acting the part of a great commander was more important than actual success on the field of battle, though Washington had confidence in his own abilities. Young Washington now understood the value of playing a role to secure advancement in colonial society, irrespective of the ability to perform that responsibility well. If his compatriots wanted him to play the part of a conquering hero and defender of Virginia, then that is how he would act.[10]

Regardless of this revelation, reality soon reasserted itself and diminished his enjoyment of the accolades. While treated kindly by Americans nursing a keen sense of pride, he was likely viewed by the British army officers arriving in the colonies as just one more unprepared militiaman. One prominent British general characterized Americans as "the dirtiest most contemptible cowardly dogs you could conceive." His assessment came mainly from the unnerving tendency of colonial militia to desert their posts. Gen. Edward Braddock, soon to command another expedition in the Ohio region, held Virginians in disdain because "their slothful and languid disposition renders them very unfit for military service." And during the French and Indian War, British major general James Abercromby described colonial troops as "the rif-raf of the continent." It was quite clear to regular army officers that colonials were not up to the task.[11]

To this point, Washington had done little to challenge this viewpoint, since he had yet to be involved in a military expedition that had actually succeeded. On his first adventure, he had completed a parley only after exposing English weakness, thereby ensuring that the initiative failed. On his second outing, he had helped to start a world war by attacking a diplomatic mission. Setting aside this record, he assumed that, given the state of war, his Virginia militia would be accepted into the king's army with himself as its colonel. He could not have been more mistaken. Dinwiddie and the Crown decided to break up his command and, in what was perhaps the worst insult of all, decreed that colonial officers who did receive a commission would rise no higher in rank than that of captain.[12]

If one looks at the situation with an objective eye, the English offer of a commission as a captain was reasonable even if it fell short of Washington's expectations. Like many other colonials, Washington's social standing did not warrant a colonel's rank in the king's army; those positions went to moneyed British professionals. That a colonial would be allowed to rise to a captain was a considerable concession on the part of the Crown. But it also indicated how the British, clinging to their belief in an officer corps of gentlemen, viewed the colonials throughout the war effort. The British looked upon them with disdain. In turn, the colonials looked upon the British policy as wholly unfair. Were they not British subjects as well, the provincials asked? Here was a strong hint of London's feeling towards its colonies.

With his ego bruised, Washington resigned his commission and resolved to begin his life as a planter, his goal from the start. He rented Mount Vernon from his late brother's widow, Anne, so that by the end of 1754, at the age of twenty-two, Washington had achieved his boyhood dream of becoming a gentleman planter, something he had been striving for at least since he first met the Fairfax family. Nevertheless, at the time he noted that his heart desired a military career.[13] These sentiments revealed Washington's dissatisfaction with the outcome that had led to his resignation. Quite quickly, an opportunity presented itself that Washington believed he could use to resurrect his military career.

In February 1755 General Braddock arrived in Virginia with two regiments of British regulars charged with the task of moving west and harassing the French on the frontier. Braddock realized he needed help to negotiate the frontier with such a large force, especially one traveling with heavy cannon and mortars. The general looked for a guide, and it was not long before he heard that Washington was the most skilled person in the colony when it came to the backcountry. After a meeting, Washington signed on as a civilian adviser to Braddock's staff.[14] Because of Braddock's connections and clout, Washington could hope to use this experience to advance beyond the position of a mere captain. Perhaps after a successful campaign with Braddock, the general would recommend him for regular commission as a colonel.

Confident of victory, Braddock set out from Fort Cumberland, Maryland, in mid-May with over 2,000 men. Progress was very slow, and the column faced multiple hardships due to the terrain and frequent harassment from Indians. Nevertheless, by July the British were within twelve miles of Fort Duquesne, the French stronghold in the area (located in what is today downtown Pittsburgh). The army had followed Washington's path of the year before, enlarging the road as it advanced, and it now stood poised to capture the fort and drive the French out of the Ohio valley. Washington had not accompanied the main force for much of the journey due to one of his frequent bouts of illness. He rejoined the advance party, now numbering 1,200, in time to see it ambushed. Washington had warned Braddock that the French in this part of the world would not fight in the style the general was accustomed to facing in Europe. Heeding the advice, Braddock had deployed skirmishers ahead of the advancing army on both sides of the trail. However, he was ambushed at a river crossing, the lone instance where he had not taken precautions. As a consequence, the British were ill prepared to face the determined French and Indian attack that followed.[15]

The result was a disaster. On July 9, 1755, a French army comprising 250 French soldiers and militiamen and more than 600 Indians attacked Braddock's vanguard, sending it fleeing backward into the main British force and sowing confusion there as well. Hopelessly disorganized, British resistance quickly collapsed despite stout efforts by the officers to maintain ranks and stand and fight. In the Battle of the Monongahela, fought in the territory north of the junction of the Monongahela and Youghiogheny Rivers alongside the Ohio River, Braddock was killed, and his army suffered more than 900 casualties, including at least 456 dead. The French and their Indian allies lost no more than 40 men killed or wounded. Washington was left not officially in command but exercising such authority on an emergency basis. He again displayed much courage, rallying Braddock's troops while having two horses shot out from under him, all while he was ill. Past experience served him well as he led what remained of Braddock's decimated column to safety.

For his actions in the battle, Virginians once again hailed Washington as a hero in the midst of defeat. Finding acclaim out of military debacles seemed to be somewhat of a pattern for him. This time around the tribute was even sweeter because this military defeat could not be blamed on Washington; Braddock had marched his regulars to disaster. Partly in recognition of his prior service to the colony and partly because of this recent heroism, Dinwiddie named Washington commander in chief of Virginia's military forces with the rank of full colonel. Washington gladly accepted the post that made him the highest-ranking colonial officer in Virginia.

Still but twenty-two years old and with his early debacles behind him, Washington began to enjoy some military success. British regulars were absent from the Virginia area for the remainder of 1755 and much of 1756, and Washington, using colonial militia and a personally trained Virginia regiment one thousand men strong, was able to defend the frontier against French raiding parties. This was no insignificant accomplishment. The small size of Washington's forces made it extremely difficult for him to defend such a large area. Moreover, he was ill supplied by the civilian government. Yet the greatest challenges came when British authorities interfered with the defense of the Virginia colony, such as when one British official threatened to place the Virginians under the command of a rival colonial governor, and when a British general ordered Virginian militia to South Carolina. Such actions stretched Washington's meager resources even further, testing his patience. Moreover, dissatisfaction with his pay and his eventual failure to win a regular commission estranged him from his patron, Dinwiddie. He threatened to resign his commission on numerous occasions. Yet successfully dealing with these issues taught him important lessons that he would carry with him in years to come. He persevered, even overcoming another serious illness. On balance, he defended the colony successfully.

In 1758 British attention again centered on Virginia, and the Crown elected to mount another offensive to drive the French from the Ohio valley. A new British general, Brig. Gen. John Forbes, led an army of six thousand troops to the attack, but he proposed to do so along an avenue of advance north of the disastrous route of 1755. Washington accompanied this force while enjoying a temporary rank of brigadier general. Forbes found him obstinate and difficult, believing that Washington "put his 'attachment to [his] province' before 'the good of the army.'"[16] But Forbes recognized Washington's expertise in frontier warfare and therefore assigned him to command one of the lead units on the march. Washington feared disaster, arguing that this new route would present overwhelming obstacles due to the rugged terrain that would slow down the army, leaving it vulnerable to ambush or exposing it to the harsh winter should it not reach its destination in time. His fears were well founded, and the English army made slow progress. In November, still some distance from Fort Duquesne and weighing the advice offered by a council of war, Forbes considered halting the advance until spring. Even in the best of circumstances, the hardships imposed by wintering in the backcountry would test the endurance of British regulars. Could they emerge from winter an effective fighting force? It would be impossible for Washington's contingent of Virginians to remain encamped near the French stronghold since enlistments would soon expire. To this dreary prospect could be added Washington's fear that once his soldiers headed for home, he would lose his command and another chance at military glory.

Here was a dangerous predicament for the fate of the army and for Washington's ambitions. But strategic imperatives prevented these forecasts of disaster from becoming realities. British military successes in Canada cut off reinforcement and resupply of Fort Duquesne. Consequently, the French evacuated and burned the fort in an attempt to consolidate their troops, revealing the waning French commitment to the Ohio valley. In November 1758 the British finally captured the French seat of power in the Ohio valley, Fort Duquesne, without firing a shot. The war would not officially end until 1763, but French power in the Americas had been dealt a severe blow.

Washington recognized the sea change resulting from the success in the Ohio region, and he resigned his commission, since his mission was essentially accomplished: the French no longer posed a threat to the Ohio territory.

Better still, Washington could rest on his laurels, the war having ensured his fame as the man in Virginia most responsible for achieving this outcome. With this acclaim, he also relished some social advancement. Election to the House of Burgesses bolstered his social standing, as did increasing his land holdings, now possible due to the outcome of the hostilities. All in all, he had profited immensely from England's war against France in the Americas, and he saw little to make him believe otherwise. If some scholars track the success the English enjoyed in the Seven Years' War as the root of the American Revolution, the tension went unnoticed by Washington, save for his rebuffed attempts at receiving a British commission.

Besides, he had other things to think about. Acquiring land was one thing; working that land was another. Improving his property holdings, as well as those of his mother, engaged much of his time. In 1759 he married the wealthy widow Martha Dandridge Custis, gaining a wife and two stepchildren. It did not appear an amorous marriage—more an arrangement typical of eighteenth-century colonial society.[17] Still, the union would survive some tough times, including the lack of children that Washington could call his own. Instead, he learned to enjoy the company of his adopted children, and he did so to a great degree, although he was careful to leave most parenting decisions to Martha. The brash colonel from Virginia, so eager to advance himself and gain the security of a comfortable position in high society, would soon realize that his status of gentleman farmer would put him on a path that would require him to act the part of the savior of republicanism. It was an unexpected role, but one he soon came to realize could bring him more acclaim than he ever had dreamed of attaining, if he played the role right. The power attending such a performance would be expansive as well. Always a quick study, a man trusting in his instincts, Washington would make the most of his opportunities and in the process, help give birth to a nation.

NAPOLEON

Napoleon Bonaparte's autocratic fame contrasts sharply with that of the republican Washington, so it is surprising that Napoleon's early years closely parallel the Virginian's. Like Washington's, Napoleon's is a tale of a youth living at the fringe of a great empire, an ambitious man from middling circumstances who envisioned far greater things for himself than his social rank suggested. And like his predecessor across the Atlantic, Napoleon saw a chance at advancement through military service and took it. His audacity would be rewarded tenfold.

Napoleon's birth on August 15, 1769, came at a time of great unrest in Europe. France, under the Bourbon king Louis XVI, was only a few short years away from renewing its war with England. On the island of Corsica, the ethnically Italian population chafed under the French boot. The island folk were not alone in their agitation. All over Western Europe, radical thinkers were spreading new philosophies about the nature of man and the world, challenging the existing social order with "enlightened" thought. How many of these ideas reached Corsica is uncertain. Probably very few. Here was a population that clung to resentment and pursued family vendettas reaching back several generations. Yet, unconventional times were not necessary to stir the people to action. They needed little encouragement to fight one another, let alone a foreign army. Consequently, the island, like much of Europe, was in a state of excitement at the time Napoleon was born that August, since 2,500 Corsicans had joined with Pasquale Paoli, the great Corsican independence leader, to fight to free themselves from French control. Among them were Napoleon's parents, Carlo Bonaparte and Letizia Ramolino.

The effort came to a halt in 1770 when a French army of occupation defeated the Corsican rebels. It was a bitter end to over a decade of independence. Paoli had assumed a leadership role in 1756, pushing the island to embrace what many observers labeled an enlightened social experiment.[18] However, even after the island freed itself from the control of the city-state of Genoa, Paoli never did foster unity among his fellow Corsican patriots, let alone all Corsicans. This did not go unnoticed in France. When Louis XV had looked for an easy conquest to assuage French humiliations in the Seven Years' War, the island became his target. Whether it was from the tradition of resistance to foreign control, or whether it was from the taste of freedom from foreign control and wanting more, Corsicans rose to defend their island. The easy French conquest initiated in 1764 turned into a lengthy guerrilla war. Only superior French numbers and a generous amnesty offered to all those who had stood in opposition to France brought the island under control five years later.

In 1769 Paoli fled to England, but those who had served under him now had to decide how best to get along with the French. Napoleon's father was one such individual. Carlo had loyally served Corsica's nationalist leader. Now he made a different choice and decided to collaborate with the French. It was a pragmatic decision for a man otherwise prone to grandiose schemes that seldom came to fruition. For his newly expressed loyalty to the Bourbon crown, French authorities awarded this minor nobleman the position of royal assessor in the region of Corsica's capital city of Ajaccio. In this capacity he earned an income of 900 francs per year. This salary was not enough to raise a family that eventually totaled eight children. Napoleon was the second child to survive birth. But as it turned out, Carlo's small means, coupled with the traditions of the day, would prove momentous for Europe. Using his connections to the royal French government, Carlo set out to equip his offspring to face the world. In late 1778 he left Corsica for Paris with two children in tow: Joseph (his oldest) and Napoleon. After meeting with court officials, Carlo persuaded the French crown to educate them. Joseph was bound for the seminary, a career in the church being a respectable position for an oldest male child. Ten-year-old Napoleon was sent to a military academy. For a son to pursue a military career was also respectable, even expected, in a family of aristocratic background. Perhaps unknowingly to both father and son, it was a good fit.

Napoleon's experience at the royal military school located to the east of Paris at Brienne demonstrated at an early age the kind of man he would become. The most often cited characteristic the young Napoleon demonstrated was a problem with authority resulting in nearly constant punishment. The boy was his own person. He paid close attention only to matters he deemed essential. If he believed something was superfluous, he invested as little time as possible.

The tendency to learn on his own terms produced an uneven education. Math interested him, so he excelled at it, but he neglected the finer points of his education. For example, literature bored him, but he liked history and would bury himself in the study of ancient Greece and Rome among other topics. It would be no accident that in later years Paoli, when sparring with Napoleon for control of the direction of the Corsican revolution, exclaimed, "There is nothing modern about you, Napolione. You come from the age of Plutarch!"[19] The remark was intended to belittle what Paoli dismissed as the romantic dreams of glory that filled Napoleon's head from his love of the classics. These thoughts, Paoli believed, rendered Napoleon incapable of adapting to the ways of the world in which they now were living. Paoli, as others would, underestimated the man. Napoleon indeed discovered inspiration in the classics, but the lessons he drew from his studies were to make his own rules and try to bend the world to his whims. It is incredible how well this philosophy served his life.

The second most often cited characteristic Napoleon displayed while at Brienne was his concern with his social standing. For instance, in 1781 he wrote to his father requesting an allowance, not for the purpose of spending the money on treats or comforts, but simply to demonstrate to the other boys that he could have the money if he so desired. This request was denied tersely. "We have no money. You must stay where you are," his father wrote in reply.[20] This must have been a startling revelation and a painful one, since it reinforced his status as a minor nobleman and an impoverished one at that. But he had other worries. His Corsican accent maligned his French and made him a target of ridicule by the school bullies. They saw not Corsican nobility but a foreigner aspiring to be French. Napoleon responded in obstinate fashion. Throughout his life, his French never became fluent, perhaps a deliberate act of defiance on his part. Moreover, for much of his youth, he spelled his name Buonaparte, the extra vowel retained as recognition of his proud Corsican ancestry. All the while, the tormented youth shouldered the jeering and taunts of his classmates in silence, save for occasional outbursts that stunned his peers. Privately he took solace in grand schemes to liberate Corsica from French tyranny. The objective was obvious and natural. What better way to strike at his fellow students than to lead his island people to freedom? Such revenge, even if it lay far in the future, eased the torment he endured in the present. In the meantime he studied hard and sought retribution where he could. Most notably, when engaged in snowball fights in the school courtyard, Napoleon's ammunition supposedly contained rocks. It was a way to retaliate against those who persecuted him the most. Assuming there was such a fight (since the record left by those who knew the great man in his youth was almost certainly embellished after the fact), the boy must have taken notice of the benefits of such martial prowess.[21]

Whether or not Napoleon suffered more torment than any other youth in similar circumstances is a valid question. His persecution may have been of his own doing. Reclusive, moody, and brooding, yet proud of his heritage and disdainful of others, his behavior did much to make him a target. But this response called attention to his sensitivity to social status, and overcoming his background—a clear obstacle to his career ambitions—remained important to him as he grew older. In his endeavor to advance himself socially, the French crown again came to Napoleon's aid. His performance and final evaluation at Brienne had earned him enough attention to merit an appointment to the École Militaire in Paris. In 1783, now fifteen years old, he entered the French military academy as a "gentleman-cadet" in artillery. An artillery officer needs outstanding mathematical skills, something Napoleon certainly possessed, but the appointment was a mixed blessing. Artillery was a relatively new arm of military service and not one coveted by members of the French aristocracy, who instead valued the time-honored cavalry. His new training would make him a better soldier, but it was not designed to advance him much beyond the rank of colonel.

Consequently, at this new school Napoleon was in an interesting situation. He had earned his way into the officer corps of the French army, even though he did not consider himself a Frenchmen. Nor did his peers accept him as a French aristocrat. Should he remain an officer for twenty years, he could expect only a modest existence, since he was unlikely to advance very far in rank. For a man as headstrong and ambitious as Napoleon, this must have weighed on his mind as he set his long-term goals. Naturally, he fumed as he confronted the reality that royal birth trumped merit, joining with those of lesser birth to fight those of higher birth.[22] Napoleon fretted about the chasm between rich and poor. He thought it strange that cadets training for army life should be allowed to live so comfortably. Napoleon believed it better that cadets be forced to live an austere army life while in the barracks, but he was dissuaded by a trusted teacher from putting his views in writing and formally sending them through government channels. He appeared to be one of the few willing to live this Spartan lifestyle.[23]

Things for Napoleon did not soon improve. His father died of stomach cancer in February 1785 at the age of 38, eliminating the family's income. It was a difficult blow for Napoleon. He felt much affection for his father despite the infrequent contact between the two after Napoleon began his education in France. He also faced more immediate difficulties. Napoleon assumed his father's position as head of the family, brushing aside his older brother, Joseph. Now family obligations spurred him to action. For the moment he could do no more than apply himself to his trade and send what little money he could to his mother in Corsica. His frustration increased, as did his hardships.

During this time, Napoleon continued to develop a strong sense of nationalism, specifically of the Corsican variety. He refused to accept French control of the island as anything but transitory, and he spurned those Corsicans who collaborated with the French there. This, of course, included his father. Despite Carlo having sided with the hated French, Napoleon loved his father.[24] His mixed feelings revealed that he was painfully aware of the contradiction he was living: a French officer in training planning to free French territory from French control. And when he put aside his nationalist ambitions for Corsica, he recognized that the French government had done much to improve his life, including making possible his own military career. In September 1785 he celebrated his commission as a second lieutenant in the French Royal Artillery with a small party at a friend's house in Paris.

While he was now an officer, Napoleon still faced the fact that there was no real future for him in the king's army. He simply lacked the family background to elevate himself to a position of great command and authority that would satisfy his desire for social advancement. Contemplating what he considered to be his bleak future led him to consider suicide, though his "innate drive, superior intelligence and curiosity," as one writer put it, led him to decide against it.[25] He talked himself out of taking this drastic step and instead he spent a year in menial garrison duty in Valence in southeastern France while studying treatises on leadership, history, and the nature of nationalism. He also kept to himself, due possibly to lack of money and personal preference.

Napoleon applied his studies to his obsession with freeing Corsica from French control, resolving to return home and reacquaint himself with the island. In September 1786 the army granted his request for a five-month furlough after only twelve months of service. He was now seventeen, and it was his first visit to the island in six years. Once there he extended his leave on the grounds of having to assist his family struggling with financial problems. These concerns were genuine enough, and he strove to put the family affairs in order. With four young children to raise, his mother welcomed the young man home. Napoleon, working in tandem with Joseph, who had also returned home after withdrawing from the seminary, accomplished very little, however. Schemes to maximize the agricultural value of the Bonaparte estate went nowhere due to a lack of capital. He did spend much time roaming the Corsican countryside, and he started writing a history of the island. His visit clearly reinforced his desire to see a free Corsica. He returned to France in late 1787, having spent more time in Corsica than at his army post.

In January 1788, after a short stint with his military unit, Napoleon was back in Corsica, this time to witness the island's reaction to the unfolding French Revolution. It was unclear to him and many others what direction things would go. Napoleon resolved to become a part of the action, to make something of himself at home by unbridling the French yoke from his native land. The Revolution clearly gave him an opportunity to do just that. Consequently, on this third trip back, which began in September 1789, Napoleon set ambitious aims. He first joined the mob in a clash with the French garrison on the island. This was treason.

Then, working with Joseph, he resisted the cautious tactics of Paoli, now back in Corsica trying to secure for his people the benefits of revolution. Although no one could agree on what these benefits were, it was clear that Paoli held the power on Corsica. Napoleon strove to come to terms with him but fumbled badly. When he first met with Paoli, he offended the revolutionary by critiquing Paoli's military dispositions when he had fought the French on the island in 1768. Then Napoleon wrote a letter to a Corsican delegate in Paris that urged a stronger Corsican stand in favor of the Revolution, in effect criticizing Paoli's leadership. The letter made its way into the hands of Paoli, who reprimanded the young soldier. Napoleon's impetuous actions ensured that the Bonapartes were now at the center of the political intrigue on the island, but how or if they would benefit from this situation remained unclear.

Napoleon extended his leave as long as he could until he had to return to France in February 1791. At this time great changes were occurring in the French army due to the Revolution, developments that would help make his career possible. For one thing, artillery had increased in importance. For another, individual initiative became a praised quality, and Napoleon could expect advancement based on his merit in this regard. Finally, military leadership experimented with a drive toward better organization of the army into self-supporting units, something that would become a norm of Napoleonic warfare. In short, the great changes created previously unfathomable opportunities, especially since larger armies required every available officer.[26]

Napoleon paid no attention as he endured a frugal existence and kept his eyes fixed on Corsica. Determined to seize any opportunity that might present itself there, he was again granted leave, and he set out for the island in September 1791. He met with yet another disappointment when Joseph failed to win election to a local political office. Their ambitions were undone by none other than Paoli, who, not surprisingly considering Napoleon's temerity in 1790, had backed the opposing candidate. Furious, Napoleon took matters into his own hands and had himself elected a lieutenant colonel of the Second Battalion of Corsican Volunteers. In this capacity as a leader of militia, Napoleon would get his first taste of command in the field and yet another lesson in power politics.

Unfortunately for Napoleon, he soon met strong resistance from his fellow Corsicans, as the island's political forces fractured into various groups. The most intractable foe remained Paoli, who now considered inviting English forces to the island to help his army expel the French. Napoleon could not discern the waters clearly. His support of the Revolution, and therefore France, met resistance on the island because the French revolutionary government had adopted an antireligious posture, going so far as to close the monastery there. Now two Corsican groups, comprising most of the island's population, opposed him: those loyal to Paoli, and those devoted to Catholicism. Napoleon soon added a third: the French Army. On April 8, 1792, Napoleon, the man who would capture Moscow within twenty years, attempted to capture the Ajaccio citadel, the fort protecting the island's capital. He led his volunteers against the French garrison, but the attack failed, sputtering to an inglorious end in short order. This was a rash act that assured his place as an enemy of Paoli, who had opposed any such attack, and also placed him in open rebellion against the French on Corsica. The tide had completely shifted, Napoleon's schemes alienating him from all factions on the island.

Napoleon fled to France for safety in May 1792, but living there was also somewhat perilous. He had attacked French forces on Corsica. This was bad enough. Worse, he had not extended his leave during this last sojourn to the island, and even during these turbulent times, the weight of French bureaucracy was in effect. The French War Ministry considered him absent without leave. In short order he had committed an overt act of treason and in the process become a deserter. Only a man willing to gamble everything could have made such errors. His actions to this point suggest that he was convinced that Corsican independence would be at hand if he simply pushed hard enough.[27] He was willing to take the risk, but he had failed. He now had to resurrect his career with his adoptive country.

Fortunately, as much as he had been a victim of revolutionary chaos on Corsica, he now benefited from this same disarray in France. In Paris he met with influential members of the Legislative Assembly and managed to convince them to drop all charges against him, a remarkable feat. He capped this performance by gaining reinstatement to his old unit and a promotion to captain. Only a chaotic situation could explain this turn of events. In June 1792, while still in Paris, Napoleon observed the disintegration of the French political situation firsthand when a Parisian mob sacked the Tuileries Palace and then in August 1792 overthrew the monarchy. Hardly encouraged by this violence, he formed a lasting hatred and fear of mobs.[28] He also understood that the Revolution had become as dangerous as it was potentially profitable. He proceeded more cautiously after witnessing these displays.

Once back with his regiment, he could not stand still as the pace of events quickened. He believed he had to act to seize whatever opportunities arose. Corsica again filled his mind, and he had the audacity to ask for leave yet again to return home. That it was granted again speaks to the confusion rife in the French army. He reached the island in October 1792. Paoli, at this point teaming with the French forces and needing a military man, assigned Napoleon to the modest invasion force gathering on behalf of the Revolution to strike at Piedmont's Sardinia. Paoli's willingness to employ Napoleon is an example of Paoli's political shrewdness as he successfully continued to play all sides. In fact, Paoli had stayed on good terms with Napoleon's mother in the hope of lessening the family's opposition to his policies. Turbulent times made shifting allies.

Napoleon now had the chance at military action he had been craving. But again it fizzled out before it began. As the small flotilla approached its target, a few islands off the Sardinian coast, the commander of the fleet inexplicably ordered a retreat. There would be no attack despite the fact that some French forces already had landed and Napoleon had deployed his guns. Paoli had ordered the expedition's commander to risk nothing, and so this man followed his instructions to the letter. Paoli never had considered Sardinia a threat to Corsica and had opposed the attack as a foolhardy move. His half-hearted effort was meant to appease the French authorities in Paris, nothing more.[29]

Paoli also feared a military hero returning home and competing with him for political control of the island. Clearly, he recognized Napoleon as this potential threat. The utility of aborting the attack became clear after the expedition returned to Corsica and Napoleon's luck ran out at last with Paoli. Incensed that the invasion had been called off, he complained by letter to Paoli. This step made it clear that he considered Paoli a personal enemy, a momentous shift in his thinking in light of his previous admiration for the man. It took a family effort to alienate Paoli completely, however. Unknown to Napoleon, his younger brother, Lucien, safely ensconced at Toulon in southern France, denounced Paoli to local revolutionary activists as a traitor for scheming with the English; his evidence was the aborted attack at Sardinia. His complaint soon made it to the newly established republican government in Paris, the National Convention.

Understanding the folly of this move by his brother, Napoleon wrote the Convention and argued in favor of Paoli. He was too late. That body ordered Corsica's hero arrested. Blaming the Bonapartes for this outrage, the island's populace rallied to Paoli's side. He now moved to break with France, citing the dangerous Bonapartes as evidence of French designs on Corsica. Soon Napoleon was a wanted man on the island, so he and his family fled for the safety of France in June 1793. His dreams of achieving Corsican independence had failed and almost gotten him killed. If this was no surprise, given his eagerness for heroics, the fact that his end almost came from his fellow Corsicans must have upset him. He irrevocably cast his lot with France.

A return to French soil meant a return to garrison duty with one big advantage that had previously been lacking: an opportunity for advancement. As the Revolution gained momentum, France faced numerous threats from abroad. Defeating a foe of the republic could earn one a fast promotion. Napoleon certainly hoped so, and he soon got a chance to do just that. One of the most serious foreign incursions came at the port of Toulon. Here English forces landed and joined ranks with French citizens loyal to the deposed king. The town stood in rebellion to the French revolutionary authorities and boasted a strong garrison of 15,000 English, Spanish, Neapolitan, and Sardinian soldiers fighting alongside its French population. Because of the size of the forces defending Toulon, reclaiming the town for France would not be easy. But it had to be subdued because of the importance of the city as a base for French naval operations in the Mediterranean. Furthermore, the city's defiance and the foreign aid it had received meant that it challenged the very legitimacy of the Revolution. To eradicate this blight, the French government dispatched a sizeable army of some 15,000 men.

Personal connections and a bit of self-promotion would bring Napoleon to Toulon at this opportune time. A fellow Corsican, Cristoforo Saliceti, was one of several figures who oversaw the assault on Toulon on behalf of the Committee of Public Safety, the decision-making arm of the Paris government. As a political appointee, Saliceti enjoyed great latitude when it came to naming commanders to key positions. He now selected Napoleon to serve as a replacement to an injured artillery officer. It was a safe, even wise, decision. Saliceti knew that he and Napoleon shared similar views on the Revolution. They had previously discussed the fate of Corsica in early 1793, and both men agreed that the island's future lay in alliance to France. If Saliceti was aware of Napoleon's earlier plans to free Corsica from French control, this revolutionary official put them out of his mind at the time. Saliceti also needed an artilleryman, and Napoleon possessed these skills as well.

Napoleon made sure Saliceti remembered both of these facts by forwarding to the politician a copy of his literary piece, *Le Souper de Beaucaire* (*Supper at Beaucaire*), a fictional tract that acknowledged French internal divisions but appealed to French solidarity to ward off foreign invaders and so avoid a return to despotism. It was a political advertisement that he was ideologically in step with the Revolution, and it was designed to curry the favor of revolutionary leaders.[30] More than this, it offered a comment on siege warfare by stressing the importance of artillery in such a battle. Saliceti had every reason to believe that Napoleon could not just fill the vacancy in command but be able to help force a decision at the port to win a key battle for the Revolution. Such a victory would make Saliceti look good by validating his selection of Napoleon in the first place.

Napoleon strove to make the most of this opportunity at Toulon. He joined the attacking army in late September 1793, the siege now almost a month old. By the time he arrived, the investing French forces had accomplished almost nothing; they had sealed the city off from the rest of France, but the English navy supplied the fortress with impunity. Another month passed. After familiarizing himself with the terrain, Napoleon recommended in late October to the French commander, Gen. Jean François Carteaux, a plan to capture the city. It was simple enough: drive out the British fleet to complete the isolation of the city and begin a siege. The way to force the withdrawal of the English navy was to control the hill that commanded the harbor, Point L'Eguillette. But Carteaux ignored the plan, and Napoleon found himself repeating it in some detail to the Paris authorities three weeks later.[31] Again no action was taken.

This was but one complication born of the confusion on the French side due to the rise of unqualified revolutionary "generals" such as Carteaux to positions of leadership. The other was a lack of organization. Having vented his frustration about Carteaux's timidity, Napoleon also fretted in his missives to Paris about that man's failure to unify command of the artillery, derisively noting poor gun placement. Individual gun commanders situated their weapons as they pleased. In this state, even if his plan were adopted, he was doubtful that it would succeed. The haphazard deployment of the artillery persisted. The following month, another meddling political officer ordered one of Napoleon's batteries into action prematurely. Napoleon had insisted that this battery remain silent until a coordinated assault on Toulon could be launched. Instead, once discovered, the English sallied forth and overran the position. However, so exposed was this force that the French response, under the watchful eyes of Napoleon, expelled the English from the battery and captured the man leading the attack, the commander of the garrison, British major general Charles O'Hara.

In the aftermath of this engagement, a frustrated Napoleon complained to the minister of war in Paris that the chaos generated by the Revolution had disordered the army to such an extent that he did not have enough officers to direct his guns. In the battle plan he had sent to Paris in late October, he felt compelled to remind the Committee of Public Safety of the importance of artillery in siege warfare. He proposed that it send a senior artillery commander to ensure that this branch of the military be used effectively.[32] Resolving to do this himself, he slowly assembled a siege train, a difficult task by his own admission. What cannons were available were few in number, with Napoleon counting two 24-pounders, two 16-pounders, and two mortars as well as a few field guns. He soon requisitioned eight guns from the nearby Army of Italy (a French field army), as well as an abundance of ammunition. He lacked equipment of all descriptions, so he dispatched a trusted man to secure axes and spades from Grenoble and Valence and wagons from Lyons. Still needed were pontoon bridges, signal rockets, and incendiary shells, so he sent this same man back to Lyons in search of these items. But finding cannon and other materials proved only the first phase. Transporting this equipment to the city became the next task. Napoleon demanded horses from Nice, Valence, Montpellier, and Marseilles to drag the weapons to the city. He next created a base camp near Toulon at Ollioules to house the technicians and materials needed to keep his artillery functioning. Finally, he commandeered lumber from La Seyne sur Mer and La Ciotat, and he ordered sandbags to be made in Marseilles to construct mortar platforms and protect gun emplacements. By early December he boasted a siege train of 200 guns, 11 batteries alone directed against the key position of L'Eguillette. It was a swift and important step toward ending the siege.

Weapons still needed a plan to put them to good use. Since he had been rebuffed by the commanding officer, Napoleon had to wait almost two months—an eternity for the impatient Corsican—before seeing his plan realized. A new commander, Gen. Jean François Dugommier, a professional soldier, recognized the merit of the attack at once. It was formally adopted on November 25, 1793. In the meantime the English had recognized their vulnerability and reacted swiftly, reinforcing and fortifying L'Eguillette. Now implementing the plan became much more difficult. An infantry assault presaged heavy losses unless Napoleon's newly created artillery arm could prepare the way and minimize casualties. Other diversionary bombardments and feints would hopefully distract the garrison.

On December 17, 1793, the French attacked. Soon the key hill was in their hands but not without difficulty. Napoleon was slightly wounded in the thigh, but his personal bravery had much to do with the success, since he directed the placement of the guns that now commanded the harbor.[33] The English admitted defeat, evacuating the city the next day. French forces entered Toulon on December 19.

Thus the wisdom of his plan had come to fruition. Perhaps the greatest significance of Napoleon's success at Toulon was that this battle meant that he had now come to the attention of important political leaders in Paris. This could be both good and bad, and the ebb and flow of Napoleon's career over the next few years reflected the volatile times. First, his benefactors in Paris, notably Augustin Robespierre—brother of the virtual dictator of France, Maximilien Robespierre—ordered him to inspect the coastal defenses in southern France to rebuff potential English landings of the sort that had occurred at Toulon. Conducting a thorough review, Napoleon declared the defenses lacking and did much to improve them. Other tasks produced more complications, however. Augustin sought his advice regarding French invasion plans in Italy. Napoleon soon authored a series of battle plans but presented them in such a brusque manner that he offended many, including Saliceti. When the Robespierre clique fell from power a short time later, Saliceti, no doubt remembering this slight, ordered Napoleon's arrest. Many such Jacobin generals faced similar treatment or, worse, execution. But the charges against Napoleon did not hold. In fact, Saliceti soon faced his own inquisitors, and his fall from power helped ease the case against Napoleon.

Released after two weeks of confinement, Napoleon now had to chart a return to favor and do so without knowing exactly who were his benefactors, let alone his enemies. The new leaders of the Committee of Public Safety looked to checkmate this obviously ambitious soldier by sending him to the Army of the West, a military force whose principle duty was distasteful: suppressing a revolt in the Vendée in western France. But Napoleon ached for command in the field, and this position assured him at least a brigade of his own. On the other hand, he hesitated to accept the post because he did not want to make a reputation killing Frenchmen. Moreover, he understood that Gen. Louis-Lazare Hoche, commander of the Army of the West, had largely succeeded in ending the rebellion. There was little glory to be gained on this front, requiring only some mopping-up operations. Yet Napoleon had to figure that turning down the appointment might incur the wrath of those now in power and possibly land him in jail again or cause a sterner rebuke in the form of a sentence to the guillotine. He stepped carefully.

Napoleon decided to accept the position but remain in Paris as long as he could. Perhaps the changing political tides would net him a reprieve from the Vendée assignment and land him something better. Pleading illness, he dallied in the capital throughout the summer of 1795. By early fall a new assignment did come: an appointment to the army's Topographical Bureau. The bureau served as a planning staff answerable to the Committee of Public Safety, so the new assignment was a blessing to him. Now Napoleon could remain in Paris indefinitely and keep a close eye on the events of the fast moving Revolution. He was in a fairly enviable position from where he could be recognized for high command or for more overtly political assignments that might help bring him the military fame and social advancement he craved.

The latter came before the former. Fortunately for Napoleon, several individuals were now scheming to control the government in France, and many of these men viewed him as a potential tool to be used on their behalf; a military man could help them secure political power if he could be controlled. Napoleon soon demonstrated his usefulness to the satisfaction of Paul François Jean Nicolas, vicomte de Barras, the latest strongman to emerge in the tumultuous revolution. Barras summoned Napoleon in October 1795 and ordered him to help defend the government located in the Tuileries Palace from the Parisian mob. Having witnessed the mobs' overthrow of the king in 1792, Napoleon accepted this order and soon positioned cannon to defend some of the most obvious approaches to the palace. The mob, perhaps 80,000 strong and including sizeable detachments of national guardsmen, posed a great threat. When it moved his way and approached his strong point, he ordered the guns to open fire, killing at least 1,400 men and women. The throng stopped in its tracks and dispersed. Napoleon was a hero to Barras and to a few others for helping to save the government, and the "whiff of grapeshot" soon won him promotion to general and command of the Army of the Interior.[34]

With this ugly spectacle, it was clear that Napoleon had arrived. The Corsican now tried his hand at politics, an endeavor that soon produced surprisingly positive results. Staying close to Barras, the man dominating the new revolutionary government, the Directory, Napoleon quickly developed an attachment to one of his mistresses, Marie Rose de Beauharnais. This woman, soon renamed Josephine by Napoleon, was a survivor, much like her Corsican suitor. A woman of humble nobility in title and means, one who had escaped the wrath of the Terror even as her husband was guillotined, she remained viable in high social circles by presenting herself to powerful men. Although Barras was her latest provider, he noticed the attachment his new general had for her and welcomed the match, presiding at their hastily arranged wedding. Napoleon and Josephine's union was unlikely in several ways, most notably in the increasingly upward trajectory of Napoleon's career compared to the fading beauty—and therefore means—of Josephine. But Napoleon hardly noticed, pursued her tirelessly, and was proud to have her as his wife. Only slowly would Josephine return this affection. But she offered Napoleon support in another way once her two children, Eugène and Hortense, came under his sway. If only his by marriage, they would provide Napoleon with support in the future, often surpassing that of his brothers and sisters. He would need whatever help he could muster, because his original aim of remaining in Paris near Barras soon paid the dividend he most sought: command of an army in the field. The general was to have his chance at military fame after all.

SHAKY BEGINNINGS

The gruesome spectacle of Napoleon ordering his soldiers to fire on the Parisian crowd appears to put great distance between him and Washington. Yet Napoleon's hatred of mobs was shared by Washington, whose own violent demonstration against such rabble would come after he became president and rode with the army once more to put down the Whiskey Rebellion in 1794, the year before Napoleon's assault on the Paris mob. The uprising that Washington faced fizzled out with almost no bloodshed, but again the shared outlook on mobs and the military steps they took to deal with them are pronounced and similar.

Both men's inauspicious first tastes of battle and command were littered with the mistakes and misjudgments of youth. Napoleon's first command resulted in a defeat so bad that he was forced to flee from Corsica. This is to say nothing of his poor judgment. He undertook the endeavor to free Corsica from French tyranny while absent from his French military post. Only the chaos afflicting the French army prevented it from tracking his whereabouts and singling him out for court-martial. It was due to the turbulence of revolutionary times that he was able to regain his post back in France and even secure a promotion; France needed officers. Not content with having escaped this trouble, Napoleon again took up the cause of Corsican independence. His brief time soldiering on Paoli's behalf ended badly as well. The Bonapartes alienated the island population to such a point that he and his entire family had to flee to France for safety. He had gambled and lost. The full measure of his failure lay in the need to find safety in a country tearing itself apart in revolution. That France was safer for him than his native Corsica speaks volumes.

Napoleon's military defeat at Ajaccio, his uneventful seaborne invasion of Sardinia, and his two flights from Corsica in fear of his life all indicate a rash youth recklessly seeking to advance his military career and earn his way to greater stature in life. His first two battles were small ones. Toulon presented him with a greater opportunity, and indeed he helped organize the French defenses to successfully end the siege. His personal bravery also helped spell success. But his tendency to promote himself in writing to all those who could help him, both in getting his chance at Toulon and in adopting his plan to force out the English fleet, also manifested itself. In this sense he was as self-promoting as Washington, who published his journal of his diplomatic mission to the Ohio Valley, even if it was Lieutenant Governor Dinwiddie who insisted on its publication. The acclaim Washington earned for this act was substantial. Moreover, Napoleon's local troops on Corsica were akin to the colonial militia Washington had commanded in Virginia. And, much like Washington, Napoleon was a local man of stature who could wield just enough influence to be elected to a position of military leadership.

Washington fumbled his first mission in the wilderness as he needlessly antagonized potential allies and galvanized longtime foes. He compounded diplomatic errors with military ineptitude when his expedition met humiliation at Fort Necessity. It was a bad combination. While he gave a better account of himself during Braddock's disastrous advance the following year, Washington's contributions to England's military excursions along the Virginian frontier put himself and his colony in great danger. Yet he undertook these risks willingly. He, like Napoleon, was an ambitious youth, unsatisfied with his station in life. Each man saw in the military a way to advance in society. Both men capitalized on family connections in an attempt to gain entrance into the upper echelons of society. True, their first commands ended in failure and for similar reasons: their egos had led them to overreach themselves. But, more than ego, they shared a desperate motivation to make something of themselves in societies that otherwise promised limited opportunity for men of their station.

Significantly, both men learned that defeat could paradoxically elevate their military careers. Washington was dubiously christened a hero in Virginia early on but earned this label when defending that colony in 1755 and 1756. Napoleon, a bit wiser after his failed adventures in Corsica, made good use of his opportunity at Toulon. While brash dreams of military glory had not come to fruition at this point in their lives, both would get what they wanted from a military career: social advancement, respect, and eventual political power.

2

A TRIED AND TESTED FORMULA
In Search of Decisive Victory

I n centuries past, a number of generals have made the transition from the battlefield to the field of government. Napoleon Bonaparte's personal hero, Julius Caesar, had been such a statesman. After George Washington and Napoleon, men such as Simón Bolívar, Antonio López de Santa Anna, and Sam Houston would emulate the general-statesman path these two towering giants blazed. It remains a popular route to political power, a chance for military men to fulfill their ambition and achieve lasting acclaim. For Washington, one war would cement his reputation in the eyes of his fellow citizens. He would ride this fame to the presidency. Napoleon's wars proved too numerous to follow this path. The irony was that after gaining his throne, Napoleon risked more with each successive battlefield victory—his army, his empire, his seat of power. In the end, his ambition undid his military career, and his empire came crashing down about him. Ultimately, it mattered most which general best understood his strategic necessities and could use that understanding to survive. Washington did not win his war so much as he persevered to its end. Napoleon won many wars but could not survive the totality of the conflict of the age he did so much to create. In the results of each man's actions sits the true measure of success and failure on the battlefield, a reckoning that ultimately favors Washington.

WASHINGTON

In the United States, Washington's reputation as a general is equal to his reputation as the father of his country. He was commander in chief during the Revolutionary War and during his presidency, and following the XYZ Affair in the late 1790s, which strained relations between the United States and France, he was appointed "Lieutenant General and Commander in Chief of all the armies raised, or to be raised in the service of the U.S.," a post he would hold until his death.[1] When he died in the winter of 1799, his countrymen gave him a soldier's funeral. Militiamen marched behind his riderless horse accompanied by muffled drums, fife dirges, and the spectacle of artillery salutes. There were probably more cannon fired upon Washington's death than he himself could muster in many of his military campaigns. Lest there be any confusion as to Washington's stature in the pantheon of American military history, two centuries later in 1976, as the nation celebrated the bicentennial of the Declaration of Independence, Congress posthumously named him General of the Armies of the United States by passing Public Law 94-479, declaring Washington's precedence over all other grades of the army, past or present. This appointment ensured he outranked some distinguished names of the past, including General of the Armies of the United States John Pershing and Generals of the Army Dwight D. Eisenhower and Douglas MacArthur. Thus, Washington will forever remain the highest-ranking general in the history of the United States.

Americans are still taught that Washington epitomizes the American citizen-general: the selfless farmer called away from his plow at great personal sacrifice and who returned to the farm when the crisis abated. This simplification deserves more scrutiny, given his pivotal role in forging the United States through battle. The early part of Washington's military career was marked by a mixture of failure and success in the wilds of western Virginia. During the Revolutionary War, however, Washington came into his own as a military leader. While he frequently acted as though he were completely unaware of the limitations of his army, he was able to grasp two fundamental aspects of the American campaign. First, Washington came to realize that strategic realities in the English colonies dictated the consequences of all tactical success and failure. Second, Washington eventually embraced the strength of his army. Unlike European armies, the Continental Army was not the military expression of a monarch's divine right to rule. Rather, it was the personification of a uniquely American definition of sovereignty as that of self-rule. When belief in the American cause was strong, support for the army and, consequently, troop levels ran high. When there was doubt about the chance for this self-declared nation to succeed, troop levels and support for the army were low. As time wore on, Washington accepted the centrality of the army to the cause—that the army was the embodiment of that cause. He realized that it was wiser to have the army in the field avoiding battle than it was to risk it in a cataclysmic engagement, since, with his army intact, the war would continue until the strategic soundness of his position handed him victory.

Washington had come to the cause of American independence as the inevitable outcome of his sense of self-importance. He spent the late 1760s trying to capitalize on the just-completed Seven Years' War by laying claim to the best tracts of land in what could be new colonies. But after defeating the French, Parliament passed a number of acts to recoup the costs of that expensive war. Washington grew alarmed by how the empire could restrict the financial freedom of those in the colonies. The apparent arbitrary nature of these acts led him to rally against the Crown. By 1774 Washington was convinced that Parliament was attempting to "fix the Shackles of Slavery upon us." Acknowledging his growing role in the movement against Parliament, Virginia's House of Burgesses sent Washington to the First Continental Congress in 1774.[2]

From one success came another. The Continental Congress appointed Washington to the top post in the army in June 1775, and the Virginian expressed humble gratitude for the opportunity in light of what he admitted were his limited qualifications. But Washington had reported to that assembly in his military uniform, a message lost on no one. He wanted the command. His impressive attire combined with his imposing physical presence ensured his nomination, the self-effacing comments he uttered primarily underscoring his assumed role: that he only reluctantly accepted such an important position.[3] All parties present understood the act. All parties probably failed to realize that the act captured the reality a little too accurately. Washington was ill-fit for the command in many ways, but the Continental

Congress had limited choices. His selection was a risk worth taking, both politically (he represented the largest colony, thereby giving credibility to the still-blossoming cause) and militarily (even with his limitations, he was still one of the most experienced commanders the colonials could find). While circumstance and necessity defined this exchange, so too did Washington. At the time of the Revolution, he was the same man he had always been, still seeking to reach the pinnacle of colonial society. Only this time the stakes had dramatically increased as Washington now played at being a general and thereby risked the well being of the nation he hoped to forge. This fight was not purely ideological; this was for personal success as well and the ends justified the means. The opportunity that military command afforded him was that of leading this struggle, allowing him to gain the admiration of his peers and secure personal advancement.

From the moment Washington took command of the rebel army outside Boston in July 1775, he had the opportunity to display a trait essential to his success as a general. During the siege, Washington molded the band of New England militias and those from other colonies into a semiprofessional fighting force, eventually forming a core group he would command for years to come. Of course, the siege also gave Washington ample time to display some of the brashness, impatience, and poor tactical judgment that had been his trademark as a militia colonel. Regardless, Boston appeared to be a stunning success, and in fact it was, although the victory came with its share of good fortune.

By the time Washington arrived in camp that July, the initial military engagements of the Boston campaign were for the most part over. The clashes at Lexington and Concord outside Boston in April 1775 had left the English confined to the city, besieged by a hastily formed American army. The English had tested this cordon in June by striking at Breed's Hill, a strongpoint that overlooked the Charles River and Charlestown and therefore dominated the northern approaches to Boston. The British commander, Gen. Thomas Gage, ordered a headlong assault on the prepared American breastworks to take this important high ground. Facing the relentless and well-aimed fire of the American militia under the command of Col. William Prescott, the British advanced, broke, rallied, advanced again, broke again, rallied again, and finally stormed the entrenchments, taking the hill on the third try. All told, in what became known as the Battle of Bunker Hill, the British suffered a total of 1,150 casualties, including some 220 killed; the Americans had 441 total casualties with only 115 killed. Since the losses amounted to more than forty percent of the attacking force of 2,500, it was the textbook definition of a Pyrrhic victory. The British could not go on "winning" such damaging battles and expect to keep their army intact in Boston, let alone subdue the colonies.

Because of Gage's inability to close the Boston wound, Prime Minister Frederick North, 2nd Earl of Guilford, sacked him soon after the Breed's Hill debacle. Gen. William Howe, the officer who had led the British assault on that strongpoint, succeeded Gage as overall commander in October. He was soon joined by his brother, Adm. Richard Howe, in charge of naval operations in America and also serving as peace commissioner to the colonies. Admiral Howe's mission was to de-escalate the conflict. Both he and his brother outwardly expressed confidence in ending this war, but how they intended to do so—by employing military force or attempting reconciliation—was less clear in their minds. In fact, when facing the rebels, this confusion of purpose continued to plague these two men, and a timid approach or at least a hesitancy to act with certainty arose on frequent occasions, inhibiting their ability to defeat the Americans.

This hesitancy was present from the start. General Howe's reluctance to risk a repeat of Breed's Hill meant that the British had little intention of coming out of the city to fight. Consequently, they would give Washington nearly a year to create a force capable of survival against the British. The Americans could count themselves lucky that their enemy had decided against another assault on the colonial army that ringed the city, because such an offensive would have almost surely succeeded in routing the poorly trained militia force, despite the results of Breed's Hill. There were too many American weak points that would have led to a break in the siege should the English attack. But the British did not come, and Washington benefited tremendously from this fact.

Once in camp, Washington was dismayed by the quality of this "Continental Army," described by one historian as "a frighteningly inept mass of humanity."[4] First, it was continental only in name. The regiments in attendance were solely from New England, and since most of the troops came from local areas, they were difficult to keep at their posts when the siren calls of home and hearth were just miles away. Second, since there were no uniforms, those regiments consisting supposedly of regulars were indistinguishable from the colonial militia that was also helping to hold the line. Washington must have found this fact particularly troublesome. This was, after all, the same man who took pride in the buff-and-blue uniform of his own Virginia regiment, which he himself had designed. Third, the vast majority of his New Englanders possessed an independent streak that led them to elect their own junior officers in some cases. This practice was popular but terribly prone to abuse. Rather than enforcing necessary military discipline, officers elected were more likely to give orders that curried favor with their soldiers. Here was an example of a revolutionary practice that would cause real hardships if pitched fighting broke out during the siege, a very likely possibility. The appointment of senior officers by Congress and by various state governors proved just as problematic. Washington would have none of this revolutionary morass and made introducing proper discipline and subordination the first order of business. He proved mostly successful in shaping the maturation of junior officers and in purging the worst of the congressional appointments.[5]

While it appears obvious in retrospect that the Continental Army required discipline and officers who were not beholden to their men through elections, it was not so to the men serving under Washington's command. The rank and file who met Washington at Boston consisted of some of the same men who had turned back the British at the battles of Lexington and Concord. These were revolutionary soldiers fighting under the banner of liberty, and Washington faced a great challenge imposing his will upon them, which he met by striving to rule his army with a firm hand. He prohibited gambling in camp. The latrines in the encampment bore special attention. Before Washington's arrival, it was common for open pits to be used throughout the American positions. Seeing the possibility for spreading illness, Washington made sure these latrines were covered up. In what would appear to be an obvious move towards professionalism, Continental soldiers were no longer permitted to make conversation with British sentries on the other side of the lines. Another serious problem that had eluded the elected officers was a lack of paperwork. Consequently, Washington's army had only a general idea of how many muskets, how much powder, and the quantity of other resources it possessed. Washington made great efforts to ensure that his quartermaster kept pace with the army's needs, a monumental task. To make such regulations stick, the general threatened his soldiers with prison when paperwork was completed late or improperly. Recognizing these issues was not necessarily the mark of a good general, but enforcing the changes was, and Washington did this, clearly establishing him as a general capable of leading. He took the title His Excellency, a sign to that band of militia around Boston that Washington intended to lead a European-type fighting force.[6] Creating this army was a crucial first success.

The experience at Boston also gave Washington ample time to nearly squander his opportunity of command by committing tactical blunders. These arose from a combination of circumstances. Only a few months after he had arrived, Washington faced the troublesome problem of his men's enlistment status. Most were on short-term assignment and did not intend to stay in camp past the date of their enlistment. If the great majority of his militiamen returned home at the end of 1775, Washington would be forced to start anew with his training efforts, just as it seemed he was making progress instilling discipline and martial skill. Even if he could find new men and quickly forge them into a fighting force, what did such rotation say of his ability to keep the British at bay, let alone to force them out of Boston? This siege, and possibly the Revolution, could end in the New Year, should the British emerge from the city and test his new army or should England remain in control of Boston indefinitely. Either way his command, and with it the Revolution, would be discredited and the cause of independence dealt a fatal blow.

The need to act before most of his army returned home prompted Washington to put forward an operation that had all the hallmarks of a failure in the making. In September Washington proposed to his officers and representatives of Congress that the army launch a frontal assault on the strong British works guarding the Boston Neck, the isthmus connecting Boston town to Roxbury. While his main force was assaulting this position, other units would use whaleboats to perform amphibious landings nearby to flank the English lines. If he could procure the necessary artillery, he would bombard Boston from the unoccupied Dorchester Heights to the southeast. With the prospect of destroying Boston—the spiritual center of the Revolution—with such an artillery barrage, Congress, not unexpectedly, delayed a decision until December 22. By then, Washington's troops had begun to melt away as their enlistments ended, and he had insufficient troops to mount such an attack. The delay was fortunate since the attack would have almost surely failed. It was the inaction of Congress that saved Boston and probably the Revolution itself.

Not content to remain idle, Washington proposed a new plan of attack in January 1776. By then, his force was significantly smaller, numbering perhaps 8,500 Continental regulars supplemented by some militia troops. On the positive side of the ledger, Henry Knox had arrived with cannon from the captured Fort Ticonderoga, although the army lacked the powder to make much use of them. Washington cared little. Tired of waiting after nearly a year of stalemate, he virtually harangued his officers into accepting the necessity of taking Boston by storm. The plan, however, again showed Washington's tactical shortcomings. This time Washington would send the army attacking to the west of the city across Boston's Back Bay, which was frozen solid, and flank the British positions defending the Boston Neck. Washington estimated that the Continental Army's strength of 16,000 men would be more than enough to attack the 5,000 British soldiers he claimed defended Boston at the time. His plan called for the artillery to remain mostly silent, since the guns were too short of powder to conduct effective fire support. In a reversal from his previous plan, he now dismissed the importance of his artillery, claiming it would only harm the town and not do much damage to the British garrison. In sum, Washington's daring attack would rely on his unseasoned troops executing a complicated plan over ice without artillery support. It was pure Washington, a plan full of diversion and complication to the point of folly. It also inflated his capabilities and minimized those of the enemy. Although Washington's own troop level neared 12,600, Howe had closer to 9,000, rather than the 5,000 troops Washington claimed garrisoned Boston. His plan was a formula for disaster.[7]

On February 16 he put the plan to a council of war. The result was not what he had hoped. Gen. Horatio Gates put a fine head on the issue, stating, "Our Defeat, may risque the entire loss of the Liberties of America forever."[8] Gates had been a major in the British army during the Seven Years' War and had served admirably with the ill-fated Braddock expedition. This veteran officer seemingly already understood what Washington would learn soon after this campaign. This army, Washington's army, was all the Americans had. If it were routed, captured, or otherwise destroyed in an attack on Boston, there would be no more revolution. There was too much at strategic peril to risk a tactical failure. That Washington had considered such a foolish offensive twice shows his continuing bent toward tactical remedies beyond his material means. Although he became a better general as his army became better trained, his true contribution to the Revolution would be his ability to keep his force in the field, often in spite of his own inclinations. Good fortune would serve him well in this respect.

Although his council had vetoed Washington's original attack plan, it agreed to a more limited attack, one within the army's capabilities. On the night of March 4, 1776, he seized Dorchester Heights. The British awoke the next morning to see American breastworks there bristling with cannon aimed at their fleet. Howe at once ordered an attack to take the heights, and an eerie repetition of Breed's Hill loomed. Bad weather forced the attack's delay and then its cancellation; too much time elapsed for the British to consider the attack possible without frightful casualties. Washington's limited offensive soon proved decisive, since the British realized that having forfeited this high ground, they could no longer supply their army with impunity via the sea. The English saw little need to remain in the port anyway, a revolutionary center and a location where it was hard for them to act decisively. Instead, they evacuated the city and retired to Halifax in Nova Scotia to lick their wounds and develop a strategy for ending the war. Still, claiming the strategic initiative was a far cry from claiming victory, something Washington could do since he now entered Boston in triumph. It was a singular accomplishment.[9]

The British evacuation of Boston was a shrewd move in that it presented the colonials with a question regarding their military strategy: where would the enemy strike next? Targets could be found up and down the long American coastline, and the British command of the sea was nearly complete. They could attack with impunity virtually anywhere they wished. Still, there was one area that both sides recognized as vital to winning the war, and that was New York City. This site had all the markings of a strategic lynchpin, since it was one of the largest colonial cities and the seat of American commerce. It also functioned as a gateway to the Hudson River valley. If the British controlled access to the Hudson and advanced up that river, they would be able to split the American colonies in two, separating New England from the other colonies. Recognizing this potential, Washington had sent Charles Lee to take command of New York's defenses in February 1776, a good month before the British evacuated Boston. Lee was a good choice as, along with Gates, he was one of the few American officers who had experience in the British army. That he had dispatched Lee so early to make plans to hold New York was evidence of Washington's growing strategic ability.

By April Lee had devised a plan to defend the city. While it pleased Washington, historians have found it lacking.[10] The plan called for the colonials to establish a series of entrenched positions scattered about Manhattan and Long Island. Nearly all these positions were vulnerable to a flanking movement on land and therefore subject to isolation. Furthermore, the Americans lacked the artillery necessary to defend against British naval advances in the various rivers and bays that surrounded the islands. If the British attacked, they would surely flank and therefore overrun the American positions, because at the very least, they would be able to make amphibious assaults behind the American lines. For the moment, however, the British remained in Halifax, and Lee continued planning his defense.

At this point in the war, Washington still sought a repeat of Breed's Hill, where the British had slammed their forces upon American breastworks, wasting valuable troop strength. Such a tactical defensive engagement would at worst create another Pyrrhic victory for Howe. Of course, the British leader would do everything in his power to avoid spending his superior military strength on such harmful attacks, preserving the army for a decisive battle. That Washington thought he could goad the British into relinquishing this caution seems foolhardy, but to a great extent that was his expectation and this mind-set shaped his strategy when defending New York. Washington did not realize his positions designed to win a tactical engagement in New York meant that any such victory would need to rely more upon British arrogance than colonial defensive engineering. The British command was running low on arrogance, at least at this time.

His confidence in securing this outcome explains his lack of concern when word came that the remnants of Benedict Arnold's American army, sent to Canada the preceding winter to take Quebec, were retiring down the Hudson River with a British invasion force following closely behind. Then from Halifax, General Howe sent a poorly supplied British force of 9,000 men to New York on June 11. He himself arrived off Staten Island on July 2, quickly causing the retreat of the small American garrison there. On July 9 Washington learned that because of reinforcement, the British army in the New York area now numbered at least 25,000 men, with fresh stores and supplies coming in very short order. Dividing the colonies in half appeared to be the British objective. Washington was unfazed by this possibility, predicting that the British "will have to wade through much blood & Slaughter before they can carry any part of our Works, If they carry 'em at all, and at best be in possession of a melancholy and mournful victory."[11] The American general expected the battle for New York to be exactly what he wanted it to be: an encounter where the British wasted themselves on American breastworks, leading to an American success that would redeem the deteriorating strategic picture.

Washington's New York campaign would not be a repeat of Breed's Hill, however. Instead, it was a virtual rout of Washington's forces, producing a crisis of the first magnitude. From the moment of the first British landings on Long Island on August 22, a move that signaled a general offensive in the region, Washington's defensive plans went to pieces. After the British attacked, Washington committed the American army to the defense of the island, and the battle was on in earnest by August 27. The British easily turned the dangerously exposed flank of the American position fronting Brooklyn Heights, and the fleeing colonials exacted little in the way of British blood.

The collapse of the American defenses left Washington and the remnants of his command clinging to the heights, trapped between the advancing British in front of them and the East River to their rear. Under the direction of some junior officers who looked to close the noose around the Americans, the British army approached by land and the British navy from the water side. As luck would have it, however, Washington was spared. Howe pulled back his junior officers and his men and did not deliver a fatal blow to the

Continental Army; he would not risk another Breed's Hill. Instead, wishing to save the bulk of his force, he laid siege to the heights. When rain started on the evening of August 27 and continued for two days, it produced what historian David McCullough called a "providential" fog, a cover so thick that it allowed Washington to quietly retreat across the East River to Manhattan on August 29, escaping undetected with his much-depleted army.[12] The American commander had been swiftly and soundly beaten, his soldiers nearly captured. Yet his concept of a Breed's Hill–type battle had come true in a way, although certainly not how he had imagined or hoped.

Deprived of his entrenchment strategy and now fully aware of his dangerously exposed position, Washington struggled to set things right. He looked to stand and fight in upper Manhattan at Harlem Heights, surrendering New York City without a fight and resisting Gen. Nathanael Greene's call to burn the city. He did follow Greene's advice to mount a defense that required him to separate his forces in the face of a numerically superior enemy. Howe soon took advantage, isolating and destroying Greene's command at Fort Washington and then threatening the remnants of Washington's army with encirclement. A short time later, Washington embarked on another desperate retreat, abandoning the New York theater of operations altogether.

Certainly it was through little more than good fortune that Washington was able to retreat with his forces first to Manhattan, then into New Jersey, and finally across that state to the Delaware River, where he withdrew into Pennsylvania. It was a low point in the war. Washington had had 20,000 men on the rolls in New York to Howe's 25,000. Against entrenched defenses, Howe should have been forced to expend more men and effort to displace these troops. In the right location, Washington could have achieved his Breed's Hill or something close to it. Making a stand on Long Island against the British army was clearly difficult, but Washington's actions revealed his continued tactical shortcomings. Lacking an eye for choosing key tactical terrain, the defenses he prepared were wholly inadequate for the battles he sought. His only redemption came through miraculous retreat.

From this low soon came a high. Washington's campaign in New Jersey conducted during the winter of 1776–1777 has become something of a legend. After his disastrous New York campaign and the dash to bring the army to safety, few suspected that Washington had much fight left in him. Howe surely did not think so. He settled the British army into dispersed encampments in and around New York, well separated from one another but in places surprisingly close to the Americans just across the river. It could prove a dangerous situation if the Americans sallied forth and attacked one of the exposed British garrisons, but Howe did not expect such an attack. For him, the year's campaign was over. For Washington, it had just begun. The campaign Washington envisioned that winter was not driven by tactical aims but by strategic ones. For the first time, Washington would show his understanding of the strategic needs of the American cause and set his tactical deployments to match this larger aim.

When Howe put his army in winter quarters, it was December 1776. Part of the reasoning behind the British halt was weighing heavily on Washington's thinking as well. In but a few short weeks, the American army would once again dissolve due to expiring enlistments. For Howe, this circumstance meant that after the devastating blow he had dealt Washington in New York, he could simply wait for the remaining American soldiers to lay down their arms and go home. From his point of view, the revolution was nearly at an end. Washington believed otherwise. He meant to act before his army turned from soldiers back into farmers at the stroke of midnight on December 31, like some sort of nightmarish fairy tale.

His plan was as bold as it was necessary. He would attack the British encampment at Trenton, New Jersey. Washington knew the stakes of this attack. If he did nothing, the Revolution would probably not survive to the spring of 1777. If he attacked and failed, then his force would in all probability break up days later, and that would be the end of the Revolution as well. However, if he defeated any British force, he might buoy the sentiments of the colonials and keep his army together. Here Washington consciously tied the fate of the Continental Army to that of the Revolution. Learning from the failures of the New York campaign, Washington accepted that his army must remain in the field, a fighting force challenging British arms so that the Revolution could continue. It was a gamble: an attack in the dead of winter that demanded tactical success. But Washington reasoned he had no choice if the American cause were to endure. The general sent orders to his officers outlining the attack. The password for that night was "Victory or Death."[13]

Crossing the Delaware River during the late evening of Christmas Day, Washington's 6,000 troops surprised the British Hessian garrison at Trenton early on December 26. The Germans offered little resistance, and Washington captured 893 of them while losing only 2 of his own men. Using the victory as a springboard, Washington paid a bounty to any man who would stay another month with the army. His appeal netted a favorable response. With 6,500 men, he marched on Princeton and won a significant engagement there when the Americans drove several British regiments from the battlefield and occupied the town. It had been a good campaign. Washington had achieved his objective of sustaining the Revolution through military action and in the process had proven to be tactically capable.[14] He was maturing as a general.

In the next phase of the war, Washington would continue to team his sound strategic thinking with a newly acquired tactical adequacy and mount the campaign that the American theater demanded. Instead of seeking to entice the British into assaulting his defensive positions so that the enemy won only a Pyrrhic victory, he looked to another ancient model, that of Quintus Fabius Maximus Verrucosus Cunctator, also know as Fabius the Delayer. Fabius Maximus won his military fame by defeating Rome's archenemy, Hannibal. Having witnessed two great Roman defeats, Fabius refused battle, looking simply to outlast the Carthaginians, who were fighting far from home. The plan was not necessarily popular with the Romans, but Fabius, serving as a temporary dictator, had his way, and the strategy worked. Hannibal, unable to force an end to the conflict and facing a deteriorating strategic situation that undermined his previous tactical successes and any potential new success, eventually quit Italy. Notably, when the crisis had passed and Fabius's term as dictator ended, he restored consular government.

Washington's tactically successful campaign in New Jersey in January of 1777 now placed him in a similar position to that of Fabius centuries before. The American general had proved to be a commander who could fight and win. But after the New York debacle in 1776, Washington asked Congress to make changes to the American military structure. He wanted to end the one-year enlistments and pass legislation to keep an American army permanently in the field. This demand clashed with those patriots who believed that militia was the best tool to fight this war, but without such a change, Washington believed the cause was doomed. Additionally, he argued that it was unreasonable to send every request governing the army's actions the great distance to Congress for debate. He needed more freedom of movement and more control over military affairs within his sphere of operations. The general also wanted to extend his power into the civilian domain, including the authority to arrest suspected loyalists or those who would not resupply his army.

After Washington's successes in New Jersey, Congress relented. For a time equal in length to the term of a Roman dictator—six months—it granted him broad authority over the lives and property of Americans of all stripes. Congress may not have agreed that his new authority constituted a dictatorship, but some army officers did, and they favored the action so that Washington could ensure the survival of the army.[15] The limitless military authority granted here provided an ominous sign that would resurface at war's end. For the moment, such fears were unfounded. In the late spring of 1777, when his authority expired, Washington relinquished his temporary powers, expressing satisfaction with the newly trained army he now commanded.

With this quality force, Washington set out to enact what John Adams openly called a Fabian strategy.[16] The army was to avoid a pitched battle but still be kept in the field harassing the enemy. However, Washington had not completely accepted the Fabian rationale, deviating from this approach once it became clear that Howe's main objective that year was the American capital. Philadelphia was not easy to defend, and there was really very little purpose in doing so. In the previous year, when it appeared the British would capture Philadelphia, Congress simply abandoned it for the safer Baltimore and were willing to do so again. Both sides understood that the city's loss would not deal a crippling blow to the American cause. Still, when the British advanced to take Philadelphia, Washington mounted a spirited defense at Brandywine Creek and Germantown. It appears that in so doing, he hoped to test his army—and his own ability—more than he looked to hold the city. In fact, at Brandywine, he sent the army's baggage train far to the rear to ensure that it was not captured.[17] And he did not mount a last-ditch defense of Philadelphia. When on September 26 the British took that city, Washington's troops were over forty miles away, too exhausted to contest its fall. While Washington achieved only mixed results when defending

Philadelphia, the more important strategic reality of the Fabian nature of his campaign remained intact, and the war continued.[18]

Retiring to winter quarters at Valley Forge led to another trying time for the American army. Congress had not seen properly to its needs, and thus the men were undersupplied and forced to endure much hardship. Some things had gone right that year, however. At Brandywine Washington had lost the battle but preserved the bulk of his army, a triumph of sorts in light of the initial English success at again turning his flank. At Germantown American troops had gone on the offensive and stood toe-to-toe with British regulars, proving that the commander in chief's improvements to his army were having a positive effect and that his own generalship was getting better as well. Moreover, General Gates had captured an entire British army at Saratoga in eastern upstate New York, giving the Patriot cause a much-needed boost of confidence.

Gates's success in the North in 1777 produced trouble for Washington. After this victory, many in Congress advocated for Gates to supersede Washington as commander in chief. This rumbling became known as the Conway Cabal after Thomas Conway, an Irishman who had served in the French army and was now a major general in the Continental army. He had written to Congress on behalf of Gates suggesting this change. It had been a key moment, as Washington's continual deference to civilian authority threatened to undo his position at the head of the army. Had he not always insisted that he was unfit for command and had not sought the position in the first place? And had he not always welcomed advice from his officers— Gates among them—because of his awareness of his own inadequacies as commander in chief? His dissembling worked to give his detractors the chance they needed to replace him. But General Washington did not remain passive. In fact, from his encampment at Valley Forge in the winter of 1777– 1778, he complained bitterly to Congress about its meddling in army affairs that endangered not just his ability to command the army but, he believed, the fate of the Revolution.[19] In this case Washington actively sought to keep his command, and he won this internal political battle. Washington's prestige was still too great and Gates's motives still too unclear for the plot to gain any momentum beyond causing more worry for the commander in chief. He weathered this storm like many others.

Despite the difficult conditions at Valley Forge, Washington's army broke camp in the spring of 1778 a more effective fighting force than the year before. Most experts attribute this development at least in part to Baron Friedrich von Steuben, a Prussian officer serving the revolutionary cause. He had trained the American army throughout the winter in the European style of fighting, leaving Washington with the professional nucleus of soldiers he had long desired.[20] But a new confidence also emanated from the commander in chief. Having withstood the political machinations whirling around him, Washington would begin to show an independence of command earned over the past years in the field. He would still hold councils of war, as Congress decreed he must, but he would effectively preside over these bodies rather than deferring to their advice. Washington the general had arrived, and the American cause was very much alive as a result.

By this point in the war, the British were beginning to lose the political will to continue the effort to control the colonies. The Americans' Fabian strategy had begun to pay off, assisted by French entry into the war, which added to the worries of leaders in Parliament, since even the British navy was not large enough to face the French in every conceivable theater of action. Concentrating naval forces in North America would leave British merchant shipping open to French attacks elsewhere. For instance, without a strong navy to protect them, the British colonies in the West Indies were extremely vulnerable to attack. As he pondered his options, Prime Minister Lord North allowed the Howe brothers to retire. While victorious on land and sea, they had placed Great Britain in this worsening strategic position by not finishing the war.[21] Despite his own failings, Washington had beaten that formidable duo.

In 1778 the Americans had the opportunity to once more enact the Fabian strategy thanks to London's decision to compel General Howe's replacement, Henry Clinton, to move his forces from Philadelphia to New York so he could then detach a large contingent for assignment to Florida and the Caribbean. The British retreat gave the colonials the chance to damage Clinton's forces as they moved about the American countryside. Washington now had to make a decision whether to remain faithful to the Fabian strategy or attack the British army in the open. A council of war, with the exception of General Wayne, recommended that the army shadow the British retreat and harass them when possible but not accept battle. The Fabian approach was to remain intact. This advice Washington heeded, for a while. The British retreat began in earnest on June 18, 1778, and the American army followed, stalking them. Many British died from heat exhaustion and at the hands of American sharpshooters.

This situation continued until June 24 when the British were just days away from receiving supplies from the Royal Navy at Sandy Hook on the New Jersey coast. Washington again called a council of war. Should there be an attack now, or should the army continue to shadow the British column? His advisors decided against attacking, but this time Washington overruled them. Instead of continuing to watch the British retreat, Washington ordered an assault on their rear guard at Monmouth. It was a step the general deemed worth taking since he might eliminate a sizeable portion of the British army and force the war to a conclusion.[22]

On the morning of June 29, Washington ordered Charles Lee to lead the attack, although the commander in chief offered nothing in the way of an actual plan. In fact, the objective was in flux. Was Lee to provoke a general engagement, mount only a probe, or simply pressure the British forces he encountered? Washington's lack of clarity was compounded by Lee's unfamiliarity with the terrain, and Lee clumsily advanced and dangerously exposed his positions. Clinton turned and counterattacked. Soon Lee was near retreat. It was another moment of crisis born of tactical failure.

When Washington arrived on the battlefield, however, he soon set things right. He rallied Lee's men and put them into a defensive line. Clinton's troops continued to hammer the Americans, nearly driving them from the field. Through his personal strength of will and by using superior artillery covering fire, Washington was able to fight Clinton to a draw before nightfall ended the battle. Both generals claimed a victory, but Washington considered it a validation of his strategy, since he had bloodied Clinton's force before it went into hiding in New York. Thus, for Washington, the Battle of Monmouth indeed was a significant victory, and for larger reasons than merely holding his own during the fighting. Gone were the risks of accepting battle and the fear that defeat would end the Revolution then and there. Despite British claims of success, Washington had won the day by demonstrating that the Americans no longer feared battle, refusing to accept that defeat would end the Revolution then and there, and wounding the British army as it fled to New York.

The remainder of Washington's war in the North followed textbook Fabian strategy. Once the British retreated into New York City, they appeared inclined to remain there on the defensive. Their inactivity left Washington with little to do. He was not strong enough to assault the city, so he positioned his army nearby to keep an eye on the enemy. The Virginian realized that complete inactivity in his area of operations might weaken American resolve to finish the fight; the lull before New York may lead some Americans to conclude that the war was near its end. To avoid this potential pitfall, he encouraged a guerrilla war in the middle colonies, particularly in New Jersey. While having tied his fate to the regulars of the Continental Army, a surplus of militias hung about the army and employed themselves in harassing British patrols and detachments. At first dismayed by the less-than-honorable nature of this fighting, Washington now accepted its value in further sapping British will to carry on the fight in the colonies and in furthering American claims of success.[23] Guerrilla warfare had added another component to his Fabian strategy. With the manpower decidedly in his favor because of his dual military assets—a regular army and a host of irregulars—Washington reflected on the evolving nature of the fighting and accepted its import: the British could only suffer defeat given the current circumstances of the war and sooner or later would have to give up the fight.

Once the British withdrew to the safety of New York City, the southern colonies became the focus of their military operations. The goal was to cripple the American resistance by driving a wedge into the fragile alliance that made up the future United States. If Clinton could find local support in Georgia and in the Carolinas, then he could march northward and bring the colonies back into the fold one at a time. Until 1780 southerners had been supporting an essentially New England–based war, and Clinton hoped that reports of southern war weariness and Crown loyalty were not exaggerated.

The early portion of Britain's campaign in the South in the spring and summer of 1780 went very well. In May Clinton captured the port city of Charleston, South Carolina. It was a short battle. The American commander, Benjamin Lincoln, was overwhelmed by superior British numbers and surrendered five thousand Continentals and militiamen. Outnumbered or not,

Lincoln had put up a poor defense. After this brief foray apparently capped with overwhelming success, Clinton returned to the North to face Washington, leaving a force of eight thousand redcoats under Lt. Gen. Charles Cornwallis to continue the new southern strategy. With the initial British success, Clinton expected victory in the South to soon lead to victory in the war once Cornwallis pushed north and joined him in the New York area.

To redeem Lincoln's defeat, Congress in July of 1780 appointed the hero of Saratoga, General Gates, to rebuild the Southern Department. Gates's appointment soon proved to be an unmitigated disaster. Far from repeating his success at Saratoga, Gates allowed his army of 3,700 regulars and militiamen to be destroyed by Cornwallis's detached force of 2,100 men at the Battle of Camden in South Carolina in late August 1780. By going head-to-head against trained regulars, Gates had placed his mixed force in a very vulnerable position. It broke and ran, and the remnants of his army were dispersed by the English pursuit. Consequently, less than two months after his arrival, Gates had compounded the defeat of Lincoln at Charlestown and so worsened the American position in the South that he threatened the entire American cause. It appeared that the British were winning the war with their new southern strategy.

There was, however, a silver lining in the defeat at Camden, although it was unknown to American leaders at the time. Cornwallis had come to completely despise militia forces, loyalist and rebel alike. At Camden the loyalist militia he had recruited after the success at Charleston switched colors at the approach of the rebel army. The locals favored whatever force appeared to have the upper hand, and this fleeting allegiance made them difficult to rely on from a military point of view. For this reason, he would go to great lengths to distance himself from their use.[24] His resolve on this issue worked to greatly isolate the British army from the local population, a mistake that would have important repercussions in the coming winter campaign against a new American commander.

Washington replaced Gates with Gen. Nathanael Greene, who arrived in the South in December 1780 after Gates had shown his true worth by abandoning his shattered army and covering 170 miles on a flight from Camden to Hillsborough, North Carolina.[25] Greene was an inspired choice to lead the Southern Department. His experience with recruiting and equipping men as quartermaster of the Continental Army would prove valuable now.

Following the complete annihilation of the southern command, Greene was in a difficult position, virtually commanding no army at all. He would have to work a miracle to create a fighting force. He also was a trusted officer, allowing Washington to issue Greene broad orders that meant the major general had the option of continuing to give battle at every turn, or he could rely upon the strategy of attack and retreat that had served the army so well in the North. With this faith extended to him by the commander in chief, Greene headed south.

Greene embraced what he called a "partizan" war in the South.[26] Adapting to these circumstances, he immediately committed a cardinal sin in military terms, dividing what soldiers he did have at his disposal in the face of Cornwallis's numerically superior army. It was a clever move, however, since this forced Cornwallis to do the same if he hoped to catch and destroy the Americans. Greene ordered his forces to give ground but attack baggage trains and supply columns when possible. Cornwallis chased the disparate American forces, resulting in a series of small engagements. His army was first bruised and then slowly broken as a result. Greene's forces suffered as well, but he always had enough men to keep fighting, since the southern population backed Greene more often than Cornwallis, thereby providing the American commander with a steady influx of militiamen and irregulars. In contrast, the British army rapidly dwindled in numbers.

After a few months, Greene felt confident enough to risk a general engagement. Though defeated by Cornwallis at the Battle of Guilford Courthouse in March 1781, it came in textbook Pyrrhic fashion. Cornwallis lost nearly 500 men killed or wounded of a force of only 1,900. It was too high a price to pay, particularly since the war went on and Cornwallis disdained any loyalist militia reinforcement that could be found. The actions of Cornwallis's men did not help matters. Most notorious in this regard was the infamous Col. Banastre Tarleton, whose Tory Legion savagely attacked rebel troops, failing to give quarter on more than one occasion and committing atrocities against helpless prisoners. Such actions galvanized support for Greene's partisan warfare. Admitting defeat a short time after Guilford Courthouse, Cornwallis moved north, hoping to interdict the rebel supply base for the Carolinas in Virginia. Since his army had dwindled in numbers, he looked to augment his small force with two British armies located in Yorktown, Virginia.

As the war raged in the South, Washington mostly waited in the North. He was obliged by Congress to send a sizable armed force against the Mohawk tribe in New York, a campaign that Barbara Alice Mann has labeled genocide in *George Washington's War on Native America*.[27] The harsh tactics helped quell the violence afflicting the western frontier as the British successfully incited native insurrection among the Iroquois. Primarily, however, he hovered near New York and the main British force. Notably, he did not lay siege to the city or try to assault it—he simply waited. So long as he remained there with an army, the American cause was alive. If he could maintain a stalemate, it might be possible to claim a strategic victory over time. The British could not say the same. They needed to eliminate the colonial army, and Washington's presence outside of New York reminded Clinton—and London—that he had not been able to do that. Waiting also gave Washington time to look for a weakness and build up his forces. After Greene caused Cornwallis to seek shelter in Yorktown, it appeared that the waiting had paid off at last.

Washington almost failed to grasp the opportunity at hand. Hesitating to abandon his positions around New York, he continued to believe that he needed to attack the main British force there. But his officers persuaded the general to act otherwise. Thus, he set about formulating a new plan for a decisive battle in Virginia. It was a gamble, but his hope was to isolate the British army in the Chesapeake Bay area once he teamed with a sizeable French land contingent and the French fleet. On August 14, 1781, he received word that the French fleet would be off the coast of Virginia in the weeks ahead but that it would have to leave by late October. Had the fleet come further north, Washington may have given into his own inclinations and disastrously attacked New York. Instead, he decided to try and lay siege to Yorktown and capture the British army there. Four days later, he began the nearly 400-mile-long march from New York to Virginia.[28]

In no mood to contest his advance, the British allowed Washington to approach Yorktown from the land side. Sure of the tenability of their position and able to be reinforced and resupplied by sea, the English were completely surprised when the French fleet arrived on September 5. There were now some 9,000 Americans and, when counting the sailors in the French fleet, 29,000 Frenchmen present. With the English trapped on the Yorktown peninsula, the siege was short, lasting only thirty-four days. Washington's influence in this battle was understandably limited, since the commander in chief had no experience in siege warfare. He did issue a large number of directives, but these were mostly unnecessary and ignored by his soldiers manning the trenches.[29] Once again, Washington was out of his tactical element, and it was French engineers who directed the siege. The English did the rest. In fact, it was the British commanders, Clinton and Cornwallis, who had created this disaster by underestimating the size of the French fleet, thereby dooming any chance of saving or relieving the beleaguered garrison in Yorktown. As if by some act of providence, on October 19, 1781, just days before the French fleet needed to leave, Cornwallis surrendered his force of 7,700 soldiers. With the only other large British force having been ordered to stay in New York, the British forfeited a significant part of their field army. The cost was too much for London to bear, and the war vaulted forward to a conclusion. Through Fabian tactics, by staying in the field year after year, and then procuring a decisive victory, Washington had beaten Cornwallis and possibly Clinton as well. When the English sued for peace in April 1782, Washington's victory was complete. It had been a remarkable accomplishment.

NAPOLEON

Napoleon Bonaparte is the most famous soldier in Western history, but he earned this title from a record of failure. Knowing this contradiction is the key to better understanding his military career. His wars cost him his throne, a sure measure of failed diplomacy given the extent of the empire that he assembled with military conquest. He simply fought too many wars to sustain his power abroad, leading to the invasion of France and his fall from power by an allied coalition under English sway. Complete defeat on the battlefield was only part of the measure of his failure since Napoleon had little else to commend his struggles. He created no innovation in terms of battle, no originality when deploying weapons. He left no treatise detailing his military secrets despite being recognized at the time, and certainly to posterity, as a dean in military affairs.[30] This omission may be due to his understanding that he had fought some sixty battles but still met with ultimate defeat. What could he offer after such a result?

Plenty. Before his career ended, he led French armies into all the major capitals of Europe, from Madrid to Moscow. He plied his craft with some success in Egypt, and he contemplated world conquest. Could a final result of abdication and exile undo such exploits? The answer is no. His record is not mixed so much as it represents an inevitable progression. Not having grown and nurtured the tool of his military exploits, the French army, he naturally abused it. He did so despite being a product of this creation, the advancement of French military arms, in particular the artillery, of which Napoleon was an especially eager convert, making his career possible to a great extent. But always at the center of his motives was ambition, the desire to use his military career to further his social standing. Of course, he could not and did not believe his goal was to become emperor of France. Here was a beneficial overreach derived from his willingness to advance himself at any cost. And so his chief tool to pursue his fortunes, the army, eventually collapsed under the weight he ascribed to it. The great general ended his military career in defeat because he had created a new limitation in making war: success in battle fueled an ambition predicated only on more military conflict.

War engulfed Napoleon, and he relished it. However, it served him well for only a portion of his career. Undoubtedly, military success was the leading factor in putting him in charge of France. This result came from a series of early campaigns that established his military reputation, two in Italy and one in Egypt. Yet these wars were hardly successful. A run of good fortune was at the heart of what defined his accomplishments in Italy, such as they were, and this same good fortune extracted him from the Egyptian folly. Of course, his wars in Italy would mirror other campaigns in Austria and Germany: military success leading to more wars. Through 1807 Napoleon proved his mettle on the battlefield, but the returns were clearly questionable. And the aura of fate, a "good" in his mind, rose so often that his belief in his "star" led Napoleon to risk too much in these wars of alarming frequency.[31] War was a step France became increasingly unwilling to take, even as Napoleon had the opposite reaction and sought out wars that clearly bore ill omens. Given the increasing stakes of his battles and the inevitable reversal of fortune awaiting him, that Napoleon lasted as long as he did is perhaps his greatest accomplishment in terms of military exploits.

Clearing out the mob from the streets of Paris in October 1795 and protecting the Directory, the latest installment of the French revolutionary government, was a success that propelled him in the direction he wished to go, a command in the field. The new government awarded him the control of the French army fighting in Italy. It was not a promising assignment. In a minor theater of war, these troops were ill equipped, ill fed, and poorly led at the highest levels. Horses were weakened from half rations, as were the men, and only some sixty guns remained operational.[32] Napoleon's chances of whipping this force into fighting shape appeared hopeless, especially since some older, talented officers resented his posting at only twenty-six years of age. Regardless, legend describes Napoleon as winning them over in a matter of days, gaining their approval with his decisive plan of attack. Shortages in supply would be made good from campaigning in the rich lands of northern Italy. His was a measure of certainty that the army badly needed, and so a willingness to follow the new commander emerged at least as long as the French army suffered no reverse.

Napoleon formally launched his military career with the conquest of Italy in 1796–1797. It jumped forward in mid-April, when the French forced Piedmont to the peace table in ten days. More difficult was defeating the Austrians seeking to remain custodians of northern Italy. Austria possessed a larger army than Napoleon's total of some 37,000 men, and even early French victories meant more fighting. But the tally came rapidly and was impressive: Lodi, Milan, Mantua—all these towns and cities fell to the French. Still the Austrians remained in the field, and Napoleon sought a decisive battle to end the war. This objective led to some tense moments in the campaign. Dividing his forces, Napoleon expected to be able to unify his command when the crucial moment arrived. At times he courted disaster, such as defending Mantua against several determined Austrian counterattacks. He eventually did bring superior numbers to bear on the enemy, but not before nearly meeting defeat at Arcola in November 1796. In fact, the future emperor risked much during that engagement, including his own life when he exposed himself to enemy fire while encouraging his men to cross a key bridge to split the Austrians defending the opposite bank. The Napoleonic legend was born there at Arcola and for the most part deservedly so, although he probably did not stand alone leading the charge over the bridge. As he frequently would do, Napoleon altered the official record to make himself the hero that day.[33] He did direct the French forces, however, that despite inferior numbers had repelled a number of Austrian offensives and forced that empire to give up Italy. It was a significant accomplishment, and the French nation hailed the liberation of the region as a victory for the Revolution.

But Napoleon was still fighting, since the Austrians refused to make peace. The Corsican now proposed to take the war into the heart of the Austrian empire. Once the French were in possession of Leoben on April 7, 1797, a city only seventy-five miles from Vienna, the Austrians at last asked for peace, undoubtedly astonished that this upstart commander and his small army had turned a secondary theater of war into the most important battlefront, one that ended this round of French-Austrian confrontation.

Equally astonished was the Directory. Napoleon had no authority to march on Vienna, but his success prevented a formal reprimand. In fact, the money and art treasures he sent from Italy to Paris in a steady stream from the onset of the campaign proved equally effective at silencing any would-be critics in the capital. Still, the French government could not ignore the symbolism of one of its generals negotiating a peace with an enemy of the Revolution, largely on his own and without consulting them. He was welcomed back in France as a hero, but the Directory now looked to rid itself of the clearly ambitious Napoleon.

Its members chose a sort of banishment, offering Napoleon command of an expeditionary force. Its target: Egypt. He relished the chance, passing on an opportunity to lead an army assembled to invade England, something he deemed as unrealistic at that time. True, a war in Egypt took him away from France, and his absence over time might diminish his newly won acclaim. But he judged the upside too advantageous to pass up, a chance to follow his historical heroes Alexander the Great and Julius Caesar by gaining fame in the east. The glory he coveted again underscored his ambition. Here was a chance to immortalize himself in history, but the immediate gain of such an end clearly tempted him as well and perhaps more than any would-be paean to the annals of history. A conquering hero in the east could so disrupt England's hold on commerce that the French nation would gain a decisive advantage over its foremost enemy. A return to France after accomplishing this feat would enhance his reputation and advance his political fortunes as well. It was a reach, but his romanticism overcame his judgment, and he remained convinced of the wisdom of his decision and of the great prospects before him. A few sly smiles from members of the Directory saluted his departure, convinced they had outfoxed the man who now chased dreams of conquest that only tangentially impacted France. This action also had the sanction of the Directory's foreign minister, Charles-Maurice de Talleyrand, who desired that France cease its wars on the continent and so bring an end, or at least a pause, to the wars of the Revolution. Getting a man like Napoleon as far away from Europe as possible could only further this aim.[34]

Napoleon set sail on May 19, 1798, convinced he would return in six months. As it turned out, he would not be back in France for over a year, and under circumstances he could not have imagined. In Egypt Napoleon won the battles but lost the war. The campaign started well enough when the large French fleet of thirteen warships and a great many transports departed from several ports in southern France and arrived off the coast of Egypt on July 1, pausing only long enough to seize Malta, the island fortress conveniently in the path of the final French destination. Having had the good fortune of evading the English fleet under Horatio Nelson that was combing the Mediterranean in search of the French, Napoleon safely debarked over 30,000 men near Alexandria. Once in control of that city, he immediately marched on Cairo, his army withstanding the challenge of the sultan's Mameluke armies, easily defeating them at the Battle of the Pyramids on July 21, and seizing the capital on July 24. He then looked to complete the destruction of the enemy and did so once he caught up to the remainder of that army on August 11. In both engagements French material weight and superior tactics proved a great advantage, and the mostly horse-bound enemy was easily defeated despite its great numerical advantage.

The news was not entirely favorable to the French, however. Nelson had located the French fleet anchored at Aboukir Bay and immediately attacked and destroyed it. After the Battle of the Nile on August 1, 1798, Napoleon was stranded in Egypt and facing an untenable situation. At first, his resolve was absolute. His land campaign simply had to assume larger dimensions; he would have to accomplish more with less. He set off to conquer Palestine, hoping its occupation would cause the British much worry should his offensive compel Turkey (allied with England) to abandon its war against France as well. A march on India could follow such a success.

The French advanced successfully until reaching the fortress of Acre. There, the Turks and the English fleet combined to withstand his assault, and his invasion of the east came to end. A retreat to Cairo followed, a setback that paled in comparison to his abandonment of his army there and his return to France with but a handful of his staff members. The romanticism of the venture had faded, and a desperate Napoleon took his leave of Egypt to try his fate back in France.

It was a bold move, even if militarily dishonorable. He had no permission, no orders. Nor could he be certain of his reception. Would France welcome back the liberator of Italy but the failure of Egypt? Circumstance would favor him. In the first place, he evaded the patrolling British fleet on station in the Mediterranean Sea, and after stopping briefly at Corsica, he did make it to French soil on October 9, 1799. Second, France had just learned of his last victory in Egypt, a rebuff of a Turkish army at Aboukir on July 25, so the full dimensions of the complete failure of the expedition were not yet understood. However, once the French authorities had been informed of his return, Napoleon faced a stern reckoning. Instead, one more favorable circumstance fell into his lap, and that was that France was again under attack from foreign foes and the Revolution in need of a capable general. Who better to lead in this struggle than the man who had proven himself in Italy?

In fact, Napoleon returned to France in time to witness and participate in the latest internal political struggle at home. The Directory wobbled in looming dissolution, its enemies accusing it of mismanagement, leading to debt at home, and an inept foreign policy producing a new round of wars abroad. Many observers realized only a push was needed to topple it. Of the many plots hatched to secure this outcome, the one involving Napoleon would prove the most successful. Teaming with Emmanuel Joseph Sieyès, an influential member of the Directory, he was installed as First Consul. The return from Egypt had been fortuitous indeed. However, the difficult task was to remain in power, an end that was all the more challenging with France again at war with Austria and other members of the Second Coalition, another alliance forged by England. Already Italy had been lost to Austrian forces that were now in position to threaten France.

As First Consul, Napoleon benefited from being in overall command of the French army. He assigned the commanders and dictated the deployment of the French armies defending the homeland. After considering his options, he again looked to Italy as the most important theater of action and departed for that front in April 1800 with a reserve army and his personal guard. He ascended the Alps and debouched upon the valley of the Po in northern Italy in grand fashion. Napoleon again courted dreams of grandeur, having followed the footsteps of Hannibal, who had crossed the Alps before attacking Rome during the Second Punic War in 218 BCE. Operating on familiar ground, Napoleon engineered a swift campaign. In a matter of months, the Austrians were maneuvered into another decisive battle, this time at Marengo on June 14. As in the previous campaign in Italy, Napoleon risked much in the field, and again only after the timely reinforcement of his hard-pressed troops did he win that key battle. The Austrians met defeat after nearly tasting victory, but this near success counted for little. The British-led coalition collapsed in the face of this French martial success. Napoleon was again master of Italy.

Lauded by the French people for his exploits in the field, the First Consul now took steps to shore up his position at home. Revolutionary violence had left wreckage throughout the countryside, in the cities, and especially in the psyche of the French people. Understanding that France needed a respite from war, Napoleon tried his hand at diplomacy, and a peace with England signaled the start of a new era. France had lacked capable leadership to this point, a failing remedied by Napoleon. Indeed, he had come far in a short period of time. His personal gains were soon rewarded with his elevation to emperor in 1804.

Yet the new monarch of France had to defend his throne and his title from yet another European coalition. England and France had gone to war again in May 1803, as the island nation found willing participants on the continent to contest French arms. Austria readied itself for another round against France and was bolstered by the armies of Russia. This formidable combination prompted a Napoleon offensive, and the attack he orchestrated in 1805 was to be his best campaign. In a swift advance, he encircled an Austrian army deployed far in advance of the oncoming Russian forces and destroyed it at the Bavarian city of Ulm in October. The Russians moving forward to meet this now-defeated Austrian army swiftly retreated, and the triumphant French soon occupied Vienna. Still, Russia continued the war, and Napoleon sought a decisive battle. In December at Austerlitz, a town north of Vienna near Brünn, capital of the Austrian-held Moravia, Napoleon defeated the Russians and the remnants of the Austrian forces in a single day of action. Some 15,000 enemy troops perished, with another 12,000 becoming prisoners of war; the French lost but 7,000 killed and wounded. The Austrians immediately sued for peace and on Napoleon's terms, while the Russians retreated eastward. The French empire under Napoleon had survived its first great challenge of arms, posed by the Third Coalition.

The problem with this "decisive" battle is that the war continued. England still opposed France, bolstered by its own great military success at sea at the Battle of Trafalgar in October 1805. Off the southern Spanish coast, Nelson had caught up with a French and Spanish fleet and destroyed it, although the famed admiral perished in that battle. Thanks to this success at sea, Napoleon's decisive battle at Austerlitz and, it would turn out, any subsequent decisive battle would fail to secure a long-lasting peace. Perhaps Napoleon did not seek this end now or at any point in his rule as emperor. Certainly in 1805, success meant more wars and therefore more battles. The following year, Prussia became the target of the French juggernaut on the slightest of pretexts. King Frederick William III had deployed his famed army in a forward position, an act Napoleon classified as hostile, apparently forgetting the constant insults and humiliations he had heaped on Prussia since the beginning of the year. The campaign began in October, and a smashing round of French victories at Jena and Auerstädt decimated the Prussian army; the French pursuit eliminated it altogether. This great success did not end the war, however. Russia again entered the fray and advanced into Prussia, eventually facing the French armies in twin battles in Poland, first at Eylau in early February 1807, a two-day engagement ending in a veritable draw. The second was at Friedland in June, another decisive French victory. After this defeat, Russia sued for peace, and the war ended, to a degree.

In the aftermath of Friedland, Napoleon met with the Russian czar, Alexander I, on a raft in the middle of the Neman River at Tilsit, where the two monarchs forged a peace. However, the durability of this formal treaty of alliance in July would prove fleeting. A chastened Alexander absorbed much of the Napoleon worldview, a vision of spoils divided between the two of them on a grand scale: Napoleon in control of the west, Alexander the east. The French emperor's humiliation of Prussia's king and queen, who were only observers during the proceedings, signaled to all who wished to see it the heavy hand of a Napoleon peace. The invitation to the czar to act as harshly when making war away from Europe certainly would have appealed to him if only it had not come by French invitation. Defeated in two campaigns that spanned just under two years, the young Russian czar was not ready to quit the fight. But at the same time, he did have to face the need for a pause. After contemplating the French emperor's grand designs, Alexander agreed to only that which would not cost him a chance to act with greater independence in the future. That chance was to come in 1812.

Napoleon expressed satisfaction in the tone of Tilsit, but less so in the results. The Russians were subdued at the moment, but only because of their reverses on the battlefield. Alexander's reluctance to fully partner with the French emperor regardless of his commitment to do so increasingly absorbed Napoleon's attention in the months after this fateful meeting. He could also see a threat from the latent power of Germany, and he hoped to contain it. But dismembering Prussia and alarming Austria by siding with Russia reflected bad judgment, since it underscored the limitations of French power. England remained defiant, and French suzerainty on the continent was transitory for this reason alone. France needed allies, but Napoleon made only enemies. Despite his title of emperor, he was the petty Corsican at heart, and his personal ambition dictated policy more than did safeguarding the interests of France. This failing alone would be enough to erode his accomplishments on the battlefield, and what ensued after 1807 became the turning point of his empire, the beginning of the end centered on his fundamental failure to understand military policy. His aim would be to rule Europe through military force, even as his "victories" underscored the impossibility of this end. It was only a matter of time before the inevitable reversal, and it would come in complicated fashion over a five-year period.

Facing the new challenges—many of his own creation—Napoleon set out to consolidate his empire, a task that required more wars. In 1808 he sent his army into Spain. He captured Madrid in a month but faced a countrywide resistance in the wake of this success. Here was a war that would not end until the complete collapse of the empire in 1814. Bogged down in

Spain, Napoleon faced a renewed challenge from Austria in 1809; the war so spectacularly won at Austerlitz had resumed just four years later. The key difference this time was that Austrian forces had improved, while Napoleon's had diminished in quality to some extent since many of his most experienced soldiers now floundered in Spain combating the resistance there. Nevertheless, Napoleon again won a series of victories against Austria, culminating in the battle of Wagram in July 1809, which ended that war. However, before this victory, Napoleon had met defeat at Aspern-Essling near Vienna; the French claimed a draw. Wagram itself was not decisive on the field; the carnage was equitable, some 70,000 casualties in total. Rather, the Austrians again decided to give up the struggle in order to remove French soldiers from deep inside their territory.

The upside of this series of "decisive" battles was that by 1810, Napoleon was indeed a ruler of an empire at peace. True, England remained opposed to French hegemony on the continent and technically at war with France for this reason, but actual fighting was minimal between the two powers. Also, the war in Spain continued, a guerrilla war posing increasing trouble for France after England sent an army under the Duke of Wellington to the Iberian Peninsula in 1808. Wellington proved a capable commander, and French troubles in Spain persisted.

Napoleon, however, looked elsewhere in Europe and decided that a great test of strength with Russia was unavoidable. His intransigence on this issue set the stage for the monumental French invasion of Russia in 1812. During this campaign, a decisive battle eluded him. The Russia commanders withdrew into the interior of the country, and Napoleon followed. When the two armies finally met at Borodino on September 7, a village some seventy-five miles from Moscow, Napoleon again claimed a victory. However, even his advance into an abandoned Moscow a short time later could not turn Borodino into the decisive battle he wanted and badly needed to defeat Russia. Alexander refused to cease hostilities, and the war continued. Napoleon sat in the Kremlin for a month before ordering a retreat in mid-October. He could do little else. He had no prescription to end the war with Russia, let alone England. The retreat that followed is famous for the destruction of the French army that was forced to make its way back to central Europe under the duress of Russian forces while enduring a harsh winter.

Napoleon's rapid fall from power nominally ended his fallacious pursuit of decisive battle. His bid to retain control of Germany failed in 1813, and France faced invasion in January 1814. Napoleon managed to stave off defeat for but three months, Paris falling to the Allies in March 1814. The exiled emperor made a last bid for power in 1815, returning from the island of Elba to reclaim his throne. But these heroics (more likely follies) merely added another chapter to the story and did not change the ending. Defeated at Waterloo, Napoleon faced imprisonment on St. Helena Island in the Atlantic Ocean, having lost everything. This is where his story ends.

Yet an examination of decisive battle cannot end here. While always in pursuit of that aim, there is no question that Napoleon's tactics changed. Gone from his later campaigns—certainly absent after his conquest of Germany in 1806—was the gain from maneuver warfare (*manoeuvre sur les derrières*) that had previously characterized his operations. Rapid advances still dominated his efforts to force a decisive battle. However, the climactic battles had become bloodbaths rather than sharp pushes to decimate the enemy's forces. It was as if Napoleon's task became to herd his opponent's forces into a cul-de-sac to then grind them into pieces. This shift helps explain the rather modest success that defined the victories of Friedland, Wagram, and Borodino.[35] Perhaps this evolution was inevitable. After all, when fighting in Italy on two occasions, 1797 and 1800, he commanded but a portion of the French army, and at both times neither campaign occurred in the main theater of action. So the decisive engagements that characterized each war in Italy, Arcola and Marengo respectively, represented the battles that did follow in later years, only on a smaller scale. At this early point in his career, he merely benefited from favorable circumstance to win these campaigns.

To argue that he was undone by circumstance after 1806 is not an accurate assessment, however. Napoleon's aim remained to destroy the enemy army, and opportunities arose to do this, on a much larger scale than in the past. But mass artillery barrages followed by frontal attacks such as at Eylau in 1807 and at Wagram in 1809 defined Napoleonic strategy at this point. Absent was any subtlety, such as that exhibited at Austerlitz in 1805, where he induced the enemy to attack his right and thereby expose their center to a French counterthrust. Nor could he count on the folly of his enemies, as

was the case at Friedland in 1807 when the Russian commander Levin
August, Count von Bennigsen, foolishly positioned his army across a river.
Clearly, the Napoleonic Wars after 1806 had progressed to the point where
something more than expert tactics had to occur to net a decisive victory.
Yet Napoleon did not even try. Commanding the entire French order of battle, he could marshal his forces as he saw fit, and his rapid advances usually
meant he did achieve superiority of numbers on the battlefield. This was
usually in terms of all three combat arms, cavalry, artillery, and infantry, so
he apparently concluded that there was no need to give much thought to
changing tactics; a mere sledgehammer would suffice. In this respect,
Napoleon's manner of fighting later in his career represented a corruption
of his earlier tactics. He was spoiled by abundance.

It is remarkable to follow this evolution to its conclusion at Waterloo, a
battle made possible by some brilliant Napoleonic maneuvering. He seized the
initiative in the 1815 campaign and successfully placed his smaller force between the two opposing armies: Wellington's British troops located near
Brussels, and a large concentration of Prussians further south under the command of Gen. Gebhard Leberecht von Blücher. This tremendous feat prompted
Wellington to exclaim, "Napoleon has humbugged me, by God!"[36] Wellington,
dancing at a ball in Brussels at the time of Napoleon's advance, understood the
danger in Napoleon's accomplishment: the two Allied armies could be defeated
in consecutive battles. However, having gained his advantage and having been
victimized by some ill fortune when attempting to envelop the Prussian army
at Ligny, Napoleon reverted to form at the battle of Waterloo and assaulted the
English center. Cannon barrage followed by infantry and cavalry assault was
the plan of battle that day, and it failed to dislodge the English from the field.
Reinforcement from Prussian forces later in the day crushed the French army.
A shortage of troops and a disadvantageous strategic position in 1815 had almost returned him to the commander he had been in Italy in 1796–1797, in
Austria in 1805, and in Prussia in 1806. A corruption of tactics ensured that
he remained a general lacking any sophistication on the field of battle. It was
a crucial failure, and it led to his defeat at Waterloo.

This is particularly true when the actions taken by Wellington are considered. He had perfected his tactic of sheltering his troops behind the reverse incline of slopes to shield them from artillery fire. His left flank

remained weak, but he took this chance, since he expected reinforcement from this direction by Prussian forces. His right rested on a strong point, the Château de Hougoumont, a position that never was taken by the French that day despite repeated assault. With these dispositions, Wellington anticipated an attack on his center, and he utilized the farmhouse La Haye Sainte to bolster this part of his line as well. In short, he had created a sound defensive front, in accordance with his reputation. These subtle acts speak for themselves when it is emphasized that Wellington won this battle without a quarter of his troops engaged. Should Napoleon try to win a battle of maneuver, Wellington deployed some 17,000 soldiers away from the field of battle to counter a French thrust to his right, one designed to envelop the English positions. These soldiers waited for an attack that never came.

Napoleon's mistakes continued. Relying on artillery, he waited to begin his attack until one o'clock in the afternoon so that the ground would be dry after rain had soaked the area the preceding night. This delay would make it easier to move the guns and affect the target, the balls not burying themselves into the soggy soil. But it also allowed the Prussians more time to reinforce Wellington's weak left. Napoleon also decided to attack the center of the English line, but in doing so, he ignored the advice of his commanders not to test English stamina under fire; they had seen the English line too often in Spain, and it usually had held firm. They urged him to dislodge the English by striking a flank of the enemy position. Napoleon responded with irritation, remarking, "Because you have been beaten by Wellington you consider him a great general. And now I tell you that Wellington is a bad general, that the English are bad troops, and that this affair is nothing more serious than eating one's breakfast."[37] He was right to suspect the quality of the English army; a good portion of it consisted of recruits taken from countries previously allied to France. Their ability to maneuver was something Wellington did not wish to test; their ability to stand under fire he doubted as well, but the duke reasoned that this was the better gamble. He would stay on the defense. And having never faced Wellington before, Napoleon had every reason to be confident of victory that day. He was merely following his own maxim of planning for a campaign with great caution but executing his battle plan with reckless abandon. A powerful frontal attack might pierce the English lines and lead to the collapse of an unsteady army. Even Wellington's steadfastness could not prevent this result should Napoleon achieve a breakthrough. Victory would follow.

Too many mistakes would cost him this chance. After surveying the English line, he ordered an assault on Hougoumont as a diversion. To move on the English right is what Wellington most feared, because he doubted the ability of his army to respond to a flanking attack. Napoleon recognized this worry and feinted to his left. However, the château was easily defended, and Wellington did so with only a modest reinforcement of the position. Moreover, he was not fooled into thinking this attack signaled an advance on his right. The rebuff of French forces before this position hardly handicapped French plans, except that Napoleon allowed this portion of the battle to get away from him. His brother Jérôme, in command of that attack, soon ordered his entire corps to be engaged there, and it remained in this fight throughout the day. It was the French who weakened their main attack to support a mere diversion, a folly that cost Napoleon a valuable part of his army. When he ordered his main attack on the English center—an infantry advance by his best troops, the rested corps of Jean-Baptiste Drouet, comte d'Erlon—the French were repulsed by the still-intact English defenders, the artillery preparation having failed to do great damage. Worse, Wellington countered this opening move with a successful English cavalry charge, further disrupting d'Erlon's forces. Here was a great feat, since the English cavalry arm was inferior to that of the French, yet it bloodied the initial French attack because the densely packed French formation could not easily maneuver. D'Erlon's portion of the French army was now inoperable at least in the near term.

Napoleon then allowed his field commander, Marshal Michel Ney, to attempt to break the English lines with a series of cavalry charges. All were repulsed, since little effort was made to utilize a combination of combat arms. The cavalry advanced without light artillery or infantry support. Ultimately, Napoleon had to hope for a dramatic victory by asking his elite Old Guard to puncture the English line before the Prussian army, already menacing his right flank, forced him to abandon the field. This predictable attack on the center of the English line was easily if dramatically repulsed. Having watched Napoleon risk his Guard and having seen it decimated, the French army disintegrated and fled from the battlefield. It was the blackest day of Napoleon's many battles but a logical end to his quest for decisive battle.

Having harshly appraised the generalship of Napoleon on the field of Waterloo, a few qualifications are in order. James Lawford wrote in *Napoleon: The Last Campaigns, 1813–1815* that this battle has been dissected so often and the mistakes on both sides enumerated in such detail that one would be led to conclude that the battle and the campaign were waged by a number of idiots who had no business being in command of a squad, let alone an army.[38] Instead, Lawford stresses that the opposite was the case, that two masters of their craft met that day. And there is Wellington's admission to his brother after the battle: "In all my life I have not experienced such anxiety, for I must confess that I have never been so close to defeat."[39] Even despite Napoleon's mistakes, the French nearly won the battle, and the arrival of Prussian forces was necessary to ensure their defeat. Napoleon's lack of sophistication on the field of battle was exemplified by Waterloo, and this shortcoming stands in contrast to his earlier successes.

Even continued success on the battlefield may not have changed the final result of the collapse of the Napoleonic Empire, since Napoleon never achieved a decisive victory because he could not overcome the strategic bankruptcy of his situation. Had Napoleon been fortunate enough to win a naval victory, perhaps his empire would have survived. Instead, he met defeat, and the causes were multifarious. The incessant campaigning drained away the professionalism from the French army, particularly after 1808. Instead, conscripts filled the ranks. This need had characterized the Revolutionary armies as well, but 1808 and afterward was a different time than 1792. It would be hard to ascribe a defense of revolutionary values to Napoleon's conscript armies. The cadres that remained did instill a devotion to a cause, but it was devotion to the emperor. It is remarkable that only five months after emerging from Russia at the head of a broken army, Napoleon returned to war in 1813 and sought to retain control of Germany. His army, inexperienced though it was, quickly netted a series of victories. The first of these, Lützen, found the emperor racing across the battlefield to cheers of "*Vive l'emperor!*" from the young wounded men.[40] While the French army often uttered this call, it is important here because it indicated that the conscripts had learned well the locus of the cause: the person of Napoleon.[41]

The novelty of civilian armies had worn thin by the time of the Napoleonic Empire as other states acted to emulate this practice and use it to good effect on the battlefield. Still, their commanders lacked Napoleon's charisma. His presence mattered greatly, due to not just his ability to perfect tactics but what he represented. The Duke of Wellington paid him such a compliment by equating Napoleon's presence on the battlefield to 40,000 men.[42] It was a bad omen when French opponents caught sight of Napoleon surveying the ground, surrounded by the soldiers of the Old Guard, his cherished personal escort and part of the Imperial Guard that functioned as the reserve of the army. Of course, its devotion to the emperor was pronounced, further emphasizing that what professionalism remained was grounded in his person, not the ideals of the Revolution.

It was a good formula, since more often than not Napoleon would prevail in a fight. Undeniably, his successes became much more infrequent after 1809, this war against Austria considered by most scholars to be his last successful campaign.[43] One key reason for the decline was that he seldom listened to advice. While still early in Napoleon's career, a capable general, Louis Charles Antoine Desaix de Veygoux, arrived on the field of Marengo to convince Napoleon to continue the battle that day, saying, "This battle is lost, but there is time to win another one."[44] Napoleon embraced Desaix's almost backhanded encouragement, and the French remained in position, their success at Marengo marking a great Napoleonic victory. Move forward some twelve years from 1800, and a now legendary Napoleon was fighting for the preservation of his army deep in Russia before Moscow. During the Battle of Borodino, Marshal Ney appealed to his emperor for the last French reserve, the Old Guard. An attack by this elite force would unhinge the Russian position and win the battle for France, or so Ney asserted. The emperor refused to order the Guard forward, rebuking Ney harshly by responding, "I will not have my guard destroyed. When you have come 800 leagues from France you do not wreck your last reserve."[45] Such caution from the great gambler surprised all those present, Ney most of all. He turned away and said to Marshal Joachim Murat and all those within earshot, "[Since he] isn't the general any more, but wants to play the Emperor everywhere, why doesn't he go back to the Tuileries and let us be the generals for him."[46] The opportunity passed, and the battle marked a French victory only in the sense of entering an abandoned Moscow a week later.

Whether a more resounding success at Borodino would have saved Napoleon's forces from the trauma of the Russian winter cannot be known with certainty, so it is misleading to cast blame on him for not heeding Ney's advice. One must instead emphasize his determination to wield command alone. Yet the personal control had become too much, really an unworkable standard to implement. As his armies grew in size, it became impossible for him to coordinate attacks leading to decisive victories, a failure painfully apparent in Russia in 1812 when Napoleon could not catch the retreating Russian armies. In fact, in the German campaign in 1813, the Allies eventually shunned battle with Napoleon and looked to engage only his marshals. The hope was that a defeat of the parts of the French army not under Napoleon's control would leave him vulnerable to mass attack, which in fact transpired at Leipzig. In this, the Battle of Nations, Napoleon was overwhelmed by superior numbers more than he was defeated in battle. It was a high price to pay for the failure of his too-centralized command system.

It is not that the French army lacked men of talent who could serve well as independent commanders. Marshal Louis-Nicolas Davout campaigned independently and successfully so on a number of occasions. Napoleon elevated many to positions of command because of their proven ability on the battlefield. This was yet another Revolutionary practice he employed, since these men were often commoners. Pierre-François Augereau, Joachim Murat, Jean Lannes, Michel Ney, and others all hailed from humble social origins and had faced a career of military service with little chance of promotion until the tumultuous Revolution. This practice of naming marshals of France based on merit became the penultimate symbol of careers open to talent, as Napoleon formally labeled it, and each French soldier could believe he carried a marshal's baton in his knapsack, as the saying went.[47] Still, while the drive and bravery of these marshals and other senior commanders made them invaluable to Napoleon's cause, they lacked the master's ability to produce battlefields favorable to them. Some formal training in the art of war, at least as practiced by Napoleon, was lacking for the obvious reason that Napoleon wished these men to remain dependent upon him. He could ill afford rivals who believed him replaceable.

Principally for this reason, Napoleon made sure to appease his military cohort by teaming advancement with riches and noble titles. It was an odd system mixing both Revolutionary and royal practices, and it eventually broke down. By 1813, after the calamity his armies had suffered in Russia, his person as the rallying point was not enough to allow France to defeat its enemies, who had become too numerous and powerful to repel. The long strain of Napoleonic conquests were to blame for both this outcome and a determination to see Napoleon defeated—or at least confined to France— by neighboring countries that, prior to this point, had been content to wage a much more limited war. Napoleon had indeed exerted his influence on this age of conflict, but in a way that reverberated negatively for France. Having been served poorly by many of his subordinate commanders at this latter stage of his empire, his army collapsed beneath him, a broken force at the top and bottom, under pressure from a now-resolute foe. It was his ultimate disservice to the Revolution, the chief icon of those past days having used up the army that had done so much to make the Revolution possible.

A larger shortcoming again pointed to his strategic limitations as a reason for his ultimate defeat. Having been reared in the style of conventional fighting, Napoleon never adapted his preferred way of making war to a concomitant reality of the Napoleonic era. Indeed, while his armies swiftly overran Spain in 1808, he faced a torrent of resistance in nearly every quarter of that country thereafter. The Spaniards refused to admit defeat, even with the vanquishing of their standing army. Instead, the remnants of Spain's regular forces teamed with the emergence of a number of guerrilla leaders to contest French rule of Spain. The success of these forces combined with Wellington's army is well-known, the debilitating impact of the "Spanish ulcer" severely impacting Napoleon's fortunes elsewhere in the empire, particularly once the fortunes of war turned against him after 1812.

The extended war in Spain did more than pose a persistent drain on French manpower and resources. It represented a symptom of a shortcoming inherent in the Napoleonic style of fighting, which had not adapted to guerrilla warfare. Spain was not the only location where a variety of irregular resistance surfaced. Before the extent of the fighting in Spain became clear, another Napoleonic campaign targeted Austria and ended with French success in 1809. However, this war witnessed the spectacle of guerrilla fighting in the Tyrol, formerly an Austrian province. Although not large enough to command as much attention as the fighting emerging in Spain, here was another example of the type of resistance now frequently contesting the Napoleonic offensives into other countries. The Russian campaign of 1812 ended with a similar reality, the retreating French columns enduring repeated attacks from irregular forces that included guerrillas in large numbers.[48]

It is worth noting that the regularity of the occurrence of guerrilla warfare accelerated as the Napoleonic era advanced. Prior to 1808 it is more difficult to find examples, and certainly these examples lack the scale of the ones mentioned; the war that erupted in France in the Vendée in response to the French Revolution is a possible exception. The insight gained here is that Napoleon's successes demanded that his enemies resort to an irregular method of warfare to oppose him. They had few choices left. If mere recourse produced this option, the inability of Napoleon to recognize the shift in the nature of the resistance opposing him revealed a remarkable deficiency in his generalship. It was not enough to occupy a capital and declare victory. Even after the disasters of Spain and Russia made this clear, he persisted in his denial. Standing on the battlefield of Lützen in 1813, having dealt a blow—but not a crippling one—to the resurgent state of Prussia, he could only remark, "These animals have been taught a lesson."[49] But the battle had been indecisive. What he should and must have known is that the Prussian army had produced a *landwher* system that rallied all able-bodied males to the cause. In effect, the Prussian high command had duplicated the French practice of *levée en masse*, although his enemies soon adapted it to better fight in irregular fashion, of which guerrilla warfare was a key component. The Prussians, for instance, also declared a *landsturm*, or emergency home-guard force, to conduct guerrilla war.[50] Napoleon, the man who had most profited from this new development of popular armies, failed to recognize the danger this practice now posed to his ambitions. As a result, he did little to counteract the guerrilla warfare that grew in reaction to his preferred conventional style of fighting.[51] The French empire paid a great price for his omission long before 1813.

To note Napoleon's ample sophistication in another regard is to emphasize that Napoleon did realize his unfavorable strategic position. He understood that a defiant England would continue to raise armies to oppose him, and France could not hope to win every battle. His task became devising an end to this pattern of incessant combat, and he chose economic warfare.

His Continental System came in 1806, after he occupied Berlin. Another success of his army had less to do with the timing than did his realization that with the loss of the French fleet off Trafalgar, he could not challenge England militarily. To strike at her economically appeared more feasible. His decree forbade the continent to trade with England and declared that "island of shopkeepers" would soon have to sue for peace, or so Napoleon hoped. However, he was not uniform in the application of the edict both by choice and by circumstance. France relied on many English goods, and to appease the home front, Napoleon loosened some restrictions. This exception infuriated other portions of the empire, and many parts refused to comply with the ban on trade. When forced to do so by Napoleon, a black market flourished and undermined the decree. And there was always the difficulty of forcing states to comply that were not under the control of France.

This edict explains the invasions that occurred after 1807, not Napoleon's love of war. In trying to enforce his decree and end the war with England, Napoleon occupied Portugal, intervened in Spanish affairs, and invaded Russia. Pursuit of a sophisticated manner of seeking decisive victory would lead Napoleon to his undoing. Somehow military force was to address this strategic goal, economic by design. These ends proved too incongruent even in the hands of the master of making war on a tactical level, the strategic implications of his military policy all too encompassing in aim and therefore in his ability to achieve it. In this respect, Napoleon's struggles were tragic beyond his person, or that of France, since he was both a product of an age and its victim. The Enlightenment left Napoleon a broken man strategically, even if it had given him his tactical opportunity.

From Revolution to Power

Without the tumultuous social upheaval generated by revolution, it is unlikely that Washington or Napoleon would have been given a chance of senior command. Once presented with their opportunities, however, they overcame the deficiencies of revolutionary armies, and the similarities between the two men are astounding. Experience early in the war taught Washington that a revolutionary force lacked the professionalism of a standing army and that no decisive battle could be won without imparting this professionalism to his soldiers. He soon coveted such a force even as he learned to capitalize on the strengths of the militias that constituted most of his army. Napoleon took the French army, a revolutionary force in its own right, and professionalized it when he formed the Imperial Guard and placed around it raw troops raised through the *levée en masse*. Lost in the process of shaping this Grande Armée was the revolutionary zeal that supposedly defined the army. In fact, it faded in both armies as the war continued in America and as the Napoleonic Wars continued unabated in Europe. Ideology was replaced by a dedication to Washington and Napoleon themselves, as both men came to represent something beyond themselves on the field of battle.

The similarities cease when the contrasting outcomes are considered. Washington discovered a cure to the strategic difficulties of his situation that allowed him to defeat the mighty British war machine. The remedy was tangible enough. Washington's grasp of the strategic needs of his army reflected his innovation in command. The American general authorized attacks on enemy weak points, such as unleashing irregular war in rear echelon areas. In this way, Washington did his part to ensure that England faced the inability to end the conflict in the colonies by having to fight one more battle after the last battle. Washington's later campaigns indeed were Fabian in nature, and this innovation allowed these patriots to drive the enemy from their homeland. Though Washington's tactical command on the battlefield remained dubious and could never rival that of Napoleon, and he lost a number of battles to various British generals, the only true measure is that he won the war by outlasting them all.

This success stands in great contrast to his counterpart in Europe. Napoleon's major mistake was that he shrank from irregular warfare as a military practice. While success tactically ensured his ability to prevail in many of the wars he fought, this success was temporary in that it too much represented a formula based on his person. Here was a crucial weakness, since he clung to conventional battle that defined his success and met defeat as the ground shifted beneath his feet. He failed to respond to the guerrilla warfare that erupted in the wake of his victories, preferring a military practice that he believed could take him to victory. That he failed to see the evolution of the resistance to his armies was as clear as his failure to see how defeat awaited him in the next battle or the one after that. A strategic short-coming, it sets him apart from Washington. Napoleon could do nothing tactically to overcome this lack of innovation.

Washington's generalship was superior to Napoleon's in that Washington made sure to arrange his military priorities correctly. He would win a decisive battle that ended the war with England because of the soundness of his strategic situation. Any American victory meant the war in the colonies continued, something England did not desire. The opposite end was the English goal on the European continent. The constant wars it sponsored there challenged French hegemony. Napoleon's ability to defeat England's partners time after time certainly provided good drama but little suspense. England stood on firm ground, its economic might presenting one too many challenges to France. Napoleon's recognition and response, the Continental System, was less a breakthrough in strategy than it was an admission of the strategic hopelessness of his situation.

Fortune smiled on Washington and frowned on Napoleon. Each man understood the probable outcome: success and defeat, respectively. While Washington waited for it to arrive, Napoleon dreaded the inevitable. In terms of military command, Washington's record exceeds that of Napoleon, even if Napoleon mounted as noble a struggle as did Washington. Both men faced daunting odds but carried on "a good fight." The difference was, as Washington understood, that they fought in the age of revolution.

3

LEADING BY DEFAULT
The Chance to Wield Power

T he steps that both George Washington and Napoleon Bonaparte took on the road from military commander to civilian leader bear close inspection, because it is here that Napoleon's path seems to diverge from Washington's. The American's journey appears as sober and deferential as the Corsican's appears bombastic and vain. Outwardly, Washington established the concept of military deference to civilian authority in the United States by gracefully, if temporarily, walking away from public life in the wake of his success at Yorktown. Napoleon surely crossed this line as he advanced from general to tyrant by capitalizing on a revolutionary environment to seize power. This is irrefutable proof of Washington's virtue, Napoleon's depravity. Yet both men rode a wave that meant accepting the power thrust into their hands. In reality, the means they took to attain political power speaks more of their social worlds than of the men themselves. For this reason, both Washington and Napoleon emerged as the singular victors of their revolutionary generations.

WASHINGTON

Washington's rise to power can rightly be said to encompass the day he took his regimental commission in the Virginia militia to the day he spoke the presidential oath for the first time. He spent his entire adult life climbing from one rung to the next on the ladder of success, the eighteenth-century Virginia *cursus honorum*; oftentimes, he helped build the very ladder he was climbing. Serving as commander in chief of the Continental Army had made him popular outside the patrician circles of power. By war's end, he was undoubtedly the most famous American in the nation's brief history. This fame carried him to the presidency and to the fulfillment of his desired social success.

The goals Washington set after the war for himself are somewhat unclear. Before retiring from the army, he prevented a mutiny in the ranks, formally surrendered his sword to Congress when resigning his commission, and claimed that he was withdrawing from public life for good. However, Washington remained concerned about his reputation among his men and among the citizens of the new United States, and so he remained subtly active in politics, advocating (when possible) for a more centralized authority than the precariously federated states wanted. His regard for public opinion governed his retirement in Virginia, since his post-war plans were centered on the theory that public reputation bests all other concerns. Thus, it is important to view this part of Washington's life through the lens of his defense of his reputation and his ambition to serve it. Everything he accomplished at this time was designed to foster a lasting legacy, and he enjoyed much self-aggrandizement in the process. In a few years, Washington would once again leave his beloved Mount Vernon, this time to serve as president of the United States. His was a willing sacrifice, however, since this high office was the fulfillment of his earlier ambitions: he was now head of the government, head of the military, and a singular force of unity in a largely disunited United States. The brash youth's ego was sated.

By the end of October 1781, the major fighting was over, but peace with England was still elusive. On the ground, the American victory in the Tidewater region greatly inhibited Britain's ability to campaign there and elsewhere, but American military success did not end the threat. Clinton still controlled a sizeable force in New York that remained capable of indefinite resupply. In Washington's estimation, only an American triumph there could lead to a final victory. With the withdrawal of the French fleet after Yorktown, the commander in chief feared that any such scenario was impossible. For the Continental Army, the waiting game would continue for two more years until negotiations with the British concluded with the Treaty of Paris in September 1783. During that interval, Washington attempted to keep the American army vigilant, but he struggled to do so. The 1782 campaign season saw little action against enemy troops. The main British force stayed in New York, and Washington remained with the army, now camped at Newburgh to the north of the city. However, since the British were unwilling to come out to fight, the war dragged on in stalemate, and the relative calm began to dull the American army. The general attempted to keep his troops occupied while they waited on the outcome of negotiations in Europe, but it was of little use. Typical army grumbling began to give way to actual protests for financial compensation for service. The Congress of the Confederation did nothing. In the absence of an active British threat, the various states had little incentive to provide funds to pay the army, and the national Congress appeared powerless to secure such monies. Clearly there would be no action taken by the country's civilian leaders on behalf of the soldiers. Without pay, the protests within the ranks inevitably grew louder.

The inability of Congress to procure funding for the American army bordered on the criminal. The government owed some troops years of back pay. Aside from standard compensation, Congress had offered pensions to troops when they enlisted during the war's lowest fortunes, but now it appeared that the Congress had little intention of making good on its promises. Potentially, the most ardent patriots, and surely the most hard-pressed by service to the cause, were being discarded by the American government. Washington's own assessment of the delicate situation kept him in camp following the idle 1782 campaign season, much to his dismay. The general himself longed to return home. His dedication to the army revealed his anxiety that monetary grumblings among his men could undo the looming peace if the American army should disintegrate into an armed mob.

Other dangers surfaced, including sentiment that Washington serve as the head of the government and use the army to ensure this outcome. For example, in early 1782 Lewis Nicola, a colonel in the Continental Army, sent his commanding general a letter expressing his sincere desire that the nation be ruled by the commander in chief. While Nicola danced around the issue of titles, he did express a view not all that uncommon during the time. He suggested that "the war must have shown to all, but to military men in particular, the weakness of republics." In this letter, Nicola presented a seven-page diatribe listing the shortcomings of the American republic and the many grievances it had caused the army. Washington's effective leadership, he argued, had proven a source of stability, unlike Congress. He had beaten the British, and he had tried to provide for the needs of his officers and men—often at his own expense. Congress, on the other hand, had delayed and equivocated and denied portions of the army its pay for years. What loyalty had Congress earned from these men who had time and time again defended the colonies? Washington's response to Nicola made it clear that he would have no part in the colonel's thinking. He assured Nicola— in terms that would strike even a twenty-first-century reader as blunt—that he was not to be a king and added, "Be assured, Sir, no occurrence in the course of the war has given me more painful sensations than your information of there being such ideas existing in the Army as you have expressed and [as] I must view with abhorrence and reprehend with severity."[1]

How many in the army shared Nicola's outlook Washington did not know. In the general's estimation, what could prove most dangerous to the American experiment in republicanism was that a growing number of soldiers who had fought for the independence of the civilian government now supported strongman rule in order to reap the promised monetary benefits. An army committed to installing its commander as the "savior" of a revolution may have been the historical norm, but Washington appeared determined to avoid this fate. There would be no mutiny against the U.S. government, no creation of an authoritarian state with Washington in control or any other one person in control for that matter. He could not accept or even suffer such sentiment without rebuking the Revolution, which its architects—including Washington—declared to be about liberty and the chief expression of that liberty, civilian rule.

Early in the following year, the issue intensified. In January 1783, after the states rejected an impost sponsored by Congress specifically to compensate the army, an anonymous author distributed a circular among the officers that called for increased support of the army's intention to secure its back pay by using force. The writer threatened vague retributions by enlisted men pushed "blindly into extremities" if such calls were not heeded by Congress. Washington failed to realize that he was the primary audience of that circular until February, when Hamilton sent a letter warning him that the army may soon act without him and that to curb this discontent, Washington needed to become directly involved in the army's machinations.[2] In his reply to Hamilton in March, Washington stated his intention not to do so, apparently resigned to the current state of affairs but hoping things would not escalate to the point that required him to act.

A short time later, Washington believed he had to act when he became aware of a meeting of his officers to be chaired by his longtime rival Gen. Horatio Gates, a gathering that would presumably decide on the army's support for the civilian government. On March 15, 1783 (ominously the Ides of March, the date marking the assassination of Roman dictator Julius Caesar), Washington formally presented himself at this assembly and delivered a plea for his officers to restrain themselves. He burst into the church hall at the Newburgh encampment, where some four hundred men had gathered and delivered a prepared statement, calling the anonymous author of the pamphlet circulated in January a British provocateur and an "insidious foe" of the army. Though hostile to the sentiment expressed by his officers, Washington was supportive of the meeting. "If men are to be precluded from offering their sentiments on a matter which may involve the most serious and alarming consequences that can invite the consideration of mankind," he stated, "reason is of no use to us. The freedom of speech may be taken away, and, dumb and silent, we may be led, like sheep, to the slaughter." His speech left many in the assembly unimpressed. It was not until Washington prepared to read a letter from Congress attesting to its efforts to secure the sought-after pay that Washington quieted his men, and he did so only because of the way he introduced the letter: "Gentleman, you will permit me to put on my spectacles, for I have not only grown gray but almost blind in the service of my country."[3] The battle was indeed won.

This repudiation, by its commander in chief, of the army's ambition to shape the government of the United States best represents the thin line between the republic that was created and the strongman rule that was averted.[4] As such, it bears careful consideration. In specific terms, Richard Norton Smith in *Patriarch: George Washington and the New American Nation* points out that Washington had been wearing spectacles for some time. That he dramatically called attention to them when facing the conspirators suggests a moment of complicity on the part of those proposing aggressive action; shame clearly won the day, as the audience complied with Washington's gamesmanship.[5] When viewed in its totality, however, Washington's role at Newburgh does not appear to be terribly important. He had little choice but to oppose any such movement by his troops. Even if Washington's opposition to monarchy was not a unanimous sentiment in the colonies, it was a popular sentiment and one that he had embraced when he accepted his commission from Congress at the start of the Revolutionary War. He was honor-bound to follow the orders of Congress, and not to do so would reflect badly on him. Washington's personal reputation was, of course, all-important to him, and to risk it on the chance that citizens would accept him as a monarch was problematic. Knowing the clear American preference for self-governance, Washington would be compromised by an overt grab for power. To try for the crown or something close to this, and in the process subvert the Revolution that Jefferson had declared so eloquently to be about liberty and preventing the abuses inherent in monarchy, would lastingly tarnish his reputation. Worry over this eventuality stayed his hand. Ambition in this sense made Washington a clever man on par with the brilliant minds of his generation.

Moreover, there is the consideration of just what was being proposed at Newburgh by the conspirators. Ostensibly, it was the immediate goal of Gates, Knox, and others to get the army paid and put the government on a sound financial footing. In logical fashion, they argued that there must be a strong association between the army and the business community. Thomas Flexner derisively labels such an alliance "a perfect springboard to fascism" in the second of his four volumes on Washington, *George Washington in the American Revolution*.[6] But did such congruence in March of 1783 necessarily mean a seismic shift in the burgeoning American political life? The conspirators did not think so. The threat of force would be enough, in their view, to establish federal taxation and in this way shore up the finances of the government and pay the army. Men such as Gates and Knox believed that it was not necessarily congressional refusal to pay the army that was the problem but rather Congress's lack of authority to raise the funding necessary to pay government debts. Washington recognized these same problems, having encountered them all too often while attempting to secure supplies for his army from Congress. The issue, in the conspirators' view, could be rectified with a show of force, nothing more. In this context, what the conspirators proposed at Newburgh was not a coup d'état at all, but an effort to strengthen the authority of a recognized legitimate government. If Gates's motives in this regard could be questioned because he was a rival of Washington's and so perhaps wanted to usurp power and best his former commander, the same could not be said of Knox, who had always been a trusted Washington subordinate. There were simply too many voices involved in this movement to assume that these men desired the overthrow of the Confederation government. More likely, the conspirators wished to solve the very serious problems afflicting the civilian authority, albeit in a manner engendering potentially ominous consequences.

Finally, to view Newburgh as a military overthrow of the government seems unlikely because it was inherently impracticable. The imposition of federal taxes on the colonies by a government now overtly backed by a military hammer would amount to taxation without representation, and rejecting compulsory taxation by a hostile government was ostensibly the very rallying call of the Revolution. For this reason, any government headed by a man chosen by the army probably would not enjoy much popular support. Moreover, with what martial power did Gates intend to enforce such taxation? The soldiers in the Continental Army surely outclassed the various state militias, but not to a degree that allowed ten thousand regulars to police the nation. If the larger British army could not exact taxation at the point of the bayonet, it is unlikely that Gates's conspirators could. And what of the motivation of the troops Gates would have to use to take this action? Once they were paid, what would compel these men to continue the oppression of their brethren? Seen in its entirety, the Newburgh Conspiracy was not much of a threat at all.

Regardless of the plot's impracticality, Washington had acted to circumvent any such scheming. But what were Washington's true motivations? First, there was the issue of his personal prestige that was tied to the preservation of Congress. An overthrow of the government, while popular with some, would violate Washington's word, given when he accepted the congressional commission to lead the army and defend the government. Second, Washington must have understood the practical limitations of the use of military force to establish the rule of law. He must have known that any such plan would eventually fail without popular support, as had just been shown by the Revolution. Finally, what was Washington to gain by wearing a crown, assuming the opportunity was offered to him? He was already the most respected and sought after leader in the burgeoning nation, and he spent a considerable amount of his time corresponding with nearly everyone of importance in the colonies. As one of his biographers, Joseph Ellis wrote in *His Excellency* about Washington's role at Newburgh, "At the personal level, Washington was declaring that he had sufficient control over his ambitions to recognize that his place in history would be enhanced not by enlarging his power but by surrendering it."[7] For Washington, what could be gained by any type of coup? Nothing. What could be lost? Everything.

No, for the United States there would be no monarchy. It would not trade one George for another, and Washington vocally placed his trust in the institutions of the republic. In reality, Washington's opposition to the Newburgh proposal did turn out to be largely irrelevant. Some eighty soldiers, mostly enlisted men, made the trek from the Newburgh area to Philadelphia, where their number grew to more than four hundred. Although this small mob did manage to disrupt the sitting Congress, order was quickly restored, and the Newburgh conspiracy went no further. The outcome was unlikely to have been different had Washington supported their actions. The Revolution did not embrace authoritarianism at this time, or any other, because no such popular sentiment existed in the body politic. In this light, the hero of Newburgh was not Washington and his virtue, but the average citizen's hatred of kings. For this reason, Washington was largely an impotent figure only able to magnify the will of the American people, not shape it. Washington understood this key distinction, and by carefully playing his part in the larger drama, he advanced his own position within the new nation. Newburgh may not have been as dangerous a threat to the emerging republic as scholars writing about the event have led us to believe, but it is clear that Washington's shrewd assessment of the situation, and his recognition of his inability to capitalize upon it, did indicate where the true danger lay. The general was an ambitious man engaged in the political struggles of his age, and he intended to come out on top. The only question was that of tactics. His political sensibilities in this regard were to serve him very well indeed, certainly more so than his at times horrendous tactical abilities on the battlefield. The famed general, the leader of men, was proving to be a keen political animal, and it was unclear that the American experience could bear such a beast.

After his seemingly miraculous stand at Newburgh, Washington appeared to do what few military leaders had done: he retired from public life. On December 23, 1783, in a formal ceremony at Annapolis lasting but a few moments and conducted before just twenty or so Congressmen, Washington resigned his commission. His lone indulgence had come a few weeks before this date when he had enjoyed a dinner with a small number of his most trusted officers at a local tavern. The toast he offered on that occasion was only outdone by the fulfillment of his promise to end his public service. And so a few days before Christmas, the great American military commander gave up his authority. This act was hailed outside the colonies as a momentous one. In a possibly apocryphal story, King George III, the recent enemy, remarked that, "if he does that [lays down his sword and returns to his farm], he will be the greatest man in the world." Samuel Adams, writing for the legislature of Massachusetts, made a special point to note that the rights they had just fought for were "too often violated by Men in Arms." He asserted that in the case of Washington, the opposite had proven true, and American patriots had been right "to applaud that sacred Attachment which you [Washington] have constantly manifested to *the Rights of Citizens*." From Adams's point of view, a historical moment had indeed been achieved in the Americas.[8]

His submission before Congress served as an important symbol, as Washington outwardly established the concept of military personnel deferring to civilian authority. Such conclusions, however, ignore the fact that Washington walked away from the incident at Newburgh with a greater hold on power than if he had drawn his sword and led that march on Congress. Washington's formal exit from public life strengthened his position within society, so the end of his military career did not speak to some innate republicanism within him. Rather it was simply one more example of Washington's deference to what society wished him to be—another way to secure societal advancement because his actions gave him more public accolades.

Washington's "retirement" in 1783 must be considered in the same light. The greatest public servant in the colonies finally returned to his wife and home that Christmas of 1783, but how long he would stay there was another question. While he was relieved to be home, very soon he developed a strong sense of melancholy that could have stemmed from the boredom of running his estate or more likely arose from his fear of relatively early death. His father, his brother Lawrence, countless distant relations, and of course his recently deceased nephew were all examples of Washington men who had had short lives, and these losses weighed heavily on him. In a letter written in 1784, he confided to Gilbert du Motier, Marquis de Lafayette, a trusted subordinate during the war, how he viewed his fate: "That I was now descending the hill I had been fifty-two years climbing, and that though I was blessed with a good constitution, I was of a short-lived family, and might soon expect to be entombed in the dreary mansions of my fathers." Jefferson noted that Washington was consistently concerned with "gloomy apprehensions."[9] This strong belief that he would not live much longer fueled his motivation to establish himself as a man dedicated to the recent gains of the Revolutionary War. Moreover, his lack of an heir preyed upon his considerations of mortality and the future; the family name may not survive his death. Should this occur, his place as the founder of the country could be in jeopardy as well. Therefore, he looked to retirement to ensure his legacy in a historical sense, that is, as Ellis put it in *His Excellency*, his immortality would lie in the "memory of succeeding generations."[10]

Washington worked diligently and actively toward producing such a memory. Flexner explains in *George Washington and the New Nation*, "Less than a month after he had returned his commission to the Continental Congress, Washington wrote to ask if he could have the document back. The paper, he explained, 'may serve my grandchildren some fifty or a hundred years hence for a theme to ruminate upon, if they should be contemplatively disposed.'"[11] Washington understood the importance of the document he had bequeathed to Congress in that it served as evidence that a republican general had surrendered command when the fighting was over. But in Flexner's estimation, this aim could not have begun with his children, since he had none of his own. It is possible that the Custis children, whom he regarded with great affection, figured in his mind, but more likely the former general must have been thinking of securing his historical legacy among the inhabitants of the new nation. The impoverished and indebted Congress obliged the former commander, returning his commission in a gold box. This telling response helps to place the value Washington ascribed to his legacy in a proper light by showing the respect he had earned from the representatives of the people. It also may indicate their relief. Always distrustful and fearful of military power, to Congress a gold box was a small price to pay to enshrine the action of the former commander.

Once at home at Mount Vernon after his retirement from the army, he received all manner of visitors. Everyone from his close associates to a large number of strangers felt entitled to stay at the estate, and Washington did not discourage them from doing so. Here was a chance to further enhance his image as a servant of the people. Upon arrival, the guests encountered a man living a self-proclaimed simple life, enjoying only a "glass of wine and a bit of mutton." The meals Washington served his guests were often fancier than he let on, and Americans were impressed with the great man, even though he himself did not always attend these dinners. A few Europeans were harder to please. Gijsbert Karel van Hogendorp, a Dutchman whom Jefferson had introduced to Washington as "the best informed man of his age I have ever seen," found Washington to be "slow of perception" and "commonplace."[12] Such sentiment among some did little to deter those traveling to Mount Vernon. The stop was very popular, almost obligatory, when coming through northern Virginia. Mount Vernon soon became the symbol of the new United States, something Washington encouraged with additions to his estate and grand plans for the region. He was the acting chief executive of the nation even without holding such a post. Whether the former general's pandering to the masses meant that he merely hoped to cement his image as a successful general or planned to pave the way for a new role in the near future remained unclear.

Washington soon offered a clue as to his intentions. More important than the majority of his houseguests were the numerous artists who called on the great George Washington. Sculptors created his image using life masks, a process that was troublesome to both Washington and his wife, who also underwent the treatment. To create such a mask, the artist slathered a plaster-like substance on the face of the subject in the same manner people had used to make death masks for centuries. It was tedious and potentially dangerous if the procedure deprived the subject of sufficient oxygen. Simply going through this intensely distasteful process suggests that Washington thought it of great importance in order to ensure his image survived. Perhaps speaking to what he believed were the republican principles of the day, the sculptors themselves were of a great variety. The little-known Joseph Wright worked with Washington, as did the more famous Jean-Antoine Houdon, the latter strongly recommended to Washington by Jefferson.[13] The depiction Houdon created of Washington speaks to the reputation the general believed he had won to this point in his life, or at least the reputation he coveted. Garry Wills points out in *Cincinnatus: George Washington and the Enlightenment* that Houdon's end product was Washington's visage as a reincarnation of a Roman soldier in the likeness of the farmer turned general and then farmer again, Cincinnatus.[14]

That Washington allowed these artists to call on him spoke to his less-than-passive role in the creation of his legacy. His was a conscious effort to secure how he would be viewed by future generations. Even before the end of the war, Washington had convinced the Continental Congress to provide him with a team of secretaries under the direction of a young officer named Richard Varick to take charge of Washington's wartime correspondence. What this team produced were the Varick Papers, the first of many volumes of Washington's correspondence. In pointing out this early attempt by Washington to secure his legacy, Ellis in *His Excellency* calls it "stunning" that Washington did not consider it an expense that he should shoulder himself, especially since the general made his request at a time when Congress struggled to furnish the army with its most basic needs. In producing works like this, Washington, Ellis suggests, hoped to avoid inquires into his personal life and to avoid interviews, which he considered vanity, a quality that the general believed he lacked: "I do not think vanity is a trait of my character."[15] Washington's definition of vanity remains unclear, but to boast of its absence during the war and then mount a postwar campaign to be remembered by future generations hardly adds credence to his self-assessment.

The campaign to advance his reputation after 1783 soon progressed in another direction. When histories of the Revolution and its military hero surfaced almost immediately, Washington made sure he had a hand in them.

In the first work, produced by William Gordon in 1788, the author depicted the war as a glorious struggle won by American heroes, none more prominent than Washington. Gordon, for example, blamed General Greene for the military disaster that overcame Washington's forces in New York in 1776. As the previous chapter in this book made clear, there was a good deal of blame to go around to explain the failure of the New York campaign, and some of it ought to rest with the commander in chief. However, Gordon's account suffers most of all from the obvious influence of its still-living subject, who had forwarded a manuscript to Gordon consisting of what the retired general called "facts" to better do justice to the actors in the narrative.[16]

Washington also advanced on another literary front. While Gordon was producing his work on the Revolution, Washington hired David Humphreys, a poet and Yale graduate, to produce a "sketch," or brief account, of Washington's youth. Ellis disparages this pursuit because he notes in *His Excellency* that Washington chose to "edit out his early ambition to become a British officer and inserted slight distortions or evasions designed to conceal the controversies surrounding his surrender at Fort Necessity," thereby creating a work of "revisionist" history in that author's estimation.[17] It is clear that Washington was taking an active, and partially dishonest, role in shaping his legacy after the end of the war. The Washington produced by Humphreys was not the ambitious youth striving for respect and laurels, but a competent commander and future hero. Likewise, the leading figure in Gordon's work conducted himself as a man always confident in the outcome largely because it rested on his own abilities. This assumption of victory hardly did justice to the events of the war, a struggle with frequent moments of crisis, many created by Washington himself and his less-than-acute military ability.

A controversial event during Washington's retirement threatened to ruin all the work he had undertaken to preserve his legacy. The Society of the Cincinnati was a fraternal organization created after the war to promote the camaraderie of former colonial officers. Additionally, the society provided for officers who had fallen on hard financial times since 1783. In a way, the organization offered what many of these officers had allegedly been conspiring for at Newburgh: financial redress. Washington strongly believed in the charter of the society: to promote the brotherhood of his former officers but not meddle in political affairs. He supported it so much that when he returned to private life, it was one of the few organizations in which he remained an active participant.

The problem for the society, and for Washington by virtue of his association with it, was that it was unpopular outside its own ranks. To the uninitiated observer, the organization did more than provide a safety net to former officers. Its obvious appeal to elitism appeared hostile to the nation's call for republicanism. The organization was designed to outlive the current generation, and membership was not open to all but was reserved exclusively for the eldest male in the family line. This hereditary mandate echoed the titles of nobility transferred from parent to child in hated Great Britain. That the society had chapters in all the states also appeared sinister. Only the weak central government could boast of fostering such unity in the newly independent country, and this it did imperfectly, so much so that in the eyes of its critics, the society mounted a dangerous challenge to the government.

A number of Americans attacked Washington's association with the society, and he worried enough about this resistance to ask Jefferson to weigh in on the topic. Jefferson reported from New York that the majority in Congress were adamant that "the natural equality of man," so important to this new republic, was damaged by having the American equivalent of a peerage.[18] Of course, he added, because Washington was involved in the society, few feared its intentions. That was not the point, however. Jefferson pointed out that the society looked to continue beyond the current generation, bestowing rank and privilege on men who had not earned the right. The stake in society held by these second-, third-, and fourth-generation Americans was increased by their lineage alone. Thus, the society was antirepublican, since it bestowed honor not personally earned. Even if he was overstating the case, Jefferson's response made it clear that the organization was a problem for the young republic and for Washington.

The question of the Cincinnati indeed struck at the heart of the Revolution's ideals and the American interpretation of the Enlightenment. A peerage was not, necessarily, antithetical to the ideals of the Enlightenment, but it was antithetical to the declared intentions of the American nation to embrace republicanism. It is telling that the language Jefferson used to alert Washington to the dangers posed by the society was so Jeffersonian in content: "the natural equality of man" that Jefferson referred to was very much akin to the language of Rousseau. The young Virginian, ever the Francophile, believed that the Cincinnati would not be compatible with American notions of equality, in this case defined by a push for democracy. This interpretation presaged the fights to come between Hamilton and Jefferson during Washington's administration over, among other things, the assumption of debt accrued during the Revolutionary War and, therefore, the meaning of the Revolution as one more restrictive in its outlook or one driven by a more expansive understanding of citizen representation in a republic.

After Jefferson's warnings, Washington feared the risk to his own reputation should he remain a member. In May 1784 he attended the group's meeting in Philadelphia, where he attempted to force changes to the society's charter that included ending hereditary membership, restricting the number of its national meetings, and ensuring the language associated with it remained apolitical. Having won approval of most of these changes, Washington accepted reelection as president-general of the organization, a dramatic outcome, since he had been prepared to preside over the dissolution of the society or resign from it altogether. Still, in the wake of this "success"—and a limited one at that, since the societies in other states blocked any changes to their own organizations—he began to distance himself from the organization by not attending its meetings and functions. Too compelled by feelings of brotherhood with his officers to abandon the society completely, Washington was nevertheless able to stave off serious damage to his reputation by his effort at making changes and his increasingly loose association with the Cincinnati. Once again, he had placed the views of the majority of Americans above those ideas he appeared to truly support in order to maintain a respectable reputation and to preserve his status among the population at large.

Besides weighing the importance of the Society of the Cincinnati, Washington busied himself with other pursuits, usually related to Mount Vernon. A tour of Washington's residence today offers visitors a stunningly beautiful view of the Potomac River. Improving his property naturally consumed much of his time after he returned from the war, although he soon

tied this pursuit to his larger agenda of advancing his reputation. Before setting off for the Continental Congress in 1774, Washington had built docks
on the river to help him ship his goods to other colonies and abroad. Now,
during retirement in the early 1780s, these docks spoke to the vision he
had for greater unification among the states that would come through increased commercial contact. The first step to this integration would be taken
by Washington himself with the founding of the Potomac Company, something he hoped would become the centerpiece of his legacy. By working
through this entity to improve navigation on the upper reaches of the
Potomac River through construction of a series of falls-avoiding canals,
Washington looked to make Alexandria a flourishing commercial center.
The survey work for the plan and the engineering involved tapped jobs
Washington had enjoyed in his youth. Here was a chance to devote his energy into one all-encompassing venture from which he stood to reap a substantial financial gain. Certainly in its immediate application it was good
business, and the larger goal was a valid one as well. Henry Clay's "American
System" of the late 1820s and 1830s proposed just this, using economic
gain, including an improved infrastructure, to strengthen the bonds between
the states, proving that Washington's thinking was ahead of the times by
some thirty years.

The Potomac served as the border between Maryland and Virginia, and
Washington needed permission from both states to complete this interstate
project. He had failed to secure the necessary legislation in the early 1770s
prior to the outbreak of war. Now, given his prestige, he won approval in both
the Virginian and Maryland state legislatures. However, since the Articles of
Confederation left the states wide latitude in regulating their own commerce,
much remained to be worked out, including fishing rights, specifics regarding
the construction of locks, right of way titles, tariffs, and so forth. In March
1785 those involved in the issue of navigation of the Potomac were to formerly
meet during a conference in Alexandria. Instead, Washington invited the delegates from Virginia and Maryland to assemble at Mount Vernon, where they
eventually resolved their mutual-use issues over the course of eight days.
Before departing the Mount Vernon Conference, the delegates suggested an
annual conference to support trade relations between the two states. If possible, Delaware and Pennsylvania were to be included as well. Even though his

efforts failed to move the canal project forward because the construction techniques of the period made the necessary improvements unattainable, the meetings regarding Washington's river company grew into a call for a larger convention to discuss how to achieve a greater unity of action among the states. It was the next convention at Annapolis held in September 1786 that would help lead to the famous Constitutional Convention and bring the "father of the nation" out of retirement.

In this way, the Potomac Company became one more example where Washington's retirement worked to advance his reputation. But he soon grew conscious of the need to service something more than his legacy, a belief that moved him in the direction of reentering public life. From his vantage point, the "virtue" that had propelled the revolutionaries to declare independence had waned during the years of his retirement. Without the threat of "oppression" at the hands of Great Britain, Virginians, Carolinians, and New Englanders simply had very little reason to see themselves as one nation, let alone to support that nation in any real way. Such discord meant trouble for Washington. Even if he had no further public ambitions, as he professed at the time, he treasured the status he had earned among his countrymen. The place he occupied, after all, was at the pinnacle of society, no small accomplishment for a gentleman farmer from Virginia. In the United States, Washington was clearly without equal, even if he did not hold an official position in service to the nation. But what if there were no United States? If there were no nation to carry on the revolution he had won, then what would be his legacy? Could one be the "father of a nation" that did not exist?

Further, Washington, while in retirement, lost faith in the Articles of Confederation. This sentiment was already clear when the day before his resignation from military service, he had given a toast at a formal dinner and wished "competent powers to Congress for general purposes," implying that competency was a quality the members of that body lacked. Also, before his retirement he had told Hamilton, "No Man in the United States is, or can be more deeply impressed with the necessity of reform in our present Confederation than myself."[19] In June 1783, one of his last official reports, in the form of a circular letter to the states, had urged this reform on Congress by instilling this body with more power to better preserve the union emerging from the war.[20] Now, as he watched from Mount Vernon, Congress did little to assuage his fears. He wrote in his journal in August of 1785, "We have probably had too good an opinion of human nature in forming our confederation. Experience has taught us that men will not adopt and carry into execution measures the best calculated for their own good, without the intervention of a coercive power. I do not conceive we can exist long as a nation without having lodged somewhere a power which will pervade the whole Union."[21] Of course, Washington had previously divested himself of any direct coercive power at Newburgh, and he had done so again after retiring from public life for many reasons, including his rejection of centralized rule rooted in the military. Now, only a few years later, he was supporting a push toward some type of coercive force to bind the nation together in the name of preserving the Revolution, an appeal to defending the spirit of 1776 that was not always distinct from his own identity in the eyes of Americans.

What could be done to correct the inherent flaw in the Articles of Confederation? The former general was only too conscious that any action on his part supporting anything close to governmental coercion trespassed on his own legacy and therefore his reputation, so he rebuffed supporting a convention to revise the Articles. John Jay asked Washington in March 1786 if he would consider attending such a conference as a delegate and head off a looming crisis, since "the better kind of people" were openly discussing the possibility of a monarchy. Hamilton, in fact, would propose this very form of government at the Constitutional Convention, albeit a limited monarchy seeking to curb anarchy and tyranny by balancing an elected monarch with guarantees ensuring the liberties of a republic.[22] Washington must have been tempted to feed his desire for respect by emerging from retirement to save the day, as it were, and helping create such a position, but he declined. Instead, he noted in his response to Jay, "What astonishing changes in a few years are capable of producing." He went on to critique a regression into monarchy as "a triumph for our enemies," allowing them to "verify their predictions" that a government of ordinary citizens could not long endure.[23] When historians portray Washington as the virtuous republican, these words go far to establishing this view. Ellis, hardly an unabashed critic of Washington, argues in *His*

Excellency that Washington was genuinely retired when the initiative for a Constitutional Convention came about, that he had no desire to risk his reputation as the Cincinnatus of American history by reentering politics.[24] By declining to attend any such conference, Washington reaffirmed his retirement from public life.

While Washington did favor a stronger central government, he recognized that the people would not accept such a concentration of power without good reason. In his view, that reason came soon enough in the form of Shays's Rebellion. In August 1786, only a few months after Washington had turned down Jay's plea, former colonial officer Daniel Shays led an "army" of farmers in rebellion against the local authorities of Massachusetts. Their grievance was unfair taxation. The state struggled to put down the disturbance but eventually did so in January of 1787 by marshalling its own army to confront Shays's band and arrest several of the conspirators. However, those opposing Shays had acted without any outside support, the congressional legislators in Philadelphia being incapable of compelling a national army to march to New England and end the threat despite pleas from the Massachusetts authorities. It was a plain failure that in Washington's view exposed the Confederation government as a weak association of independent states. Jefferson may well have believed such violence to be a sign of health in a Republic, remarking to a trusted correspondent at the time of the rebellion, "The Tree of liberty must be refreshed from time to time with the blood of patriots and tyrants," but few others saw it that way.[25] Certainly Washington did not, and he grew increasingly alarmed at the state of affairs in the clearly struggling nation. The threat of open insurrection in Massachusetts frightened many political players, including Washington, who now came around to backing a play to strengthen the central government.

In his charge, a new government would be acceptable, or at least Washington hoped this would be the prevailing view. In truth, this rationale is telling of where he thought his self-interest lay. If such a convention produced a monarchy, even with himself at its head, his status as the great hero of the Revolution would be lost. The converse was as unpleasant to contemplate, however. What would happen if that convention failed, if the nation were unable to create a centralized government necessary to safeguard the Revolution? If this should be the outcome, and chaos reigned in the

United States, his reputation would also suffer. The former general had run himself into a corner. Undoubtedly he was concerned that by attending such a political convention, it would appear that he had broken his word to retire.[26] But under pressure to maintain his hard-won title as "father of the country," Washington did decide to participate in the Convention with the expectation of ensuring the transformation of the Articles of Confederation into a centralized government that stopped short of monarchy. Retirement may have had its appeal, but so too did the lure of taking center stage again. Once convinced of the overriding importance of defending his reputation by returning to public life, Washington set forth to attend the Constitutional Convention held in March 1787.

For all his hand-wringing and second-guessing, Washington's actual role in the convention was relatively minor. Elected chair by an early and unanimous vote, he presided over the debate but did not actually interject himself into the discussions. The Washington of the Convention was at best a titular leader, and he was not a force in the creation of the Constitution.[27] He may have wished he had been more of a participant, because he was not happy with the final document unveiled at the end of the Convention. In his estimation a great deal of ambiguous language prevented the document from clarifying the relationship between the power of the states and the national government. The representatives of the various states had previously demonstrated their parochial interests, and to Washington they had done so again, since the states could still impede the actions of the central government. Ellis writes in *His Excellency*, "He wanted the ambiguities clarified and the sketches filled out, at least sufficiently so to assure the creation of a national government empowered to force the states and citizenry into a budding American empire."[28] Of course, today experts consider the occasionally vague language of the Constitution a strength that allows the government to use its broad authority to force the citizenry into a national mold in much the way Washington had hoped. But in his assessment at the time, while the Constitution did contribute to strengthening the authority of the central government, and it was good that it was open to amendment, the Constitution failed to ensure federal supremacy over the states; this was a negative because the representatives remained loyal to the needs of their states' residents.

The shortcomings as he defined them were something Washington was forced to live with. The Convention made him the first president of the United States, pending approval by the states of the union. Under the pen name of Publius, Hamilton, writing in what would become *The Federalist Papers*, surely convinced more than one person of the benefits of the new Constitution and helped secure passage, but it was Washington's standing that won the day. Only he was the safe choice to move this bold experiment forward. James Monroe wrote to Jefferson and stated in unequivocal terms that "[Washington's] influence carried this government."[29] One has to wonder if by understanding this, Washington supported what he saw as a flawed document so that he could be installed as president. If so, it was a singular triumph. He now ruled the former colonies in limited fashion on paper, but, in reality, he enjoyed unbridled power deriving from the majesty of his reputation. The preservation, really enhancement, of his reputation over time had made him the most powerful person in the United States, free to interpret the new Constitution as he saw fit since the concept of judicial review would not be established until 1803. Because of the ambiguity he identified as inherent in that charter, he now enjoyed considerable latitude in defining the new powers of the government. He had accomplished a masterful gambit, assuming a deferential demeanor to place himself at the head of the new government. It was a position that "the hero of the Monongahela" could only have dreamed of reaching, but he was now there. A unanimous ballot of the newly created electoral college elected the first president on February 4, 1789, and George Washington was inaugurated as president of the United States on April 30, 1789. He now looked to add to his legacy.

NAPOLEON

The assumptions heaped upon Napoleon by those fascinated with his life today are never more misplaced then when discussing his rise to power. There is no question that his early military career soon gave way to opportunity for great political advancement. A calculating Napoleon emerges from this period of checkered French politics. Awarded command of the Army of Italy for his success in protecting the Directory, he would maximize this opportunity by trying to turn military achievement into a greater accumulation of power. He would go far, perhaps farther than he had ever expected, particularly after the ill-fated invasion of Egypt in 1799. Napoleon led this expeditionary force but soon found himself bottled up in a region that effectively removed him from the French political scene. After his flight from Egypt and sudden return to France, he discovered that he was still a desired commodity, if for no other reason than to serve as a tool for those planning to overthrow the doomed Directory. Napoleon would surpass all intriguers and come to rule France. But control of that country had never been his goal; it was his opportunity. Unsteady in his new position of First Consul, a circumspect Napoleon would plot his course to absolute power very carefully. Thereafter, he would not repeat this behavior, casting caution to the wind, since he was now convinced of the need for the French people to be led and that he was that person to do so. Still, his path to becoming emperor of France had been a long journey in a short period of time, its outcome never certain. In this light, to label Napoleon ambitious certainly hits the mark, but to consider him covetous of absolutism simplifies his accidental gain from his opportunism. France would need Napoleon more than Napoleon needed France. That this symbiotic relationship would reverse itself years later reflects Napoleon's unbridled ambition, but only after an equally ambitious French society welcomed its new master.

Ambition, talent, and drive certainly presented themselves as Napoleonic qualities in the wake of his successful Italian campaign of 1797. Yet such character traits emerged not only in his numerous military feats there but in his conduct of that campaign personally and politically. He would find that a venal streak lay in all mankind, not just himself. He remarked on St. Helena, "In my youth I had illusions; I got rid of them fast."[30] This heady lesson, more a confirmation of a suspicion on his part, freed him to act on what would become "Napoleonic." His self-discovery followed ordinary routes after arriving in Italy and confronting his newly won title of "political" general, a derisive label. He ignored the admonishing comments and, though younger than many of his divisional commanders, he offered no discussion of the forthcoming campaign. Instead he issued orders. That they were obeyed confirms the descriptions of those who remarked on his hypnotic appearance and his ability to engage with his eyes and force compliance to his wishes.[31] This certainly exaggerated ability set down by admirers in later years to commemorate his brilliance must have contained some truth in that his self-assurance surely proved contagious in the tumultuous time of revolution. Generals found themselves willing to obey the new commander, as did the French army. Napoleon's famous declaration to his troops was well received, that the offensive they were to undertake would consist of more than an advance; it would serve as a reprieve from their hardships.[32] A promise of booty, of course, always motivates armies, but to couch such an aim in the revolutionary ideals of liberation, as Napoleon did in this message, must have appeared too altruistic as well as prosaic to all those listening. After all, the Revolution was eight years old, and French armies had been fighting in other countries for five of those years. That his call to arms would in fact motivate his army must have once again clued Napoleon into the power at his disposal, power that emanated not only from his person but from the willingness of the French soldiers and their commanders to allow themselves to be led ostensibly in the name of the Revolution, even if the actuality was a more base goal: survival. The ideals masking reality must have struck Napoleon as creating his true opportunity.

After eighteen months of campaigning, he had the opportunity to dictate peace terms to the Austrians with the Treaty of Campo Formio. The Directory understood the blurring of his military command with political affairs but could do little about it. Napoleon was now too successful by every measure. He had reversed French fortunes on the battlefront in Italy. He had enriched the French government with enormous sums of treasure looted from his area of engagement, and he promised more. In a very real sense, his pillaging had averted a crisis of government at home. His reward would not be a reprimand by the French government, but a final sanction of his ambition in this campaign. The Directory approved the treaty with no changes.

Napoleon now clearly understood that a successful general could do much, achieve much, and possibly move to new heights in revolutionary France. The military career chosen for Napoleon by his father had indeed been a path to greater heights. To achieve supreme command of the French nation was hardly a goal at this point, but to reach beyond his hopes and move ahead socially—this was absolutely within his grasp. For this reason, with this end now ingrained in his mind, he delayed leaving Italy as long as possible.[33] There, he ruled his own fiefdoms that he labeled the Ligurian and Cisalpine Republics. The aim was not to act as someone who was just in command, but as someone in command who could wield a reputation that extended his influence beyond the army to become a "benefactor for humanity."[34] A reputation as an able administrator and lawgiver now defined Napoleon and was something he carved for himself, along with the new states he created out of the fabric of northern Italy. From this cornerstone could come political gain and therefore social advancement. Back in France, uncertainty awaited, since he could not possibly hope to repeat this contradiction of enjoying unfettered power in a republic. Over the course of the next several years, he would recalibrate this assumption.

First came a change in his personal makeup. The mixed results of the Egyptian enterprise completed his loss of idealism, and the shift was significant. While sailing to Egypt, Napoleon conversed with the many scholars accompanying the expedition, in one instance asserting his belief in the afterlife by pointing to the stars and saying, "You may say what you like, but who made all those?"[35] Napoleon appeared at home among the distinguished party, espousing truths that promised to make his enterprise something more than an act of force. In fact, the lasting importance of this campaign would come from these savants accompanying him in 1799. They discovered the Rosetta Stone, the key to deciphering Egyptian hieroglyphics, and advanced the study of Egyptology on behalf of all of Europe. Thanks to this company Napoleon was more than a conqueror heading east. He was a cultured man, a general wielding knowledge as well as military might, and with a judicious cause benefited all of humanity, not just France.[36]

Any such idealism, should it have been real, did not survive the expedition. The first blow came with the news of his wife's unfaithfulness. Embittered, Napoleon became more imperious and ruthless. It would be on the march to Acre that he allowed a great military atrocity to occur when his soldiers murdered almost five thousand Turkish prisoners. The second blow came when he finally accepted that he and his army were marooned in Egypt. The halting of Napoleon's military operations meant the stagnation of his ambition, a problem he remedied by deserting his command and reaching France after fortuitously evading the English navy. And he basically discarded his impassioned belief of himself as a new Alexander conquering lands that welcomed liberation. He would be pleasantly surprised that France would be more open to such a heavy hand than would the peoples

of the east. As it was, he gave his great vision in Egypt little chance to succeed, fleeing back to France once his grand schemes underscored how small
a presence he was outside the confines of Europe. Somewhat shaken by the
disasters in Egypt, he was a timid man, an individual needing a familiar setting to define his ambition. He would look to reposition himself in a France
still offering the opportunity for an aspiring general to advance himself socially due to sudden changes in the political winds. He would reap a heavy
profit from this optimism.

Once he returned from Egypt, Napoleon fended off impassioned pleas
from several of his brothers and sisters to jettison Josephine and look to
marry another. His wife had come to him largely as a gift from Director Paul
François Jean Nicolas, vicomte de Barras, and she did not relish being
handed off to Napoleon. Her many affairs while married to Napoleon hurt
him greatly but paled in comparison to the intentional disrespect she
showed him by referring to him after they were first married as simply
"Bonaparte" to her friends.[37] From the point of view of Napoleon's siblings,
she had outlived her usefulness and could only hold him back. Nevertheless
reconciliation with Josephine came in 1799; the question is, why? Later on,
once in control of France, his ambition would crowd out his feelings, particularly amorous ones. There was the memorable scene where the impatient
emperor pursued a rendezvous with a beauty and burst into her room only
to find her with another lover. The man had dallied for an inordinate period
of time, at least according to Napoleon's clock, and his devotion had upset
the Napoleon timetable. Napoleon departed abruptly, apparently denied
any companionship. On another occasion, an actress was presented to him
in his study, but he delayed his advances to complete his ongoing work, the
task leaving him disinterested in romantic pursuit. Some five hours later,
the woman found herself languishing after the rendezvous was postponed
in the name of state business.[38]

These episodes were diversions for Emperor Napoleon. For those scholars
examining the Napoleonic love life, they are correct to note his genuine attachment to Josephine.[39] He would break with her with difficulty just over
ten years later, but not now, not at a time when Napoleon still could be
swayed by outpourings of affection from this one woman. Josephine successfully wept her way back into his good graces. Still, his affections, however

defined or expressed, mattered less than did the significance his family attached to his marriage to Josephine. How was he to rise with her at his side? This question reveals the optimism of all concerned parties that Napoleon had returned at a still-auspicious time; France, fed up with the ineffective Directory, needed sweeping change; and Napoleon would be asked to implement it. He had come far from the days when his attachment to Josephine led all observers to believe that he merely looked to ingratiate himself with Barras. That Napoleon would be the man in control certainly was not the end Napoleon had in mind in late 1799. The question was how far he could go as a front man to those operating behind the scenes. Events soon amended this more limited view in Napoleon's favor.

A France withering under the guidance of the Directory allowed Napoleon to pose as the savior of the Republic. He took this to heart, moreso than did most members of the teetering government. Emmanuel Joseph Sieyès was a famous figure only because of the unlikelihood of his having become a member of the Directory. It had been a twisted path indeed, his evolution from priest to intellectual to revolutionary radical. It was Sieyès who had written the shocking pamphlet that dared to ask, "What Is the Third Estate?" His answer—that it was everything—in many ways fomented the radical turn of the revolution. This triumph placed him on the left, and he began a career authoring constitutions. An austere man, he was not suited entirely to radical politics, so he was an obvious choice by the Directory to add to their ranks to placate the vocal Jacobin opposition in the Council of Five Hundred— one of their kind but not too far to the left. Once sitting as a director, he soon proved this point, since he supported the Directory's decision to suppress radical Jacobin politics, a step that only brought the French government closer to collapse. He cared little, convinced that he could craft a new government with himself in control. It was a heady conceit, one that left him a conflicted man along with his colleague on the Directory, Barras. This sponsor of Napoleon had turned on his rank as much as Sieyès, since Barras's aristocratic background did little to prevent him from assisting the Revolution in moving forward and in the process attacking his own social class. Barras profited from the course he had chosen and soon was a powerful figure in French politics, dominating the Directory in due course. Once this arm of the government floundered, however, Barras bore most of the blame, and his success in stymieing opposition in September 1797 with the assistance of a Napoleon subordinate, Gen. Charles Pierre François Augereau, did little to consolidate his position as things grew worse for France in succeeding years. For this reason Barras endorsed Sieyès as a new member of the Directory to try and shore up a government that was in crisis, and he did so just as Napoleon returned from Egypt.[40]

Nothing pointed to the illness consuming the Directory more than the alliance of Sieyès and Barras. Dissolute in every appetite, Barras was the very opposite of the reserved Sieyès. Yet these conflicted men now looked to set France on a new course. In this context, Napoleon's ambition was no more forthright than his competitors'. This fact could be seen starkly in the plots by other generals, in particular Jean-Baptiste Bernadotte, who drew to his side as many schemers as Napoleon did. They authored a plan to overthrow the government, but nothing came of it after they were detained by Napoleon's accomplices on the day of action. Napoleon had friends in high places, and these men were confident that they could control him. Sieyès looked for a general and considered Bernadotte, but worried that he, despite his republican credentials, would turn the military against the government. When Napoleon suddenly returned, Sieyès saw him as a clear choice, Sieyès assuming he could manage any scenario producing strongman rule. A man of letters, Sieyès would frame a constitution at last worthy of the ideals of the Revolution. But it would all come a little too easy for Napoleon. Important men would settle for familiar spoils. Charles-Maurice de Talleyrand would resume his post as foreign minister, Lazare Carnot that of minister of war, and Joseph Fouché again chief of police. Barras simply self-destructed. When the decisive moment came, he stepped aside, too spent in body and mind to object. Generals accepted postings that took them far from Paris—Jean-Victor Moreau to central Germany, André Masséna to Switzerland. And so the mixed group of intriguers, with often diverging aims, demolished the Directory and established a new government of France, understanding that only one of them would profit the most. That it would be Napoleon was a surprise to all of them.

Venality or avarice cannot fully explain the motives and aspirations of this cabal of ambitious men who soon bowed to Napoleon. Something more was afoot. Indeed, the Corsican enjoyed a distinct advantage, and that was his military experience. He publicly bemoaned the Directory's forfeiture of his victories in Italy. The Austrians had returned and recovered most of what he had gained there in 1797. He said little of the public support the Italians now offered to the Austrians, meaning that French rule in Italy had been brief but oppressive enough for most of the population there to deem revolutionary reforms hollow and hail Austria's return. But Napoleon's reputation withstood this setback as well. Indeed, if one condemned Napoleon for the failed liberation of Italy, all of France would have to face the inability to export the ideals of the Revolution, a step few Frenchmen were willing to take. Admitting the end of the Revolution risked a reaction that meant all trials and tribulations up to that point had been in vain. A Bourbon restoration was likely, and a penitent France would not be in a position to dominate the continent unless the Revolution could again be directed outward.[41] But to move in this direction required a consolidation of the Revolution at home, and France faced the task of, if not ending the Revolution, taming it to benefit from its already momentous ripples. It would be this dynamic that propelled Napoleon to power.

Napoleon was slow to understand the changing tide of revolution, and his obtuseness almost cost him the chance to assume power. Circumstance again would favor him. His brother Lucien, in charge of the Estates-General, took the lead in trying to ensure that his older brother benefited most from the agreed upon coup to topple the Directory. A few of the Directors had asked Napoleon to help them save the Republic by deploying soldiers under his command to safeguard a change in government. Napoleon coyly kept his suitors at bay and guessing as to which conspirator he would support, while he secretly planned to elevate himself to power. This goal was an easy step to consider. The actualization of the plan was much more difficult, and here is where Lucien played the key role. At the time of the coup, Napoleon, very much caught up in trying to seize his opportunity, gave what contemporaries labeled an incoherent and troubled speech to the assembled senators. Louis Antoine Fauvelet de Bourrienne, his aide, pulled him to the side and demanded he stop "talking nonsense."[42] When Napoleon next appeared before the Council of Five Hundred, he was run from the building by angry legislators screaming his name and accusing him of trying to destroy the republic. Once he was in the courtyard, it fell to others to refocus the shaken

Napoleon. Surprisingly, Lucien acted the part that all the intriguers had expected Napoleon to play. Lucien shouted to a detachment of nearby soldiers that the government was in peril, best evidenced by the manhandling of the war hero who had done so much to defend the Revolution. It was now their task to empty the legislature by force of arms. Lucien's antics could not overcome the soldiers' hesitation, and one grand display remained: a feigned willingness to run his brother through with a sword should Napoleon not be devoted to the Republic. That bit of theatricality broke the spell, and when the drums beat, the soldiers engineered a coup.

Lucien's role overshadowed that played by Napoleon, but it raised troubling overtones beyond the fate of the Republic. The temptations now before the Bonaparte family were great, and Lucien did not survive them. His appointment as interior minister appeared to be a suitable reward for his key role in the coup, but he enriched himself on a grand scale and made manifest his belief that the chief function of a government official was to better himself, not France. Such maladministration had been the mistake of the Directory, and Napoleon was not about to repeat it. Moreover, Lucien's lack of personal reserve would grate on Napoleon, who, while profiting from his new position, appeared to be a modest man in light of his brother's multiple new estates, many mistresses, and absolutely unapologetic attitude toward the fumbling of his responsibilities of office. In response, Napoleon reassigned Lucien to diplomatic tasks in Spain, but when he failed there as well, Napoleon exiled him in 1804 to Italy. Lucien's anger never left him, and he convinced himself that his brother's lack of republicanism had led to his own undoing. Lucien's resentment that he had not been named First Consul himself, or even an heir to that position, eroded his supposed devotion to republican values. But it was Lucien who, while in service to France, had published a tract in which the writer compared Napoleon's new position to that of Caesar and Cromwell, dictators who had ended republics.[43] The historical import of this piece could hardly escape attention, as it undercut Napoleon's efforts in bringing order to a chaotic state by illustrating the possibility of his coveting power and so ending the Revolution. It was an inferred accusation Napoleon could not endure. In drawing attention to the uncertainty facing France, Lucien reminded Frenchmen too much of Sieyès and Barras, men Napoleon did not intend to emulate in either their personal behavior or rule—that is, if he did not wish to replicate their demise. For this reason, Lucien's role as his brother's alter ego soon ended.

Regardless of the family relations that both helped and hurt him—best captured by his interactions with Lucien—Napoleon now had to define himself as a politician. He benefited again from some fortuitous circumstances. After his elevation to one of three consuls, he was to serve first as First Consul, the order being decided alphabetically among himself, Pierre-Roger Ducos, and Sieyès. Once in this presidential capacity, he quickly dominated the new provisional government. But this aggressiveness was more a reflex than a design, although there is no disputing the opportune result that came from this instinct to assume top command. More telling is Napoleon's surprise that the Revolution could be so visibly overturned. His speech before the legislators on the first day of the coup had reflected his uncertainty in this regard, as he called for a defense of the republic with brute force but was clearly unwilling to distinguish himself as the person leading this call to arms. In fact, as First Consul, he was still wrestling with the very notion of how he was to maintain centralized power without destroying the Republic. Undoubtedly worried for his position, he no more wished to surrender his newly won office now than when he was in charge in Italy in 1797. Yet he also had to continue to pay deference to the Revolution, seeking a way to ensure that this reality remained so in France and that he did not undo its gains but define them and then present them to France. In his mind he faced a difficult balancing act. He was slow to grasp the reality before him, that France would take this step for him without him needing to do anything at all. The Republic would exist in name but not in fact, and France was willing to embrace the contradiction, even if the coldly logical Napoleon could not accept this nonsensical conclusion.

Context again gave him a reprieve. With the frequent transitions of administrations that already had punctuated the Revolution, exactly how France should be ruled was a problem of the first magnitude. The possibility of more bloodshed dispirited those gauging the next step, and a fear of more "terror" made timidity prevail. Napoleon sensed the apprehension and took advantage of it. He appeared a steady hand to the Jacobins, the chief authors of the chaos that so far was the wellspring of the Revolution. They looked to the general as a moderate, a man who could possibly threaten their republican institutions but who was useful because he would steer away from the intrigues and plots that had plagued their experiments in democracy so far. He appealed to royalists too, since he was a stepping-stone to a restoration of the Bourbon line should he return monarchy to France. Surely, they reasoned, from this step would come another, which would be Napoleon's embrace of France's rightful king, King Louis XVIII, now an exile in Europe. There was another group to consider that had contributed as much to the tumult France now faced as any other faction. The mob—the political entity generously named the "public" in true Enlightenment fashion—also weighed in and it favored Napoleon. No doubt his promise of peace stemming from law and order, really something tangible only in the cloak of his military uniform, ensured the general the support of the public. He was both ending the Revolution (to the relief of France) and embodying its foremost attributes, including the will of the majority. But for the moment, it was clear that hesitancy filled the air, as did a belief in all corners that decisive action could remedy the ills of the country, if but one capable man could be found. Napoleon understood that filling this need could keep him in power.

This outlook explains the cautious steps he took to consolidate power. Relegating his peers in office to insignificance was an obvious move to make but again was more a reflex than a conscious decision. He next acted more aggressively when his fellow consuls, Ducos and Sieyès, were replaced with new men who were reduced to unimportance by title and assignment: Jean Jacques Regis de Cambacérès as second consul and Charles-François Lebrun as third consul. Sieyès recognized the changing tide and accepted the demotion to president of a powerless Senate after the plebiscite of 1800. The first of the famed national elections during the Napoleonic period that would mark each step to accumulating greater power in Napoleon's hands earned him the position of First Consul for a ten-year period and was, in a sense, a second coup.[44] France now looked to Napoleon for its lead; in the public's eye, his decisions mattered most.

Napoleon made sure that reality reinforced this hierarchy. He ended the conflict in the Vendée by pleading with those occupying what he believed was a "middle ground" to side with France, which they did. He looked at this success as a map for his conduct in general, saying that by "shunning left and right he could drive down a large path in the middle." Maybe so, but in this case, the middle ground became defined through trial and error. He had ordered punitive military actions against those fighting in the Vendée, but the harsh measures proved ineffective, as had been the case under previous administrations. Special tribunals offering legal standing to dissenters mollified the resistance much more effectively. So Napoleon found middle ground somewhere between military force and revolutionary practices.[45] It was an early lesson in mixing the two means, and he was quick to realize that he would have to perform more such balancing acts to be successful.

His appeal to the center made for good politics, an amorphous stand that symbolized everything and at the same time excluded radicalism. He indeed had stumbled onto the method of ruling a dying Republic, even if the actuality of this stand during his tenure in power was still uncertain in his mind. He simply hoped that the middle road would be enough for now. In many ways, the Directory made his task easier, since it had attempted to find some middle ground of its own. Its call for a more efficient fiscal system to end the economic malaise gripping the nation, for example, had appealed to the propertied class now dominating the Revolution, who were moderates in that their wish was a government that could consolidate the recent changes rather than making more. The push toward achieving economic prosperity placated this group, as did assurances that their property and place in French society would remain intact. In many ways, the Directory drove down this road.[46] After all, the Directors had held on to their positions largely because they had earned the label of moderate in one way or another, regardless of pasts that painted most of them as radicals.

The government could well offer this guarantee of moderation, but the international setting remained a menacing one to France, still at war with England and its allies on the continent. Facing the prospect of a defeat that would certainly undo the Revolution, the Directory was vulnerable, its limited successes at home forgotten. Timing was everything. As the coup gained momentum in November 1799, France hit an economic nadir and could only move toward recovery. The nation needed a capable general to defeat its enemies abroad in order to at last begin a period of peace and prosperity. Napoleon represented the promise of military success. As First Consul, he faced a formidable challenge because his entreaties with England went nowhere. But his efforts to end hostilities appeared genuine, and in French eyes, it was that island nation that remained intransigent, not Napoleon. Again, his was the moderate voice. It was a surprising conclusion, given the obvious reliance on military power that he represented. In the person of the First Consul lay a veiled threat of forcing a military resolution to the ongoing conflict.

By 1800, after his victory at Marengo, he had subdued Italy for a second time, and France's faith in its new leader appeared vindicated. Napoleon looked to turn his considerable energy inward to the reconstruction of France, and he bowed to the considerable military achievements of others. Moreau's victory over the Austrians in Germany at the Battle of Hohenlinden in early December 1800 received an ovation in France worthy of that given to Napoleon after Marengo. Moreover, Napoleon had made it clear that he had only reluctantly joined the army during the campaign in 1800 when he served as its commander in chief in Italy. Before that point, he had deferred to Moreau as responsible for the main attack in Germany until that general declined to follow Napoleon's plans of advance on Austria. Italy became the main theater of action, and it was under Napoleon's direction only because of Moreau's obstinacy.[47] Nevertheless, the resulting team effort in defeating France's external enemies meant that the country was indeed at peace by March 1802, as England agreed to an end of hostilities with the Treaty of Amiens. Because of this success, something France expected of Napoleon, the First Consul emerged out from under the harmful shadow of the Directory. He would now stand on his own merits, a development he welcomed.

French relief a few years into the Consulate could not efface the troubling sign of the general eclipsing the statesman or at least overshadowing that persona. The military facet of Napoleon's rule was apparent, and it would endure beyond Marengo. Still, France could look at the man as the ultimate product of the Revolution, a creature born of Enlightenment thought and action. The nation had achieved the impossible, a republic in the person of one individual, or so it appeared. However, the brittleness of this arrangement also sent unsettling shockwaves throughout the newly minted regime. Talleyrand, for one, worried openly of what would happen to France should Napoleon be killed in battle or some other misfortune overtake him. Assassination attempts and plots were frequent enough to underscore this possibility. Napoleon again appeared a transitory figure, a stopgap between the excesses of revolution and what appeared to be the inevitable regression toward the restoration of the Bourbons. He understood the implications of the limits of his rule as well. His reply came first in a written note to Louis XVIII, responding to this cast-off royal's plea to Napoleon to reinstate his family line—i.e., himself—on the throne of France. Napoleon told him to put that thought far from his mind, that Frenchmen would never accede to such a move, and that the attempt would cost France a hundred thousand lives, such would be the resistance to his return.[48] The familiar Napoleon dualism had surfaced again in this reply, however. The prediction of casualties proved conservative; something close to a million Frenchmen would die in the Napoleonic Wars. But the majority of these losses came from retaining Napoleon as head of state, and one has to wonder if Napoleon's reply to Louis meant less French resistance to a Bourbon restoration than it did portend the costs of maintaining himself in power. By 1800 France may well have forbidden a move to a Bourbon restoration. When and if the mood shifted, this problem would beset the Napoleonic regime for the duration of his rule.

Once he was established as First Consul, caution slowly dissipated as Napoleon gained experience and confidence. This growing assertiveness made itself plain when he confronted rivals, imagined or otherwise. Moreau was soon immersed in a royalist plot to retake the throne of France. Only intrigues with Bourbon sympathizers could have blemished Moreau's record, but the general claimed to know nothing about the individuals supposedly relying on him to implement their coup. The First Consul's role in springing the trap that undid this general was one of capitalizing on this vague situation where the conspirators may have been nonexistent. When sentenced, Napoleon expressed amazement that the punishment was but a long prison sentence. He intervened and banished Moreau to America.[49] Moreau's rapid downfall greatly aided Napoleon's grip on power. Now there was only one military master in France, a general living somewhere between the legacy of the Revolution and France's new destiny, something yet to be decided; Napoleon was sure to call it a middle path. Moreover, it was clear that Napoleon could not be so easily undone by the political intrigues circulating within France. He again had weathered a storm and gained considerably from it.

If good fortune helped remove Moreau from the picture, the First Consul had a direct hand in removing another potential rival, the unfortunate Louis Antoine, duc d'Enghien, a Bourbon possibly contending for the throne of France. In early 1804 Napoleon ordered d'Enghien seized in neighboring Baden, Germany, and thereafter tried and shot for the dubious accusation of plotting to assassinate him. The First Consul's instructions were obeyed, even to the point of violating the neutrality of that principality, and the heavy-handedness of the decision appeared evident, the push to tyranny revealed. But mostly, Napoleon's instinct for self-preservation shone through, a gut reaction that prompted Fouché's lamentation that executing d'Enghien was "worse than a crime, it was a mistake."[50] Still, little shocked the French, although royals plotting additional moves against Napoleon were taken aback and intimidated to a great extent by the execution. The life of one man, and a royal at that, was not going to end France's love affair with its First Consul. France had come too far in too short a period of time to raise an outcry against Napoleon. Because of this acquiescence, nothing could undo his meteoric rise to power. He watched and learned, absorbing the lesson that France would countenance centralized authority so long as its citizens appeared to be free. Clearly, political freedom meant less to them than did the freedom inherent in civil liberties. In this respect, executing a potential Bourbon leader spoke more to this combination than it did to signaling the advent of absolutism by Napoleon. Frenchmen would more likely gain—or, to be precise, retain—the fruits of the Revolution under Napoleon more than they would under any royal restoration. The civil liberties of the masses mattered more than did the life of a royal. Napoleon continued to represent France's new freedoms; his execution of d'Enghien was a sign of his commitment to this end, not a herald of an advancing tyranny in the name of Napoleon.

Success nourished his ambition. A more belligerent First Consul who looked to establish himself permanently in power was a great deviation from the presidential role at the heart of the constitution designed by Sieyès. The shift was possible because of Sieyès's own fears and therefore circumspection. In trying to strike a balance between Jacobin radicals and royalist intriguers, Sieyès had to find some middle ground that stayed clear of one more pitfall, that which had undone the Directory. Too many ministers and ministries had made the Directory moribund, and it died due to its inability to get out of its own way. The solution, to Sieyès, was a compartmentalization of the government, staffing its branches with Notables. These dedicated republicans would ensure that the government ran smoothly despite the still largely divided apparatus that defined it. In forging this practical idealism, something Sieyès was famous for, he willingly restricted democracy, since the Notables were elected by peers, not the body politic. Even with the most talented public servants discovered and put in office, the fragmentation of the administrative bodies required some oil to run smoothly. Therefore, the government gravitated to a centralization of power and found that oil in the consulship.[51] This was acceptable, even provided for, since those serving as consul were to rotate in and out of office. In this way, the talented were elevated and the most ambitious held in check. The constitution appeared a worthy document.

That Napoleon never surrendered this power after becoming First Consul is an extraordinary thing that reflects favorably on his ability to capitalize on all that came before him. Relishing the idea of Notables, he fostered the creation of a Council of State, an advisory board on which sat the most gifted men in all areas of civics. He pulled ideas from this group and implemented them.[52] He also encouraged the idea that neither the Council nor France would function as well without him because he was the most capable of overcoming endless theoretical discussion by ruling over the Council and implementing their ideas. When he then extended the use of Notables to include prefects who ran each district of France, his authority became more pronounced as France became better governed. To demote the First Consul soon risked too much, and France had to consider what it valued most, democracy or efficiency. The Notables had already made this decision for the nation, since their compliance with continued Napoleon rule did not deface democracy—it validated the best of the Revolution, given that so many of these men now occupied positions that were possible only because the Revolution had ended the acceptance of primacy of birth as the determining factor in holding government office. In shaping his practical idealism, Sieyès had made Napoleon possible; actually, any man in his stead would have been indispensable. But Napoleon redoubled his workload and strove to make it clear that France could not live without him as First Consul.

Presidential power died in this way, at the hands of an aggressive statesman, something endorsed by those shaping the state because of the need for talented leadership in all avenues of government and a public acceptance of measurable results. At the highest level, Napoleon was the enlightened despot, the successful creation of a revolution espousing republican ideals in a country historically prone to accepting royal absolutism. France saw no need to try and improve on this compromise. Sieyès followed suit. Confined to the Senate, he accepted a wealthy retirement to enjoy the proceeds of having given France a presidential figure who was actually so much more.[53]

As if to underscore this outcome, Napoleon had soon shifted the seat of power from the Directory's headquarters in the Luxembourg Palace to what had served as the king's residence, the Tuileries. Once the moment of crisis had passed, Napoleon turned to his fellow conspirators and remarked, "Well, here we are in the Tuileries; let's see to it that we stay here."[54] This statement contained an element of bravado, but it also reflected a troubled mind. He was still uncertain how to make the new government work as a centralized authority that represented republicanism. Dogging his plans remained his belief that a republic must be maintained, even in absolutism. The opportunist was present, and a wiser, shrewder practitioner he was, but he continued to ponder how to resolve this seemingly impossible contradiction.

Napoleon again benefited from a France that pulled him along the path to greatness. National plebiscites confirmed his power in three steps: a push to be First Consul for ten years in 1800, First Consul for life in 1802, and, the most radical step, emperor of France in 1804. These referendums validated at crucial times his belief that France welcomed authoritarianism even as it relished its increasingly compromised republican beliefs. This meeting of minds, as it were, became most visible after the election of Napoleon as emperor. The 99 percent vote in his favor settled him on his goal of absolutism. But surely he expected such a result, since the vote was tampered with on a lavish scale, with Napoleon's advocates simply throwing out an unknown number of opposing votes. It was an established practice. Lucien, when serving as interior minister, had thrown out some three to four million negative votes in the case of the plebiscite of 1800 legalizing the Constitution of the Year VIII. Stability in the form of the Treaty of Amiens, the apparent pacification of the Vendée, and an economic rebound had produced genuine popularity for Napoleon's government in 1802, so there had been little need to manipulate the election result that made him First Consul for life. In the other two instances, Alan Schom, in his biography *Napoleon Bonaparte*, asserts that these acts constitute the greatest electoral fraud in French history.[55]

By 1804 Napoleon was feeling increasingly sure of himself and willing to take greater chances. Still, when standing for emperor, he appeared to have a great desire for self-assurance. One has to ask why, if he already knew the outcome, at least in terms of votes cast? What Napoleon strained to hear was that there had been no uprising, no act of violence to dispute his royal title. In accepting the vote making him emperor, France had embraced the clear contraction of absolutism in a republic. Napoleon's relief was in finally understanding that this referendum mattered most because he at last accepted that the political and administrative elite held over from the days of the Directory wanted strongman rule. The emperor and this new class, these "masses of granite," forced themselves upon the French people because Napoleon could best offer the results of a "civilian dictator" as well as a military one.[56] It was a profound moment of accord in France, punctuated by the acquiescence of the Notables, the propertied elite in France that could have disrupted Napoleonic administrative reform but chose not to in favor of the prospect of material gain.

After this step, it was at times hard to make distinctions between past kings and present royalty. The coronation of Emperor Napoleon in December 1804 blurred them entirely. Some 80,000 soldiers garrisoned the long parade route on this occasion, and all the finest dignitaries of France, many from other nations, and certainly large numbers of the curious public turned out to watch the lavish spectacle. The pageantry of the moment undoubtedly reminded French onlookers of former monarchs, as did the presence of the pope at the ceremony. Riding in the long procession to Notre Dame Cathedral, Pope Pius VII endured the biting comments and scornful looks that came from his newly reclaimed subjects. After all, France had repudiated Catholicism during the Revolution, even going so far as to imprison the previous pope, Pope Pius VI, who had died from that treatment. Napoleon offered an end to this religious war, with the Concordat of 1801. In one of his early acts as First Consul, Napoleon had looked to make peace with the Church, a less popular reform but one he deemed necessary to restore order to France.

Not sure of the reception, he took the precaution of announcing the Concordat in April 1802, after the Treaty of Amiens was completed in March 1802. In this way, peace with England eased French trepidation that a restored Church might threaten the Revolution.[57]

By late 1804 Napoleon's expectations had largely been realized. After much deliberation and many doubts, the pope consented to anoint the new emperor of France, giving Napoleon the added legitimacy, in the tradition of Charlemagne, that he believed he needed. The pontiff's attendance, of course, could also serve to remind Frenchmen that the Revolution had ended in the midst of this religious peace. No doubt considering this development, Napoleon headed it off in truly dramatic fashion by ensuring that a humiliated pope blessed a self-proclaimed emperor. This act was more than a Napoleonic gesture, crowning himself emperor and then placing a crown on Josephine's head. What it symbolized was that he was France, and France had crowned itself, independent of any religious sanction. The Revolution had not ended. It had been sanctified in a holy ceremony where the most renowned religious figure in the land served only as a bystander and therefore as a witness to the birth of a new creation, a new France. This novel entity, headed by Napoleon, was so powerful that even the Church obeyed it. Certainly the act of coronation was august, momentous, and laden with meaning. If soldiers lined the processional route, a symbol of the path to power taken by the new emperor, the self-coronation was a symbol of a new era for France, one initiated by Napoleon, but with a momentum all its own. The moment was a glorified spectacle for a single individual, who had picked up all of France and heaved it into the future. No king could do this; they looked to the past and to the heavens for permission. Napoleon looked to France, and its people consented.

Admittedly, some confusion remained regarding how best to serve France in this new capacity. Was Napoleon king, or was he something else? Always one to improvise in stride with events, he himself was not exactly sure either. At one time he remarked, "I found a crown in the gutter. I wiped away the mud which covered it and placed it upon my head."[58] But this statement had portentous meaning beyond an acknowledgment of restoring a type of royal authority. A reliance on oneself, a belief in his self-made opportunities—these views lurked in the statement as well and grated with a resurrection of royal authority. He was proud of his accomplishments, and rising to rule France as an outsider and one-time enemy of France was one of his proudest achievements. But the jealousy and envy that his family threw in his direction vexed him, as he knew they would be nothing without him, and he lashed out at them for suggesting such benefits were a birthright. Even though frustrated, he still elevated them to great positions of power and wealth.[59] All they enjoyed in France came from his achievements. It was hard to argue with this logic, that his abilities had steered him in the right direction and that he had earned his place and they had not. But even the "great man" understood he had not done this alone. If not aided by individuals, the self-made man understood he was a product of an age, of a revolution, and of an enlightened era. His rule was not a divine right from God. He was a man ordained by an age adhering to the virtue of intellect. While he had surpassed all others, the age he lived in had created his opportunity, and he had seized it. Truly, ambition had elevated his social status, allowing him to reach his lifelong goal. It had been a fortuitous journey indeed.

The ride had not been completely smooth, however. France, after a short respite, had resumed its war with England in May 1803, so the welcomed peace gained by the First Consul soon gave way to the wars of the emperor. Although he failed to keep the peace, France rallied to his side and fought on, even past the era of clear successes in 1806 and 1807, to the bitter end of seeing the invasion of France in 1814. To display this doggedness, something more than war had to sustain the nation, and there was something more. France relished the accomplishments of the man at home and sided with him for that reason. These were tangible enough, but it was also the glory he brought to France that was key as well. Somehow the two accomplishments—statesmanship and military success—intersected, and Napoleon recognized the congruence. In so doing he assumed great power. The balancing act of absolutism with the ideals of the Revolution endured long after his early political success, and Napoleon would carve out a legacy as a statesman as well as a soldier because of this fact.

Two Men of Virtue

The Washington who rode his military accomplishments to the presidency did so in a striking fashion, riddled with contradiction. He had earned his reputation as the hero of the Revolutionary War. Yet, as the new nation struggled to define itself, he strove to appear a harmless general determined to defend republicanism. With much foresight, he began playing this role while still in command of the Continental Army, opposing the emerging coup at Newburgh. Then, in high drama, he resigned his commission and offered his sword to a grateful Congress. But shedding his role as general was part of the act in this unfolding drama. The next step was retirement. No doubt both actions possessed a note of sincerity. The man was worn out by military service and longed to return home. Still, when at home, he obviously longed for the limelight once again, if only to better shape his image for posterity. From his estate at Mount Vernon, he kept tabs on political developments and experimented in economic schemes to exemplify how to better unify the nation. His plans seldom moved beyond the locale of Virginia, save for the overt support he offered the Society of the Cincinnatti. When his allegiance to this institution drew criticism from those who might keep him from retaining his hard-won reputation, he distanced himself from the organization. Again, when his long-term thinking is considered, it appears that political calculation accompained his every step, even if he was loath to admit it.

There could be no denying his move to the background after the war, until one considers the inevitable gain to be had from both his retirement from military life and from his interjection at times into issues impacting the nation. He now possessed the perfect credentials to lead the country. Washington knew the opinion of his countrymen all too well. His skill in playing the part of American hero is in evidence as he oversaw the writing of a history of the just-completed war and endured discomfort to have his image cast to stand for perpetuity. But was the presidency his objective? Once he presided over the Constitutional Convention, the job was his, and he seized it, even if appearing to drag his feet. He said little, letting the disquieting events of Shays's Rebellion provide the catalyst for creating a more centralized government. Still, there was no question that he was the unifying figure of the states, a significant return on feigning the reluctant leader. But would the man remain what he was in the aftermath of war—a figurehead— now that he served representative government? His reserve prior to reaching the presidency suggested to his fellow citizens that the "father of his country" was a safe choice to start the great republican experiment. It was a mandate that would be tested in the years to come.

Napoleon likewise expressed a reserve in office as defined as Washington's, but his was cultivated after his climb to power. Napoleon's reach for power was overt and contrasts mightily with the first American president. His success as a general in Italy brought him much recognition, and he only relunctantly gave up his command there. His Egyptain expedition proved a miscalculation, a hoped-for step to greater military fame, but the campaign did not fulfill this aim. However, Napoleon's reputation was not tarnished even by failure in Egypt, as he raced home to find France teetering on the brink of chaos once again, providing an opportune moment for a man seeking to advance himself in every way possible. In 1799 his ambition met political opportunity, and he grasped it by intriguing with various individuals to establish a new government, but he was determined to put himself in command. He did so, helped along the way by circumstances that could only be described as fortuitous. For instance, Lucien ensured that his brother gained the most from the coup, Napoleon having fumbled badly when looked upon to lead. Once installed as Consul, Napoleon again took steps to retain power but did so self-consciously, clearly not understanding his full opportunity: France had grown weary of the Revolution and now welcomed a capable man to balance a restoration of order with the preservation of revolutionary ideals. In this equation lay strongman rule. When Napoleon arrived on that seat of power, he did so as the reluctant general forced into duty as a statesman in order to do his nation's bidding. The result was empire.

In this way, Napoleon was just as contradictory a figure as the American general. Indeed, if power was Napoleon's mistress, that love made him virtuous when wielding that power. It appears he was capable of devotion, as he was to Josephine, whom he revered, and as he was to France. Like Washington, Napoleon could hardly have aspired for the top governmental post, emperor of France. He was carried in this direction by France, much as Washington was embraced as president by an American public. Napoleon sezied opportunities, but he must have been amazed where these opportunities took him. The same could not be said of Washington, aspiring to achieve the apex of colonial society and purposely playing a part to get to that position. While he operated in the background, his was an overt grab for power, presenting himself as something desired by the body politic, even if he wished to become something more. Washington would serve the United States as president, and his own ambition as well. Napoleon would play the part of emperor, but he did so to better serve France. This outcome underscored that the difference between them lay not within their characters but in the wishes of the enlightened societies they now governed.

4

ENLIGHTENED STATESMANSHIP
Winning the People's Favor

F or both George Washington and Napoleon Bonaparte, brilliant statesmanship decided the limits of revolution. Washington's commitment to the ideals of the American Revolution were always limited, and his tenure as president included marching an army against U.S. citizens who, in his view, were protesting a just tax. Napoleon's commitment to revolutionary ideals was much stronger, and yet he ended the French Revolution with a seemingly complete repudiation of self-rule. In each case, the national well-being was much better off for having had these men in positions of power. There were detractors, to be sure, voices that cried out about the death of idealism after the death of liberty, but these voices were the smallest minority. Still, if Washington served his nation well during his time in office by setting the ship in calm waters, his successes were not his alone. His accomplishments also belonged to the system he had helped to create. Similarly, Napoelon's failure to find that calm harbor was not his failure alone. Though he did not remedy the strategic necessities of the French situtiation, such a triumph may have been beyond the reach of any leader on the continent. And he offered his own good service to the French nation, securing the best ideals of the French Revolution while ending the excesses that had led to the Terror. In the end, each man presented a noble story of the general-statesman, determined to use governmental power to secure the "will of the people" but also prepared to render such service to sate their own ambitions.

WASHINGTON

Not only was Washington an effective statesman, but he was also probably the best choice Americans could have made under the Constitution of 1789. The presidency was a potentially dangerous position from which an individual could threaten the new nation's liberties, given the vaguely defined executive authority. Even with the much sought-after checks on the power granted this office, there were real questions as to the extent of executive license. In the wrong hands, such power might undermine the very republican government that the Constitution granted to the citizens of the United States. Considering the often self-serving nature of Washington's presidency as a means of catering to his ambition, his administration ought to be viewed in this light of posing a looming danger to the office.

His peers widely believed that it was Washington's personal support that allowed the government to come into being in the first place and had he actively opposed the new compact, ratification likely would have failed. But with his support came a price: supporters of the Constitution had to accept the former commander of the army as the first president. Ironically, despite his military background, one historically inimical to representative government, people trusted Washington to wield executive authority because, as historian James Roger Sharp wrote in *American Politics in the Early Republic*, Washington had a "well-known commitment to republicanism."[1] The depth of this commitment is suspect, however.[2] Though effective both in administration and in preserving republicanism, sometimes ruthlessly so, Washington was a more dangerous threat to liberty than is remembered.

Several major questions faced the chief executive of the new government, including how to hold the new nation together. During the era of the Articles of Confederation, many expressed a wish for greater internal unity, a view opposed by an equal number determined to ensure that no governmental entity be allowed to amass potentially oppressive authority. The new president's most discernible political goal during his presidency was to increase concord between the states and therefore overcome this tension gripping the new nation. It was this aim that Washington claimed had brought him out of retirement to support the Constitutional Convention and then serve as the nation's first chief executive. But in protecting the new republic, he also hoped to serve his personal ambition. The unanswered question as he took office was to what lengths he would go to protect his legacy. Was this goal more important to him than fulfilling the Revolution and its promised liberty, or could both aims be accomplished at the same time? It would fall to Washington to strike a balance.

He had reason for optimism. The success Washington had garnered for himself in the new nation became manifest during the journey he took from Mount Vernon to New York, the seat of the new government. He was sent off with cannon fire in Baltimore and at every stop on the week-long passage was beset by well-wishers and local dignitaries. He arrived to ceremonial groups of riders in Philadelphia. When he crossed the Schuylkill River at Grays Ferry fifteen miles outside of that city, a laurel wreath was literally placed upon his head. According to accounts, Washington brushed off the wreath, refusing to accept such adulation.[3] He was not a king, and the hero of the Revolution would not accept any such mandate. Of course, the wreath was probably offered to him because it was understood, even expected, that he would not accept it. But the wreath did signify respect for him as a person and for his reputation. In playing the part of chief executive, Washington feigned the rejection of all things royal even as he accepted the noble tidings heaped upon him. The balance he struck at Philadelphia would have to continue long after his triumphal entry into New York City on April 23, 1789. As if to underscore this point, as he made his way through the city, enthusiastic admirers feted him with a verse set to the tune of "God Save the King."[4]

His first act upon his arrival in the capital was to accept the presidency and to do so in a way befitting the public's understanding of its hero. Washington's inaugural address on April 30 was interesting in as much as it was the first and therefore a novelty. He began his speech by reminding the crowd of his limited ability, a judgment he had offered when he had accepted many of his public duties in the past. Moreover, he emphasized his modesty by referencing the possibility of succumbing physically to the demands before him and therefore failing to complete his important work as president. As if to lighten the load, he offered neither great policy initiatives nor any general course for the government to take. While citing the clause from the Constitution that the president ought to pursue those measures he finds expedient, he recommended no actions other than to suggest that the country avoid partisan squabbles and party animosity. In effect, he left the act of governing to the other elected officials serving the nation. Such was the duty of Congress. Washington did offer one specific and that was to continue his policy of free public service, requesting only that he be reimbursed for expenditures that he made in service to the government.[5] With that speech, the new government officially came into being.

Washington's presidency almost became one of the shortest in American history. As he began to govern, he was struck down by a nearly fatal tumor. For most of his first summer in office, the new chief executive lay in New York, incapacitated and seemingly on his deathbed. The crowds that gathered outside the presidential residence to pay him homage remained quiet, lest they disturb the convalescing man. The illness lent credence to those pronouncements of ill health made during his acceptance speech. Lucky to have a full recovery some forty days after surgery removed the mass from his leg, Washington again commented privately to Dr. James Craik, a close friend, that he expected to die early in life.[6] Though this illness seemingly had no immediate impact on his presidency, Washington's stamina and mental fitness would become a political issue in time. Upon taking office he was already fifty-seven years old. But in 1789, with his health restored, Washington set about shaping the executive branch of government.

His appointments illustrate the true managerial greatness that he aspired to and largely achieved. Most importantly, he placed Alexander Hamilton of New York at the Treasury Department and Thomas Jefferson of Virginia at the State Department. These were top political figures in their own states, so in this sense they were very good selections. But they were also two men who soon distrusted each other and then actively plotted against one another, a growing rivalry that threatened to disrupt the new administration. In making these appointments, Washington strove to balance the needs of the nation by reflecting the country's strong regionalism. Hamilton represented an important northern state, and Jefferson, from the South, was from the largest state in terms of influence and population. In this way Washington looked to allay the sectional rivalries and loyalties present from the founding of the colonies. To create the working unity he desired, he would prove that northern and southern sensibilities could be brought together in the name of the national cause. Unfortunately, Washington's hope that competing points of view would not mean competing ends proved to be naive. Still, in his own way, he was confident that he could make things work, and by setting a precedent, the same would hold true for future generations. If safeguarding his reputation had deliberately gotten him to the presidency, he now put his legacy at risk. It would be a tall order to see into the future, but if he did not succeed in this regard, it is to his credit that he took the chance.

The first year of Washington's administration was eventful in that projects with long-term significance were initiated. Hamilton, at the Treasury, was busy in April 1789 during the first session of the first Congress (1789–1791) that was convened under the Constitution, putting together the necessary arguments to begin what would be an important test of Washington's commitment to republican idealism: taxation. The authority of the national government to tax was an especially prickly issue considering the formerly contentious relationship between the colonies and the British Parliament over this very subject. Most late eighteenth-century Americans wanted to curtail the power of taxation in the hands of their central government. While the lack of centralized political control protected local sovereignty, this arrangement created significant difficulty in actually governing the nation. The ship of state had too many skippers. For Washington, he needed to only remember the difficulty Congress had in securing pay for the Continental Army during the war years. Perhaps with this experience foremost in mind, as president he increasingly ensured that expediency and practicality won out over allegiance to ideals when it came to this issue and others.

Washington's support of Hamilton's plan would require him to take a definitive stand regarding the national financial debate, a concrete position he tried to avoid. The treasury secretary completed his proposal in December 1789. It was nothing short of revolutionary, consisting of two main parts: consolidation of all debt and the funding of that debt with the creation of a national bank that would manage financial transactions. From the outset Hamilton believed that the national government should assume the foreign, federal, and state debt that he estimated totaled at least $75 million dollars. Hamilton won widespread support for meeting the entire obligation. After only the briefest consideration, Congress agreed with the secretary that the payment of this debt was crucial to the international credibility of this new government.

But assumption of the Confederation's debt raised the question of discrimination. Who would be paid the money owed on the debt issued under the Articles of Confederation? Would it be the current holder, who was now most likely an investor or speculator, or would it be the original holder? For a time, James Madison in the House led a serious effort to pay at least part of the value of the note to the original holder. The theory, imminently democratic and populist, was that the honor of supporting the Confederation and the war effort was borne by the original purchaser. Thus if the debt was to be repaid, it ought to be repaid to that virtuous citizen. But in practice discrimination was completely unworkable because finding the original purchasers of the government certificates was nearly impossible. The debt would have to be paid to the current holder of the note, whether that was the original holder or someone who harbored less republican zeal. By February 1790 Madison's bill had been defeated, allowing Hamilton's proposal to gain momentum.

The assumption part of Hamilton's plan was the most controversial, since the arrangement called for the national government to assume the debts that the state governments had incurred during the Revolution. Hamilton argued that by making state debts part of the national debt, the United States would be in a stronger financial position on the world stage. Foreign investors could deal with one borrower in place of thirteen. And by assuming this debt, the federal government also would further bind the states together in common cause. What was awkward here was that some states had paid down their debt while others had let it fester. The issue became, in a land of liberty, why should one state be taxed to pay the debts of another? Privately, Washington rejected this view. He believed that if Massachusetts had surrendered to the British rather than incur the great debt it did to continue fighting, the states that had amassed a small amount of debt or that now had only a small amount remaining to pay would have lost their independence long ago. He agreed with Hamilton that these were shared debts because they were created in a common cause.[7] In this respect it little concerned the president that many southern states had gone to great lengths to pay off their debt in contrast to several important northern states.

The clash over federal assumption of state debt brought forth the regional infighting that Washington had looked to avoid. The sectionalism between North and South evident from this issue accentuated the still tenuous union of the nation. However, the problem was settled, not through Washington's will or leadership or through a convincing argument for the cause of assumption, but by political compromise. The national capital would be moved from New York to a permanent site on the Potomac River in exchange for the federal government assuming state debt and funding it as national debt. Such a move satisfied southern politicians who believed they had won an advantage in any future political clashes with those representing northern interests because of closer proximity to the seat of power. Conversely, while northern access to power would decrease, the business elite acquiesced because assumption would become law, which it did by the summer of 1790. Now financial elites stood to reap considerable reward from Hamilton's new system.

Even with the legislative successes of defeating discrimination and passing assumption, the tensions arising over the nation's finances continued as Hamilton's effort to create a national bank met vigorous opposition. Here was the last chance to thwart the aims of the treasury secretary; without the national bank, assumption and funding of the debt could go nowhere. Madison (leading from Congress the strenuous opposition to Hamilton's plans), and Attorney General Edmund Randolph and Jefferson (both serving in Washington's cabinet) filed legal briefs arguing against the constitutional authority of the U.S. government to establish a bank of the United States.[8] Tendering banknotes supported by government bonds to secure debt backed by the federal authority was problematic from a legal sense because it would serve to create a type of paper currency. Article I, Section 8 of the now-standing Constitution gave Congress the exclusive right and obligation to coin the money of the United States. Article I, Section 10 also made it illegal for any state to offer anything but gold or silver as a tender of payments on debt. Hamilton's plan appeared to violate the prerogative of Congress by allowing the national government to produce currency that was not gold or silver but was backed by faith in the government's ability to pay. The issue boiled down to favoring explicit or implied powers of the Constitution, the three Virginians supporting the former position by adopting a strict constructionist view in order to defend southern interests they saw as threatened at the hands of the predatory northern businessmen who would dominate such a bank.

In an idealized light, those opposing Hamilton on constitutional grounds hoped to limit the centralization of governmental power by defining republicanism as something that was possible only when special interests were kept in check. Washington's presence reassured them that they need not fear the accumulation of the monarchical power they believed inherent in debt consolidation, but what would happen after he was gone? Washington, for his part, had leaned in favor of discrimination, believing it would benefit many of his former soldiers, but he had quietly supported assumption as a means of unifying the nation. On the banking issue, the president eventually decided that he had no choice but to back his treasury secretary. The new nation needed a sound system of finance in order to remain united and grow. Strict constructionism impinged too much on this developmental process. Washington had experienced poor financial situations throughout his life, both personally when managing Mount Vernon and during the Revolutionary War when serving as commander in chief. Thus, it is not surprising that he chose the practical needs of the nation as presented by Hamilton over the clear objections of some important figures from his home state. After Hamilton secured passage of the Bank Bill in early February 1791, Washington signed it into law on February 25.[9]

It was no small accomplishment to finish the national financial debate and to end it in the president's favor. But this compromise, if it could be called that, could not mask the sectionalism that spoke to the deep-set philosophical debate about the nation's future. Was America's simple agrarian society to evolve into a complex commercial enterprise or remain lodged in that pastoral setting? When weighing in on government finance, American leaders ensured that the U.S. Constitution played a key role in the struggle to define the Enlightenment as an ideal that should be fixed in time once attained or become merely a signpost of how modern society should evolve. The debate was impossible to rectify completely in the abstract. Meanwhile,

Congressmen and government officials increasingly defended opposite views on the matter and thereby fostered a partisan political environment that Washington abhorred. In this case, the president's drive for practicality could not avert the disruption of the very premise of his administration: seeking internal harmony by rising above factionalism of any kind.

The second key domain where Washington proved to be an able, practical statesman was handling issues arising due to the French Revolution. This cataclysmic event reached beyond Europe and affected the United States, a nation that in 1789, the year the French Revolution erupted, was looking to leave its revolutionary past behind it. The French tendency to reference the American Revolution for any number of reasons meant the Americans could not quite break free yet. More tangibly, practical problems arose that tested both the new U.S. government and Washington, problems that would have challenged any leader. Loyalties to France, trade relations with Britain, and, in general, the extent to which the United States should become embroiled with revolutionary France were all open questions. If he did not step carefully, Washington believed that a war with France or Britain was possible and that such a war would prove disastrous for the United States. In avoiding a conflict with either nation, Washington showed himself an able statesman but one not strongly committed to the ideals expressed by his countrymen. He would soon find himself out of step with the majority of the American public.

Once the French Revolution occurred, a good portion of the population of the United States became enamored of all things French. Democratic-Republican societies sprung up in the various states that espoused support for the French cause. The South Carolina Republican Society even secured membership in the Jacobin Club of Paris. Newspapers and clergy were often writing about the kinship of ideals between the American and French Revolutions.[10] This view continued even as France veered down a road producing radical changes. By 1792 the country was engulfed by a political storm, its government besieged on all sides by both conservative reformers such as the former hero of the American Revolution, the Marquis de Lafayette, and more extreme elements within French society. At the end of that fateful year, the combination of malcontents and radicals, either by design or happenstance, succeeded in abolishing the French monarchy, executing King Louis

XVI on January 21, 1793. In the United States this news met with approbation from a large majority of the populace that considered regicide a continuation of the spirit that had ended the reach of the British monarchy onto American soil. In the French revolutionaries, more than a few Americans saw their philosophical brothers and sisters straining against the chains of oppression, so U.S. support of France remained widespread regardless of the increasingly radical nature of that movement.

Washington was far less enthusiastic about happenings across the ocean. There were a number of personal reasons for him to be concerned. Lafayette—his longtime friend, surrogate son, and a valuable ally during the war—had eventually been made an outcast in France and, after fleeing, was imprisoned in Austria. He was still thought too French for the Austrians to view him as anything but an enemy. And the convulsions in France accelerated attacks on Washington at home. He was viewed as too formal by many of those now openly supporting the French revolutionaries and their goals. For instance, the *National Gazette* criticized Washington's "fastidious" behavior.[11] Although a journal hostile to Washington and in the employ of Jefferson, it had not directly insulted the president before, which weighed heavily on the mind of one who viewed his service as a call from the people. The journal strained to make its point, however, since only after the French Revolution grew more radical and the Terror promoting a supposedly classless society, could Washington's manner, in comparison to the developments in France, be construed in a way that appeared overly reserved and monarchial.

Aside from the personal concerns and the increasing affronts to him that the growing conflict in Europe created for Washington, there were questions of national policy. The president reasoned that to become directly involved in the ongoing struggle between Britain and France would be harmful to the interests of the United States. Britain was the young republic's primary trading partner, and any interruption in that trade would be troublesome in the extreme, possibly resulting in financial insolvency. England's naval power ensured that it could bring such economic pressure to bear on the United States should hostilities resume between the two countries. Furthermore, Britain retained considerable military power within the boundaries of the United States. The Treaty of Paris of 1783 had called for evacuation of British forts in the Ohio Valley, but by the beginning of 1793, this still had not occurred. Clearly, there would be difficulties at sea and on its own soil if the United States went to war against Britain.

Making the diplomatic scene more difficult for Washington was that France and the United States were formal allies. The Treaty of Alliance between them was left over from America's Revolutionary War when French assistance was greatly needed. The treaty committed the United States to material aid should the French request it, specifically with regard to defense of French territory in the Caribbean. Further, a separate commercial treaty granted French privateers the right to operate out of American ports and use the same ports to set up French prize courts. These two documents, so long as they were in force, gave the French the ability to conduct a great deal of their war effort in the Americas from bases on U.S. soil and shield their military activity behind the stars and stripes. Since Britain would not tolerate American facilitation of French war aims, Washington faced a great challenge as he tried to avoid entanglement in a war he did not want to fight.[12]

The president's concerns about the French Revolution proved to be prescient. As soon as war broke out between France and Great Britain in early 1793, Washington's administration, now entering its second term, confronted the problem of maintaining American neutrality, particularly since the French intended to utilize their treaties with the United States to the fullest. Along with the news telling Washington of the declaration of war, there came word that French consuls in the United States were issuing letters of marque to allow their ship captains to commission American sailors and ships into French service as privateers. The danger here was obvious. As James Thomas Flexner wrote in *Washington: The Indispensable Man*, "It was impossible to believe that the British would accept the veneer of legality that made these American ships seem French ships or would sit quiet while their vessels and sailors were brought as captives into American ports. Motivated by a combination of greed for prize money and pro-French idealism, a small group of private citizens were preparing, in effect, to bring the United States into the war with England."[13] Thus, Washington had an enormous problem on his hands. Since the United States had signed a treaty with France, the law allowed those Americans wishing to do so to serve as privateers in French ranks. The ideological appeal of the French Revolution, the French battle cry of liberty, fraternity, and equality being from the same mold as that which had galvanized the American cause in 1776, increased the likelihood that many Americans would aid the French in this way. The United States had been founded on the principle of guaranteeing individual liberties, so what could its new government do to stop private citizens from exercising their freedom of action, even if these actions started a war? It was a dangerous situation.

In response Washington demonstrated his practical brilliance as a statesman but at the same time clearly compromised the ideal of self-government. Washington believed the United States could not afford to go to war, so he saw it as his duty to protect the country from its own citizens by ordering his cabinet officers to produce a Proclamation of Neutrality, released on April 22, 1793, just over a month after beginning his second term. This declaration went to great lengths to compel the citizens of the United States to "adopt and pursue a conduct friendly and impartial towards the belligerent powers."[14] This pronouncement made it unlawful for American privateers to act on behalf of France. In some quarters, the Neutrality Proclamation was considered nothing more than a way to back the British by handicapping the American support of France. In others, Washington's decree was accepted as a sensible step to take during troubled times internationally. On balance, the proclamation represented the president's true desire to avoid a conflict with either nation. Through neutrality, Washington hoped to ensure that the United States would, as he put it, "improve without interruption the great advantages which nature and circumstances have placed within our reach," and in this way it would not be long "before we may be ranked not only among the most respectable but among the happiest people on this globe."[15] Such growth and happiness would not be possible if the United States were drawn into a shooting war with or against Great Britain or France. For this reason, practicality had to win out over ideology.

The policy was not without controversy in another respect. In so acting, Washington established the precedent that the executive branch determines foreign policy with an almost free hand. This view was not widely accepted at that time. The Constitution does state that the executive must confer with the Senate and secure its consent in foreign affairs, which Washington chose not to do, again for practical reasons. There simply was not time to call the Senate back into session before the privateers Washington looked to stop would go to sea. The Jeffersonian Republicans complained bitterly that Washington sought to support monarchy over republicanism by acting rashly. As with the previous attacks from the Jefferson faction, Washington was personally hurt, since he had always been driven by a desire to avoid such political infighting as now characterized his relations with Jefferson, despite the lengths his secretary of state went to in hiding his role in opposing Washington.[16]

Try as best he could, the president could not escape some fallout at home from the momentous events in France. The growing clamor among Americans to more openly oppose England soon received a boost from the new ambassador that France sent to the United States in 1793, Edmond Genêt. This man's constant reminders of the aid France had provided the colonies during its own very recent revolutionary war, his overt efforts to assure Americans that Frenchmen now walked in step with the United States given their creation of a republican government, and his charismatic appearance and speech all contributed to an upsurge in American sympathies toward France. He also brazenly attempted to mobilize America's intent on armed resistance to England and decried Washington's efforts to stop him from doing so.

The latter was Genêt's lone mistake, challenging the image of Washington in the mind of Americans. Only Washington himself could do that, and he soon did. Genuinely concerned about being forced into war against England, the president coldly greeted Genêt then lashed out at the domestic scene, condemning the growth of democratic-republican societies celebrating republican sympathies for France while antagonizing England and threatening American neutrality.[17] His ostensible effort to again stand above party factionalism succeeded more in making it clear that he stood apart from the majority of Americans when assessing the French Revolution than he did in quieting the national disposition toward France. If more subtlety would have made Genêt a better spokesman on behalf of France, a similar comment could be said of Washington, who, in reacting to the American public's clear support of France, managed to reveal a partisanship made more tolerable only by his magnanimous later gesture to Genêt. The showdown with the president forced Genêt's recall, which would have led to his certain death at the hands of the revolutionary government, but Washington granted him asylum.

Despite the rancor within his administration and the at times troubled home front, when dealing with the financial crisis facing the United States and the threat of going to war with France or England, Washington's ability as a statesman shone through. His support of Hamilton's treasury plan was important, since this approach helped create the very successful American financial system. And Washington's recognition that a war with England or France would endanger American independence was almost certainly correct. Of course, that is not to say that practicality won out to such an extent that Washington was not a man of conviction. He remained a principled leader but one who recognized that conviction is usually a hindrance to compromise, something he believed necessary to good government. In choosing compromise over conviction, he demonstrated his talent as a statesman.

Washington deserves such high praise, until another motive is considered. His push for achieving practical ends over preserving the ideals of republicanism also served—at least in part—his personal gain, since the republic had found a defender who used the nation to shore up his vanity. By this measure, practicality triumphed over ideology but only for the basest of motives. The actions taken by Washington as president suggest that he passionately supported federal authority to protect the social ambition that had followed him to the presidency. Soon it became clear that his personal reputation advanced in line with his acts supporting practicality. Therefore, he was no innate friend of republican liberty, or if he was, theirs was an accidental liaison.

Washington had a great deal to show for breaking his promise never to leave private life after the Revolution. The national hero had helped to create the new government, placed officers in its employ who might continue that government, and set in the minds of the nation the idea that there could be a central government of the United States that did not destroy individual liberty. Importantly, by 1792, Washington saw that his own presence in the capital no longer fostered harmony, and thus Mount Vernon called to the man as a shelter from a growing storm. The fact was that some renowned citizens of the country had begun to question Washington's merit, and the great general was not interested in getting into such a battle. Indeed, with the government established, Washington had largely secured his legacy as the first president of what would hopefully be a long-lasting republic. What more could Washington gain by staying in power?

This last question was uppermost in his mind as he entered the fall of 1792 with his first term winding down and presenting him with an opportunity to leave the presidency. If there was no more adulation to be had, no more public laurels to win, then surely he had no reason to continue as president. By this time he was sixty years old and showing a marked decline in his physical prowess and, more troubling, in his mental faculties. Moreover, Washington was aware of this deterioration while at the helm of the new nation, and he was concerned about it, confiding as much to his closest advisers.[18] That summer, while at Mount Vernon, Washington also was confronted by the death of his nephew and estate manager, George Augustine. After this loss, he assumed control of all his private business dealings. This added burden did not ease a growing fatigue. Even the long rides on his coveted acreage at home had begun to physically tire him, when in the past this recreation had always been a source of rejuvenation.

Yet, despite all of these problems, Washington was inclined to stay in office. And many national figures objected to Washington leaving for a number of reasons. Attorney General Randolph worried that civil war would erupt between the northern and southern states if Washington left. Voicing similar concerns, Jefferson famously quipped that "North and South will hang together if they have you to hang on." Following orders from Washington to conduct what might be called an opinion poll in and around Philadelphia concerning his retirement, Washington's secretary, Tobias Lear, determined that the president's retirement was viewed with "apprehension."[19]

It appears that Elizabeth Powel's recommendation carried the day, however. Powel, a witty and intelligent woman, and notably one of Washington's closest friends during this time, wrote to him expressing what she viewed as the general's own thinking on the subject. She thought the perpetual "diffidence of your abilities" must be overcome. Whether she considered this self-effacing tone by Washington to be an act or to be genuine is unclear, but she went on to put Washington's entire career in distillate form. Washington had a "sensibility with respect to public opinion," she wrote, and that much of the popularity thus far gained would "be torn from you by the envious and malignant should you follow the bent of your inclinations" to retire from office. Furthermore, "ambition has been the moving spring of all your acts," and thus at a critical juncture, it would reflect poorly if "you would take no further risks" on behalf of the people of the United States.[20] Washington's thinking from his youth to the verge of his second term in office had never been put so clearly then or thereafter.

Powel clearly understood George Washington. They had likely met during the summer of 1787 at the Constitutional Convention in Philadelphia. Americans today best know Powel not from her friendship with Washington but from one brief question she asked Benjamin Franklin. Upon seeing Franklin emerge from the convention hall, Powel inquired as to the type of government the great thinkers had produced. Speaking to the fragility of the new state in light of historical experience, Franklin famously replied, "A republic, madam, if you can keep it."[21] From their meeting in Philadelphia onward, letters between Washington and Powel were very friendly. She now accurately appraised the situation. The risk Washington took by taking Powel's advice and staying on for another term in the presidency was to his reputation, and she knew this vexed him most. He could fail either through maladministration owing to his declining faculties or through exposure to increasingly partisan attacks. Either result would diminish his reputation in the eyes of his countrymen, probably even if he excelled in his second term. Washington also feared he would be attacked for continuing on in office, for refusing to give up his position now that he had "tasted the sweets" inherent in it.[22] As Powel had suggested, he could overcome the fear of risk for the same reason the risk appeared; he could not sacrifice his reputation so dearly won. Thus, he was trapped by a web of his own making and he increasingly saw the office in such terms. Ambition for public laurels, both the ever-slimming possibility of attaining new ones and for the protection of the old, brought him back once more to the highest office in the land. Personal ambition conquered his fear that he might not be up to the task. A second term was a chance worth taking.

It was during Washington's second term in office that the politically expedient alliance between Jefferson and Hamilton came apart. From within Washington's administration, Hamilton at Treasury and Jefferson at State continued the battle of ideas that had emerged at the end of the American Revolution. Hamilton fought for a nation of producers and protocapitalists, while Jefferson wanted one of independent yeoman farmers. Ultimately, these two men would help create the first political parties in the United States. Washington considered such a party system to be counterproductive and dangerous in a republic because he believed—and he was not alone— it would create unwarranted factionalism and stifle the drive necessary to sustaining good government. In keeping true to eighteenth-century Enlightenment thinking, he also believed a republican government could bring the independent interests of each member of society to the most successful end, and for this reason, parties were unnecessary.[23]

That Washington has come to be regarded as the first Federalist president underscores that he did have political differences with many in the nation, even though he strained to rise above the fray. During his presidential career, he naturally found himself presiding over a vigorous debate of what best constituted republican government. On the one hand, many believed that the chief executive, chosen by the electors of the people, should be left unmolested and their decisions not subject to public scrutiny. Hamilton's Federalists believed in such a "deferential" style of Enlightenment government. The people of a state would elect the best men to govern, and these men would govern selflessly. In this Federalist view, the proper moment for citizens to express their political views was Election Day. Politics was responsive to the ideals of good government if the citizens were periodically allowed to ratify the actions taken by their elected leaders, but ratification was enough. The rest of the time, Federalists considered it uncouth for citizens to express their opinions on matters of state, since the elected representatives of the people could better handle this obligation.[24]

On the opposite side of this political debate were men such as Jefferson and those identifying themselves as Republicans, who believed the citizenry had a greater role to play in the ongoing governance of the nation. In large measure, it was this view of the political situation that had made its way into the American Declaration of Independence and had defined the Revolution itself. This radical document proclaimed that all citizens had an active obligation to thwart the aims of a government that was oppressive. More than this, Jefferson and the Republicans embraced the idea of political equality. The farmer, the merchant, the president, and the Congressman all had an equal claim to understanding a problem and offering solutions to it.

Certainly in Jefferson's mind, there simply was not a class of rulers. This lack of distinction was a major difference with Federalists and a reason for Jefferson's support of the French model of republicanism emerging from that revolution. As was the case in Paris salons, he believed that in the United States, debates, meetings, and public discussion were critical to the expansion of liberty and its ongoing defense. Thus, key figures in the United States debated the nature of the Enlightenment, and something approaching "law and order" was pitted against absolute liberty, with Hamilton and Jefferson fighting for these views respectively.[25]

The support Washington showed Hamilton's plans at Treasury, and his issuing of the Proclamation of Neutrality, suggest that his political outlook rested with Hamilton, but he said little publicly, leaving some doubt on the issue. It was a crucial area in which to maintain a vague political stand, and Washington's hope that he could avoid the growing political acrimony between the two camps crumbled when faced with another key decision that would help define his presidency. As trouble between France and England threatened to embroil the United States in a European war, Washington sent Chief Justice of the Supreme Court John Jay to England to negotiate a treaty, which he did by November 1794. The following year came the fight over ratification of the Jay Treaty, and it won the approval of the Senate in the summer of 1795. Washington backed the treaty, but he considered it flawed since the terms did not force England to suspend its aggressive and unilateral determination of the rights of neutral nations On the other hand, the president was pleased that England renewed its promise to evacuate the forts it still controlled on American soil and affirmed its recognition of American sovereignty. Here was an equitable exchange that soothed U.S.-British relations and also recognized the limits of American power and influence.[26] The payoff from this stand, however, was tangible enough: avoiding a war with either France or England and thereby gaining breathing space to allow the new nation to find itself. To make sure this did ensue, however, Washington had decided to accept a second term.[27]

A tone of practicality had again surfaced in Washington's presidential dealings, one that had to withstand the howls of protest from Republicans claiming that the United States was now committed to a pro-English policy. The charge was too categorical. The president's reaction to the so-called

Whiskey Rebellion, however, shows without question that Washington's sympathies lay with the position of deference advanced by Hamilton and Federalists. The choice to resort to military force to preserve order as the president did in this instance is surprising, and one has to believe he acted to impress upon England his ability to keep order in the new nation. A show of force that swiftly quelled the rebellion could only strengthen Jay's hand while negotiating in England. Ending the threat proved easy, but determining whether the use of force was the best course of action raised a number of questions. Washington could have chosen other methods to deal with these discontented westerners voicing their concerns about unfair taxation arising out of Hamilton's financial schemes. Many complicated mechanisms had been put into place to pay the assumed debt of the Confederation governments. Instead, Washington ignored the pleas of these farmers until their situation became so dire that they took up arms against the national government and, effectively, against the president himself.

From the start of this problem in 1790 to the time Washington ordered an approximately 12,000-man militia to march into Pennsylvania in September 1794, a series of thoroughly republican actions were taken by dissidents in several western areas. Citizens in Pennsylvania, for example, had petitioned their new government for redress, claiming that the projected excise tax on whiskey that came close to $900,000 dollars was undemocratic in that it targeted distilled spirits that were popular among a large portion of the population. It was a tax aimed at the common people but levied by those not of the whiskey-consuming class. When these petitions were unsuccessful, western Americans began protests that closely resembled the course of the American Revolution in that they elected "extralegal" assemblies to better represent the will of the people. Such organizations had precedent in the Continental Congresses and before that in the Albany Congress of 1754. The great majority of the people attending such meetings in the autumn of 1791 did not challenge the authority of Congress to enact an excise tax. These citizens merely wanted a more effective voice to convince Congress to repeal the tax on whiskey and implement a fairer tax.[28]

By 1792 not much had changed on either side of the debate. Farmers continued to oppose the tax, and Washington's administration continued to insist upon enforcement. Sporadic episodes of violence against tax collectors had taken place in some of these outlying regions, discouraging the federal government from enforcing the measure. In fact, in large parts of Virginia, South Carolina, North Carolina, and Pennsylvania, no tax was collected at all. The federal government grew increasingly impatient. Hamilton, the chief proponent of the excise tax as part of his larger funding plan for the United States, advocated a military response against these states. Washington initially chose a less belligerent course of action. He sent letters to state governors asking them to help the federal government impose such a tax, and he issued a proclamation demanding an end to the resistance, although he remained painfully aware that he now hoped to curb the violent resistance to government decree that he himself had sanctified during the Revolution. The president faced an enemy caught up in this newly created American tradition as much as in the stated rejection of a government-imposed tax.[29]

When the rebels did take up arms in 1794 with the intention of protecting their perceived rights, they had gone through all the steps that one would expect of eighteenth-century enlightened malcontents. Yet by this date, Hamilton and Washington viewed the rebellion as something altogether different from what had come to pass when they themselves had embarked on revolution almost twenty years before. Why? For one thing, four years had slipped by with little or no enforcement of the excise tax on liquor, and Washington had begun his second term in office. Now action had to be taken. Worse, the events that summer marked a low point for federal authority within the new republic when armed rebels attacked the home of the excise tax collector in Pennsylvania, Gen. John Neville. Washington asked the governor of Pennsylvania, Thomas Mifflin, to call up the state militia to deal with the rebels, but Mifflin refused the president's order by suggesting that military force ought to be the last resort of the government.

Mifflin's response altered the issue, since Washington was now faced with a significant challenge to his authority from an organ of government. While debate and deliberation had held sway to this point, it did not work for Washington any longer. In his view, state officials lacked the right to countermand or refuse an order from the federal government. Hamilton got his wish. Washington mobilized a militia culled from several states and placed them under the constitutionally empowered military chief: himself.[30] Then the former commander in chief of the Continental Army led this force of

12,000 men—larger than that which he had often deployed against the British during the Revolutionary War—into Pennsylvania to put down the revolt of his fellow citizens.

The rebels dispersed before the army even arrived, and the outcome of the rebellion was fairly anticlimactic—it ended with a whimper. Having encountered no resistance, after a short period of time, Washington sent the army home. However, the significance of this show of force was clear. The administration would stand for law and order above revolutionary principles. While the episode was not the civil war either Washington or Hamilton feared it would become, the fact that the tax had gone uncollected in so many jurisdictions in and beyond Pennsylvania suggests that the government mandate was very unpopular. State officials, as well as "the rabble," had detested the method and the goals of this particular tax. Rather than listen to the petitions of the people and lend his considerable political weight to an appeals process, Washington chose to support law and order because, in his view, the tax was lawfully passed by representatives of the people. Federalists did not find it important to acknowledge that the citizens who were expected to pay this tax had considered their representation wanting because officials elected prior to the 1790 census had passed the tax. This rapidly growing region of the country was surely underrepresented until reapportionment in 1793 added 36 new seats, meaning that nearly 1.1 million (out of 3.9 million) Americans had not been constitutionally represented when the tax was passed.[31] The representation in Pennsylvania alone jumped from eight to thirteen Congressmen based entirely on numbers already present in 1790. Of course, it had been a question of representation allowing the imposition of odious taxes that had compelled Washington and his compatriots to rebel in the 1770s. This time though, Washington's federal authority was paramount, and any challenge to him was problematic to the new central government.[32] For those citizens at the end of Washington's bayonets, he must not have appeared the personification of republican virtue. Indeed, this George, though elected by representatives of some people, was as reviled as George III by a large number of Americans.

The domestic troubles Washington faced when serving as president did not merely pull his attention toward the unruly citizens he disciplined in

Pennsylvania. Native Americans presented challenges as well, often leading to situations that required the use of military force. American expansion westward meant a war in the Ohio territory, long a Washington battlefield. Border clashes along this still-undefined frontier meant that government action was necessary, so the president dispatched two different armies each totaling some 1,500 men to force a peace. Both met defeat, the second more seriously then the first, at the hands of an Indian confederation of Shawnees, Miamis, and Delawares. Although the president attempted to negotiate with many of the tribes, the military defeats limited this option. He ordered a third campaign, this time placing an army under the command of "Mad" Anthony Wayne, an officer of proven ability during the Revolutionary War. Wayne did not disappoint. In late August 1795, his force of 3,000 men overwhelmed the native tribes at the Battle of Fallen Timbers just west of Lake Erie. Washington had won a great victory, and a conflict that had simmered from the beginning of his first term in office was resolved near the end of his time as president.

Any settlement with Native Americans was but half the story, since this clash in Ohio mitigated the impact of Washington's proclamation at the end of his second term in office. His Farewell Address, published in newsprint six months before he left office, was a written statement that, among other things, warned U.S. citizens to maintain neutrality in foreign affairs. In realty, however, his Indian war represented an entanglement with the European powers, England in particular. Convinced that England was involved in stirring up trouble with Indians, he ordered the harsh blow to be delivered in the Ohio region specifically to send a message to the European powers that the United States intended to defend itself. Of course, defense was not the best term to apply to what amounted to U.S. expansion and a continued redefinition of what, to its own advantage, constituted the frontier. Since a move westward invited a clash with Native Americans *and* with England, Washington singled out the Native American tribes for attack because they were the easier target both in martial terms and in terms of checkmating European inroads—a continued presence—in the region. To crush the natives robbed the English of their allies in a proxy war. By striking punitively and with military force at the native tribes, Washington continued American enmeshment in European affairs, only he localized the action to best serve

American interests. The accomplishment was impressive but incomplete. European involvement in continental native affairs would continue well into the next century, long after Washington left office. But his shrewd Indian policy can hardly be separated from European affairs, since England was at least concomitantly the intended target.

The defeat of Native American peoples in the Ohio area meant a further consolidation of the American experiment by the end of Washington's second term in office. The United States had benefited from this war and was now able to focus on creating political accord. In his Farewell Address, Washington stressed the need for internal harmony and overcoming the lurking sectionalism that threatened the union. Proffering commercial interaction with the world but staying free of direct ties to European powers was a key ingredient to achieving this end as well. It was a difficult goal to accomplish, however. The United States did not initially stay free of that trouble, as the economic interests of the new nation overseas meant a role for the United States in the climactic French-English clash of the Napoleonic Wars. That it would respond to this crisis in something of a united fashion came about largely because of the promise of continued expansion at home, particularly an advance westward at the expense of Native Americans. Any political accord and national unity came from this bounty, and harmony for the sake of the common good served at least for a time until westward expansion bred new rivalries that threatened to plunge the country into a violent civil war.

It is a telling irony that George Washington, the famed Indian fighter from first to last, had rested the nation on a foundation he knew best, an appeal to a uniquely American character that required conflict to sustain itself. Consequently, the path forward for the United States after Washington's time in office was as troubled as the man presenting his views in newsprint that September 1796. Here was a man who was straddling differing political philosophies defining the American political experience at this time but who had always had to curb his own ambitions to better serve the common good. In this he largely succeeded. The most laudable outcome of his work in office is that he passed on power peacefully at the end of his second term. But was it Washington's supposed innate sense of republicanism that kept the nation moving toward John Locke's "life, liberty, and estate," or was it something else? At times, Washington's actions as president evinced no true opposition to authoritarian tactics to accomplish national goals. Rather, his desire to be well respected in a society accepting Lockean views of personal liberty often stayed his hand from acting more overtly in the manner of an autocrat. He was a Federalist after all, and the value and worth of that stand rested in his person. When he finally did retire from the public scene, he took the Federalist movement with him, and it soon faded from view.

NAPOLEON

The haunting specter of Napoleonism is his hunger for power. It was Napoleon who crowed, "My mistress is the power I have created. I have done far too much to achieve this conquest to permit someone else to ravish or even covet her."[33] A bald admission, it is all the more stark when those moments of unabashed love of war surfaced as well. During the buildup to the invasion of Russia in 1812, Napoleon's ambassador to Russia, Armand-Augustin-Louis de Caulaincourt, duc de Vicence, admonished the emperor for his true motive for the proposed invasion of Russia: Napoleon's love of war. In reply, there came only a mocking denial.[34] The method worked together with the motive to cast Napoleon as the ultimate proponent of authoritative government. Certainly, in his France, the centralization of power in the man facilitated both his love of war and hunger for power, rendering peace a rare commodity in the Napoleonic Empire. War erupted where and when he desired except at those times later in the empire when an exhausted France struggled to defend itself; it then faced invasion and more war. His power rested on military success, and when the empire Napoleon constructed did come to an end, it did so due to military defeat. The master was vanquished at his own game. However, this result and the means to this end, the string of invasions and retreats constituting the Napoleonic Wars, have too often obscured the other side of the Napoleonic regime: the statesman's concerted efforts for reform through the advance of liberty at home and throughout the empire.

Napoleon could and did argue that the pursuit of power through war served the purpose of liberty. The more troubling aspect of this assertion is that it may be correct and classically Napoleon, the inexorable logic leading to conclusions that are alarming but satisfy the truth. If one aspect of his statesmanship could be condemned as a failure born of generating too much conflict, another element can be singled out and praised as a determination to advance a liberal society defining a "new" France. This latter vision so dominated its creator that war became the means to an end certainly, but only as it spoke to a dedication of serving the public welfare. Given the loss of life and destruction visited upon Europe as Napoleon sought to bridge the gap between war and serving the public, his dedication to this "good" again appears misguided until the tally of his reforms and advances while in power are made concrete and seen as undeniably beneficial to France and perhaps to Europe. In this light the great man once more shines through, since his chief obstacle to better serving Europe was England, a nation that succeeded not in stopping an ogre practicing tyranny but in preventing a visionary from advocating on behalf of the divided peoples on the continent. Europe was the poorer due to the outcome of this struggle that ended with Napoleon's defeat.

Early in his career as a statesman, Napoleon had to decide how best to redefine France. He would be learning on the job, since he lacked previous experience in bureaucratic service, but the general would prove most adept, regardless of his puerile disposition in this regard. And he certainly would prove effective in furthering his own career. Still, the image of Napoleon alone atop a government apparatus that answered to his every whim is a view too much in the favor of those wishing to see him only as a despot and is, of course, a negative one. A more accurate picture emerges from the vantage point of better understanding the problems that beset Napoleon first as consul and then as emperor. Indeed it was a fast and steep climb to power, but Napoleon was ever-conscious of the precarious nature of his rise and rule, and he moved cautiously, cunningly, even conservatively to advance his fortunes and those of France. He did not always succeed, and he eventually failed in all regards, but in the interim, for the extended period of some fifteen years, he managed to sustain himself in such dramatic fashion that his statesmanship should receive as much acclaim as his ability to make war. The entire record reveals a man serving France more than leading it, and coping with problems that neither he nor any other man in France was prepared to encounter. This evaluation could be extended to Europe. Where was there another man equal to Napoleon?

There is no denying Napoleon's drive to control. He centralized his governmental affairs as much as he did the disposition of his armies during his
military campaigns. Indeed, this tendency, while natural and understandable
in both regards, may in fact explain his ability to swiftly consolidate his rule
as consul and as emperor despite a lack of experience. But here, of course,
is the first great liability to the argument of Napoleon as despot. If the aim
of authoritarian control must be conceded, the actuality can be disputed by
asking how much control one man could exert. Undeniably, Napoleon's aim
was control. The stories of his famed work ethic are numerous and convincing on this point. He issued dictation at such a fast pace that he required
numerous secretaries to record his orders, mandates, and ideas. Indeed, all
the affairs of France flowed through him. It was an impossible workload,
and his method restricted the completion of tasks. In a vain attempt to overcome this bottleneck, he wore out even his most dedicated supporters; his
secretary Louis Antoine Fauvelet de Bourrienne, for example, had to retire
after a number of valuable years of service. That Napoleon took the task at
hand seriously can be measured by his dismissal of Bourrienne in 1802 because of that man's greed as well as fatigue. Bourrienne had mired himself
in a commercial scandal of such weight that Napoleon summoned the man
and simply said, "Give any papers and keys you have of mine to Méneval,
and leave. And never let me see you again."[35] The emperor demanded dedication, but he clearly conflated the mission of guiding France with serving
him. Bourrienne's avarice offended Napoleon in a more profound way than
is understood, and dismissing from service a longtime friend underscores
this point. In a larger sense, that man had worn out his service to France,
at least in Napoleon's estimation, and this sacred duty could stand no im-
pediment, particularly given the difficulty of having one man run the state
in the first place.

The dedication Napoleon offered France was genuine and manifested
itself clearly when he collapsed under the strain on at least two occasions.
The first came in 1806 as Napoleon prepared for war against Prussia.
Despite an announced departure date, he remained prone and inert at the
side of Josephine for a number of days. The second arose in April 1810
when Napoleon again suffered a near-epileptic fit as he prepared to hon-
eymoon with his second wife, the Austrian archduchess Marie-Louise.

Foreign Minister Talleyrand had noticed with alarm the temporary loss of vigor in the man in 1806 and asked himself what it meant for the fortunes of France. The foreign minister feared that too much depended on one individual, and the scene in 1810 probably reinforced his earlier inclination to ensure that the fate of Napoleon not remain tied to that of France.[36] Unlike Talleyrand, France's anxiety remained muted, a willingness to share the fate of the man so successful in war and in making France great. A long period of time would elapse before France buckled under the ambition of Napoleon.

Such a separation of man and station was not easy to achieve given Napoleon's ability to mask his power within the bureaucracy. Always he created a machinery of government that offered the semblance of representation, a bow to the Republic, while its functions remained at his service. For instance, when serving as one of three consuls after the coup of 1799, he immediately looked to establish himself as First Consul, and after he did so, staying in this position was no small accomplishment by the untested general. But his ambition took him in this direction, and France welcomed him. A strong central authority was needed in France, and Napoleon recognized this and acted accordingly. His ability to advance beyond this point to Consul for Life and to name a hereditary heir—these steps would have been transgressions on the Republic had the government not kept pace in other respects. The Senate, Tribunate, and Legislative Body served the interests of the people, even if Napoleon selected their members. Some institutions of representative government remained in place even when he acted as emperor. True, he dismissed the Tribunate in 1807. Here was a heavy-handed action, particularly since he had purged that division in early 1802, rendering it less obstructionist. By increasing the size of the Senate with handpicked appointees, he neutralized potential opposition from this branch of government as well. The Legislative Body could be discounted, since it only acted on laws already determined by the Council of State, another appendage that answered to Napoleon. France raised no objection, the opposition proving negligible as Napoleon first consolidated his rule and then flexed his muscles as emperor. More than this, however, France allowed its new master to become the autocrat he was because the nation was enjoying success and not willing to risk a change. After all, the checks and balances were present, but they were simply unnecessary. As Louis Bergeron writes in *France Under Napoleon*, Napoleon was the "strong personality of a philosophical ideal," an "alliance between democracy and authority."[37] Previously, government bodies had attempted to make this achievement possible. France had seen such entities wanting but now recognized this possibility in the person of one man. It was a great moment despite the humiliation of the admission that the country could not be trusted to govern itself. For this task, someone had to be found, and the French had found Napoleon.

The governmental machinery also spoke to success when wielded by the master. Napoleon stood above the state and therefore existed outside the very apparatus he had created. This feat meant that no governmental bodies disrupted his official decrees. A few brave individuals saw through the veneer of checks and balances to where power really rested, and they resisted, some from within the state. Talleyrand moved unpredictably behind the scenes in an effort to shape foreign affairs that he believed best served France and not Napoleon. But the foreign minister's ultimate vision for France was a restoration of the Bourbon monarchy and therefore a transgression against the entire French experience since the Revolution of 1789. Thanks to Talleyrand, France may well have been fortunate to have held on to its territorial stature after the Napoleonic Wars, but Talleyrand's shrewd service also extended to serving his own interests, in his case a desire for personal enrichment. Joseph Fouché, the off-and-on minister of police, would also survive the Napoleonic era with his standing and fortune largely intact, but his chief gain was that of escaping punishment for crimes committed during the Revolution and when working diligently on Napoleon's behalf. And while Napoleon was returning some sense of order to France, both men kept quiet.[38]

As Napoleon's grip became firmer, his control became gradually more transparent. Most notorious was his suppression of the press. State organs assumed the role of informing the empire, and they did so with a steady stream of good news that always surfaced, whatever the circumstances. The famous 29th Bulletin announcing the disaster overtaking the army in Russia is the best example of the positive spin now demanded of government information. While admitting defeat, this bulletin ended with the pronouncement that the emperor's health had never been better.[39] This farce Napoleon deemed preferable to allowing press that opposed the regime, and he firmly believed that "three hostile newspapers are more to be feared than a thousand bayonets."[40] Clearly, state controls were in the ascendancy, but French citizens directed at most only barbs back at the Napoleonic regime, and the obvious transgressions against the freedoms of the Republic went unnoticed, or at least unacknowledged, by France. The willingness of Frenchmen to assent to strictures in the name of empire but still cling to republican ideals did not escape Napoleon's attention. The more he pushed, the more France absorbed the majesty of empire over the fading concept of republicanism. Napoleon understood that France endorsed the trade-off, and the emperor needed to only play the game of being emperor. Napoleon did this well enough, suffering reverses only when meeting defeat on the battlefield. Statesmanship in this context became less a task of balancing republican ideals with the practicality of running a centralized state than it did understanding to what extent the French population would accept the nation's ascendancy in foreign affairs as a mollification for the loss of republican ideals. To Napoleon the depths seemed endless.

Not all of France readily accepted Napoleon's practical netting of success while often overriding the gains of the Revolution. The chief opponent in this regard was a woman, Germaine de Staël. From the capital she mounted an attack with the written word and used her influence to gain allies and subject Napoleon's authoritarianism to increasing ridicule. She soon attracted a close second, Benjamin Constant, and together they sounded the alarm about Napoleon's shift to despotism. France paid no heed. Only Napoleon listened and acted, throwing Constant out of the Tribunate and finally expelling Staël from France. These two former lovers, by then merely companions, kept up the attacks but increasingly drove each other to distraction. Still, each would survive the Napoleonic era.

It is hard to dispute Staël's chief complaint, that there was no outlet for dissent under Napoleon and therefore no voice for the people.[41] But she had missed a key point, one Napoleon recognized. Such a voice had given rise to the mob, in particular the Parisian crowd that had contributed to revolutionary excesses, including the Terror. France desired that this flirtation with anarchy be avoided, and Napoleon's authoritarian measures were a sign of his determination to keep the political far left in check. These actions of centralization were as rewarded by Frenchmen as those he took to contain the right, a clear need given the many royalist plots to assassinate Napoleon. Still, Napoleon had the resolve to guide the nation down a middle path, one undefined except for what it was not: radicalism. Was Napoleon a propagator of a new radicalism? His ability to mix state control with the successes of the Revolution said otherwise.

For Napoleon, Staël's crime was an intellectual one in that she refused to bow to the Napoleonic vision of a greater Europe under French leadership. If the aggrandizement of French power advanced Napoleon's fortunes as well, this was something the intellectuals of France had to live with as the more personal consequence of his success. They had been bested by a man living in both the theoretical world and the world of practicality, one who had been able to apply himself and achieve results. Napoleon's reserved nature should have made this dualism palatable to his enemies, particularly at home. After all, he looked unsettled as royalty, not because he thought it undeserved, since he certainly saw himself as a self-made man and was proud of the accomplishment. Rather, playing the part of royalty was a feckless use of his time. Perhaps the best example is when Napoleon went hunting, which he hated but did because it proved him "royal."[42] On one particular outing, he was beset by the very rabbits he was supposed to kill. Rather than Napoleon having to chase them down, the tamed varmints came to him looking for a handout when he emerged from his coach.[43] This incident reflected his role in the larger drama of playing the part of emperor, and though he remained faithful to this end, it too often did not suit him. He said as much after his coronation ceremony, when he murmured to his brother Joseph, "If only our father could see us now!"[44] A moment of elation certainly, it was also a moment of recognition that ruling all of France had been an unexpected windfall indeed. This high met a low in Russia. As he retreated from Moscow, he declared, "I have played emperor long enough. It is time I played general."[45] Circumstance had forced the admission, but the tiresome nature of role-playing had always been there. In this case, he rallied the remnants of his army and escaped from Russia.

Playing at royalty also estranged Napoleon from his marshals, a keen blow that advanced his isolation. He said himself that he had few friends. He wept bitterly when Marshal Jean Lannes died at the Battle of Aspern-Essling in

1809, his remorse genuine for a fallen comrade in arms. Lannes was one of the few marshals he embraced; the others he kept at a distance due to rivalry. Understanding the need for talent on the battlefield, Napoleon did his best to placate these men. Riches, fine estates, and much glory satiated most of them, but of course before receiving these accolades, they had to survive on the battlefield. These soldiers soon grew weary of risking their lives in war, wishing instead to enjoy the spoils of their exploits. As one marshal put it when he saw a friend admiring his Paris mansion: "So you're jealous of me. . . . Very well; come out into the courtyard and I'll have twenty shots at you at thirty paces. If I don't hit you, the whole house and everything in it is yours." Marshal François Joseph Lefebvre added, "I had a thousand bullets fired at me from much closer range before I got all this."[46] Others made shrewd choices. Jean-Baptiste Bernadotte accepted the crown of Sweden in 1810. His decision to do so, and Napoleon allowing him to go, speaks to the high point of the Napoleonic Empire. But the empire's peak was short-lived, lasting only till its rapid decline when military fortunes turned against it after the Russian campaign in 1812.

Military defeat undercut the success of Napoleon's statesmanship, although France and a good part of Europe had accepted him when he was on the rise. The fissures besetting his empire only surfaced after particularly disastrous defeats like the Russian campaign, Leipzig in 1813, or Waterloo in 1815. This calamity brought forth a deluge of criticism then and now, and his detractors today point to a catalogue of what they term exploitative measures—the troop levies on behalf of the empire, the increasing taxation to pay for these armies, the suppression of liberties in the name of protecting the state, and the imposition of the intrusive and unworkable Continental System. These acts, they argue, betrayed Napoleon's true motive: service to himself and his glory. This transparent motive supposedly undid the value of the expansion of the empire into Italy, Germany, and Spain, and even his accomplishments at home. While Napoleon's attempt at one-man rule made it easy to place both success and failure on his shoulders alone, the reality was more complicated. He embodied the age when he was successful, yet he suddenly embodied only himself when the tide turned against him. He was alone after all.

The limits of his one-man rule, and his realization of them, showed through at inopportune moments that revealed the emperor's struggles with the mantle of enlightened ruler. When a courtier suggested that the Austrians could be defeated again should they chose to resist the empire, Napoleon responded coldly, "It is easy to see you were not at Wagram."[47] By 1810, in the wake of the Austrian campaign of 1809, winning battles was a growing weight upon his mind as he considered that the empire he governed was perhaps too much under his individual control. The near defeat at Wagram that had ended the most recent war in Germany had clearly left this impression. His orders more frequently assumed the tenor of diatribes, perhaps even tantrums. On one occasion he kicked a distinguished guest of court in the stomach in a fit of rage.[48] And there was the spectacle of him assembling all the kings and dignitaries under his control to a meeting in Dresden prior to launching the invasion of Russia. Pomp and ceremony could not hide the lingering disrespect most directed at him, a tension stifled by the fear he generated solely because of his military might.[49] His ambition had come to fruition on a grand scale, but did he understand the rancor left in his wake? He did not in 1809, when he survived an assassination attempt by a young German. After the man was sentenced to death, Napoleon offered a pardon in exchange for an explanation as to his actions. The emperor was refused, the youth only replying that he wanted to kill Napoleon the tyrant.[50] This motive Napoleon could not understand. Nor did he understand the animosity he had engendered on the continent by 1812. He advanced into Russia with an unsettled Europe at his back but believed otherwise.

At other times the talented administrator was only too conscious of watching his self-made edifice collapse before his eyes. Already wedded to empire and stretched to the maximum, he had no recourse but to try to correct the premature decay. By 1810 Napoleon was in step with Talleyrand as the emperor joined the effort to separate the empire from his person to a degree, which he did by seeking an heir. He divorced the barren Josephine and married Marie-Louise. While conscious that she had been offered to placate "the ogre," Marie-Louise also understood her role as a political device and married the emperor and even was for some time content and happy. The couple did have a son, the future King of Rome. But the success of this move would only be clear in time, and the marriage did not prevent the Austrians from declaring war on Napoleon in 1813 in the wake of his defeat in Russia the previous year and the indecisive battles in Germany in the spring. The Austrian wish for revenge clearly outweighed any newly established fraternity between the thrones. This result can be considered only a base political outcome, typical in light of the politics driving the wars in Europe. More telling was Napoleon's effort at directing his affection to Marie-Louise while still thinking fondly of Josephine. There would be no ease of mind or political burden here, but Napoleon moved forward given the necessity of action. The fortunes of his empire were turning, and while battlefield defeat would be the final verdict in this regard, the toll of having too personalized and centralized his power was a mightily contributing factor to his troubles.

The true accounting of the success of his second marriage lay in 1812. While Napoleon was campaigning near Moscow, a small group of conspirators in Paris announced that the emperor had died in Russia, and a coup in October nearly unseated him. The bureaucracy saved his throne. Men loyal to the government and to the minister of police, Gen. Anne-Jean-Marie-René Savary, a soldier dedicated to Napoleon who had replaced Fouché at that post in 1810, quickly arrested the culprits and ended the threat. However, the tremors were enough to compel the emperor to abandon his army in Russia and return to Paris. Napoleon reestablished his control, but had to face the fact that while the bureaucracy had done its job, it had overlooked his heir, the King of Rome, just as his enemies had done. Divorce and offspring had not solidified his tenuous control by producing a Bonaparte regime, one not just relying on Napoleon but extended to his son.

If surviving this coup represented the high point of his bureaucratic rule despite the slighting of his hereditary claims to the throne, the low point came soon enough. Having lost the bid to retain control of Germany in 1813, France found itself facing invasion in January 1814. Within three months Paris capitulated in a way that stunned the Corsican. Some of his generals turned against him, including Marshal Auguste de Marmont, who defected to the Allies with an entire corps of Napoleon's now much-depleted army. Worse was the caustic stand of Michel Ney, suddenly standing toe to toe with Napoleon and declaring that the army would march with its generals, not the emperor. Marshals hoping to hold on to some of their well-earned riches help explain the turn. But the desertion of many of his

longtime comrades in arms composed but a part of what was an old con-
fluence. Poor service at the hands of his family and erstwhile associates
throwing him to the Allies to make peace were factors now playing a large
role in his fall as well. His brother Joseph prematurely surrendered his capital. Talleyrand secretly plotted with the Allies to force the emperor's abdication, and when the Senate orchestrated this step and the restoration of
Bourbon rule, it did so at Talleyrand's behest.[51] At long last France had compelled Napoleon to become part of his own government, and he did not
survive it. Here was the low.

A new high came unexpectedly in 1815 when the deposed emperor returned to France from Elba to reclaim his throne. The French people acquiesced. The Hundred Days—the time that Napoleon would spend in
charge of France this second time around—would prove to be the final
measure of his personalized authority as a statesman. Defeat at Waterloo
ensured that it did not extend very far, and his compromises with past enemies such as Fouché, who returned in 1815 as police minister, indicated
that the time for Napoleon had passed. The resentment of Napoleon by
great minds was largely undeserved, since he returned only loyalty, rein-
stating Talleyrand and Fouché time after time, even when he learned of their
efforts to unseat him. He did so because he understood their intellectual
abilities. That he could extend some grace to these men for this reason, and
they could not do the same, spoke again to Napoleon's greatness of command and, in this context, governmental rule. He put the welfare of France
before himself, even at his own peril. If the return from Elba was a selfish
act, more in his interests than in those of France, he again offered to lead in
an inclusive manner, hoping that France could mount one more rally, certainly on his own behalf, but also as a sign that the Enlightened Age had
not evaporated entirely. In 1815 he discovered that the age that created him
had at last discarded him as well, allowing men just as unscrupulous as
himself to declare France a lesser power in exchange for his final expulsion.
If the age had passed him by, so too had it deserted France. Talleyrand and
Fouché may have seen this reality even more clearly than Napoleon. They
profited from this end, and Napoleon did not, but they served their own
selfishness more than France by helping to speed their country to the lesser
status that was its chief fate with the end of the Enlightenment.

It is important to stress that the shortcoming of an overcentralization of power, so clearly advanced in historical writings addressing his strategic failings and how these contributed to his military defeat, also could be registered when assessing his rule at home on behalf of France and the empire.[52] But this latter point is virtually nonexistent in the literature. Instead, scholars stress the contribution of the administrative apparatus that Napoleon created to better control the empire. This amounted to an emperor that was almost an absentee ruler and an empire run on autopilot as Napoleon campaigned to protect his creation.[53] These bureaucrats assume a good portion of the responsibility for any tyranny or exploitation, except for the fact that too often too many local elites joined with the French. An empowered elite became formidable enough to argue that French rule outside of France at times found harmony with the standing governments and did not replace it or uproot them. If so, French hegemony under Napoleon hardly amounted to cultural imperialism, because the "Enlightenment project," to borrow a phrase, was aided and abetted by far too many non-Frenchmen. Moreover, the French civilizing mission was adjusted throughout the empire to better ensure French control. Some conquered areas were broken, as was the case in Italy where, following 1807, the French could declare the region quiescent after facing much resistance. The same could be said of France. The greatest administrative triumph Napoleon enjoyed was when the government—nominally under Bourbon authority—handed him an army in rapid fashion after his return in 1815. Here was French capitulation to the master.[54] For the most part, however, a civilian feel to the empire trumped Napoleon's militarism. His practicality of rule in turning to civilian administrators meant there was not a French nationalist crusade led by Napoleon at the head of his armies, but only a campaign to implement competent rule on behalf of Europe. Napoleon did not raise the specter of the Enlightenment to such a force that he may well have overturned that movement (meaning the Enlightenment). Instead, he took the pulse of a Europe that at times willingly acceded to that uniformity and at other times did not. The flexibility in accommodating both eventualities meant competent statesmanship.

All of this is not to deny the numerous examples of Napoleon's personal rule but rather to call attention to the burden that rule imposed on one man, raising the very real possibility that his despotism was simply undone by the impossibility of one-man rule. No better example exists than Napoleon's effort to control his empire through his siblings. He reached out to them for help, but never was such a large family more incapable of providing even the slightest asset to a dominant sibling, a failure that increased Napoleon's burdens rather than alleviating the strain upon him. His brother Louis clamored for a royal seat in Holland, received it, but then lost this position by refusing to heed Napoleon's policy decrees. That state found itself annexed to France in July 1810. His youngest brother, Jérôme, proved an inept ruler of Westphalia, and this state too came under the direct control of Paris. His sisters married men who eventually turned on their benefactor. Caroline's husband, Marshal Murat was the most notable example, as he tried to maintain his authority in Naples by declaring for the Allies in 1814 as Napoleon's empire collapsed.

Because Napoleon reached out to his siblings, his defeat reflected on both him and them. Perhaps Napoleon's judgment was at fault, however, rather than any shortcomings plaguing his kin. Skirmishes and incidents affecting him and his siblings had been manifest well before his ascension to the throne. The most frequent target was Josephine, a woman held in disdain by Napoleon's family. His sisters refused to carry her train during the coronation ceremony, and the barbs and derogatory characterizations directed at her by them persisted after her coronation. Even his mother did not rise above the fray. She spat venom at Josephine as well, joining with the family to dismiss her as "that woman" and worse.[55] However, the hard side of Napoleon would certainly have surfaced here had he desired it. He did force Jérôme to divorce his new American bride, Elizabeth Patterson, in order to remarry and assume a role in the empire. He also carried on a feud with Lucien, so they seldom spoke after 1804, a great gulf indeed for the Corsican family. No, another motive than merely sharing the spoils of success must have directed his hand when it came to doling out rewards to his family after the sudden rise of Napoleon's fortunes. The answer lay at his never-ending sense of illegitimacy as ruler of France. In the effort to remake France, an acceptance of his station outside French borders meant a permanency beyond just one man. Sibling rule certainly accomplished this in decree by extending the Bonaparte name to territories France controlled; it did not succeed in reality due to, among other reasons, family member limitations. Still, Napoleon concluded that he had few choices.

In this context the family trappings of royal rule appear to tread dangerously close to an overt compromise of the French Revolution. Was not that Revolution a repudiation of hereditary rule born of royal blood, and was not Napoleon's newly created family royalty just the opposite? Napoleon took this risk and, as usual, compensated in other areas. The revolutionary ideals he instilled in France would calm fears of a return to absolutism in the person of the emperor. These he worked hard to bring about, and he largely succeeded. Women were the better due to his command at state. True, his Civil Code affirmed paternal control of the family, and this meant that Napoleon scaled back the advances for women accrued during the Revolution. Their education remained largely a matter for the church, for instance, and the grounds for divorce restricted. However, the possibility of divorce by "mutual consent" offered some protection to women under duress in marriage. Misconduct by either spouse could end the marriage. However, within the family the man remained the dominant partner. When added to the continued denial of legal or political standing to women outside the family, the protections offered women under the Code were limited indeed.[56]

The Janus face of Napoleon's regime had surfaced again, making it hard to paint him as the ogre or the progressive reformer.[57] That he offered any concessions to women is remarkable given Napoleon's view of the opposite sex, which hardly transcended his Corsican upbringing at any point in his life. His mother he revered for having birthed so many healthy children. In fact, Napoleon believed that a woman's highest priority was having children. For instance, as he rode the bloody battlefield of Eylau, he acknowledged the loss of Frenchmen by reputedly consoling himself with the hope that, "One night in Paris will replace this."[58] He rebuked his rival at home, the intellectual Staël, by responding to her question asking who was the greatest woman by saying simply, "The one who has borne the most children."[59] For this man not to turn the clock back entirely when it came to the condition of women in the state clearly worked against his natural inclinations, and something more had to be at play here than simply a triumph over his prejudices. Certainly, the revolutionary ideals of egalitarianism and fraternity meant something to him, and he acted on them even when they countered his internal beliefs. This was statesmanship of a high order.

He also looked to restore the Catholic Church as the official religion of the state by creating with Rome the Concordat of 1801, a document he made public in France in April 1802. The agreement with Pius VII checked some of the wider abuses of the Revolution, a movement that at times looked to restart time and abolish religion. By forcing the Church to recognize the Consulate and accept the nationalization of ecclesiastical property, Napoleon agreed to return a semblance of Catholicism to France. Napoleon certainly hoped that religious structure would again bring much-needed order to the country. If this move appeared a retreat from the Revolution, it was not. Rather, the effort reflected his skill in serving the Revolution even as he ended it. In this case, Catholicism was officially decreed the religion "of the vast majority of French citizens," but other faiths were granted religious toleration as well. Protestants were allowed to perform public service on behalf of the regime, and Jews were protected and encouraged to stay. As the empire expanded, so too did this decree, and Jews in the Napoleonic Europe enjoyed a measure of freedom not usually witnessed in Europe, as did other faiths.[60] Here again Napoleon extended civil protections, thereby living up to the ideals of the Revolution.

Additionally, an embrace of Catholicism by the state checked some of the French tendencies toward creating personality cults, which had been vividly on display in the person of Maximilien Robespierre, chief architect of the Terror; now it was something Napoleon flirted with. For a man like Napoleon, supposedly consumed by a thirst for power, here was a remarkable retreat from power, restraint from enshrining himself as the "ruler" even in the name of defending the Revolution. He chose the title of emperor carefully, a label rooted in historical meaning, not in contemporary experiments. Still, what Napoleon gave with one hand, he took with the other. When confident of securing greater power, he crowned himself emperor and asked for the pope's blessing, which was granted. Such an act assuredly ended the Revolution. France had seemingly come full circle, from the absolutism of a king to that of an emperor. But this was not the case. An emperor hardly initiated a new era in France that involved but one man. The new royalty included those awarded Napoleon's Legion of Honor, a distinction initiated in May 1802 and almost exclusively granted to persons demonstrating exceptional military service. Soon a growing number of Frenchmen joined Napoleon in exalted status.

In like fashion, he named a number of his military peers marshals of France. Certainly Napoleon still stood above the entire pageantry of military honors, but all of France gained from the spectacle and would lose with its demise. Many of those ordained as royalty were of humble birth, dependent upon Napoleon's success to maintain their newly won laurels. Order returned to France for a number of reasons, among them the prosaic restoration of religious institutions, albeit under state control, and the creation of a new nobility based on merit, a much more innovative step. But in doing so, Napoleon hardly jettisoned revolutionary ideals or their meaning. In fact, he institutionalized them, and France moved forward under a centralized rule that still possessed a revolutionary substance. It was a fantastic accomplishment.

The government apparatus also spoke to other successes when wielded by the master. As First Consul, he presided over French law and created the Civil Code, branded the Code Napoléon in 1807. This effort at secularization, in which 2,281 articles were condensed and unified, was badly needed because coherency in French law had certainly been lost in the Revolution. It was a long-lasting Napoleonic reform. His success in this regard was extraordinary, since France still employs portions of this law today. While there is debate over his role, and some scholars are careful not to lay all the success at his feet, it is also true that he sat among those shaping the new laws and continually asked, "Is it just?"[61] Since his input came early in his rule as First Consul, his desire to ensure a successful body of laws was certainly genuine. In fact, he may have been more personally tied to the result than has been understood. This conclusion can be derived from the enormity of the implications of what was being done, not just from the specifics of the laws themselves. Here was a goal of civil equality, obviously one that validated his own place as head of state: a man of modest birth now ruling a country formerly controlled by an estate determined by birth. So enshrining "careers open to talent," as the Code did, was certainly a self-serving end. But so many in France shared his fate, they too having been elevated to positions of wealth and power that would have been denied to them under the ancien régime. They were as vested as Napoleon in the outcome of a code that protected universal norms of equality, liberty, and justice. The Code was the very declaration of the Revolution, and France welcomed the results. Law and order was certainly an appealing facet of the Code, but the

French were also pleased to have a society now governed by the very ideals unleashed by the Revolution. It was another tremendous accomplishment.

While France rejoiced, the monarchs of other nations did not. They recognized the Civil Code as Napoleon's foremost declaration of war. He endorsed his own legitimacy with the law, and in so doing so, he threatened to undo the monarchs still clinging to power by right of birth. His was a dangerous stand to take, given that France had a large population and expansionist tendencies. The implications for foreign affairs were obvious. Napoleon, a man proven in war who relished the act, could now use France to satisfy his personal ambition, remaining in power and doing so by attacking his neighbors all in the name of expanding liberty. The monarchs of Europe grasped the threat emanating from France, and they took steps to meet it. By repeatedly declaring war on France and teaming with England, these nations waged a struggle for self-preservation. To ensure their continued rule, Revolutionary France and then Napoleonic France had to be stopped. These monarchs were the ones in danger of losing power, at least as much as Napoleon, since the questions of legitimacy they faced when confronted by the French Revolution left them as unsteady on the throne as Napoleon. For this reason, they can be said to have borne as great a responsibility for the wars that ensued as did Napoleon.

This is certainly one view. Another redefines this push for self-defense as something else, but again hardly exonerates the nations of Europe for their role in the Napoleonic Wars. When singling out the new power of France, old rivalries dictated an order of battle that seldom included all of the states acting in unison against it.[62] Rather, competing and contrasting ends, most in line with eighteenth-century thinking, plagued any coalition so that Austrians, Russians, and Prussians could not find a meeting of the minds until 1813. When they did, the only rallying point was the defeat of Napoleon. Even here there was inconsistency. When invading France proper in 1814, the Allied states of Austria, Prussia, Russia, and England at first offered terms that allowed Napoleon to retain control of France, but France alone. The emperor rejected such a peace, and the Allies advanced to unseat him but announced that they did not make war against France, only Napoleon. It was a remarkable turnaround, an outside threat directed at one man in 1814 rather than at all of Revolutionary France as had been the case in 1793. In fact, here was a tardy enforcement of the original aims of the First Coalition, and it underscored Europe's vacillating reaction to Napoleon. Revolutionary France was acceptable if French power remained confined to France, and Napoleon was to ensure this end. When he refused and led France in war against Europe, here was the misstep that brought ruin upon him, culminating in the 1814 campaign. As Austrian prince Karl Philipp zu Schwarzenberg, who led one of the allied armies into France at that time, said with only partial veracity, "He brought it all upon himself."[63] In truth, much of Europe fostered these wars as well.

It is no coincidence that the power at the center of any European alliance against France was England, clinging to its mantra of balance of power. This foreign policy goal could not survive France leading the pursuit of revolutionary ideals. For Napoleon to conclude that he sat at the vortex of European affairs and, better still, that he occupied the most fortuitous position at that vortex—the leadership of the most populous nation in Europe, a nation willing to face the challenges of turbulent times, a nation not afraid to shrink from the costs and implications of the times—this was a reasonable conclusion. That he took drastic measures on many occasions both to try and control the course of events and to save himself and his vision, this too is understandable and less a character defect of vanity born of the corruption of power than his enemies at the time and those writing in retrospect would have us believe. In fact, far greater is the Napoleon "good" than is the concept that England advanced on behalf of Europe, a drive for a "balance of power" that was instead a push for an English supremacy reaching beyond Europe.[64] Disturbance close to home could only upset this equation and reduce England's world reach. In this case, Napoleon was the great problem, a destabilizing factor of undetermined but fearful dimensions. European affairs would coalesce around a French and English confrontation. The victor in this struggle would dictate the future of Europe in the near term and perhaps for a longer period than that. Both results did come to pass in favor of England, but it is hard to argue that English conservatism that bolstered its unfettered maritime empire in the wake of the defeat of Napoleonic France was any better than the supposed despotism of France under Napoleon.

This was the Napoleon narrative, that England opposed a burgeoning French power. For this reason, England backed one coalition after another, supporting enemy after enemy and sending them against France. Napoleon's love of war now proved a blessing for France, his wars a matter of self-defense, since he understood the death struggle that England insisted Europe embark on in the wake of the Revolution and his rise to power. But England hardly advanced the understanding that France had to be stopped. The island nation's objective was not an ideological struggle—England merely wished to ensure its economic vitality. In fact, success in this regard rallied Britons to support the war effort in expectation of a closer integration of the state. This reward held it together during the trying period of the wars against Napoleonic France.[65] This mandate may in fact speak to an economic ascendancy that England enjoyed at the expense of Europe, but it had another aspect as well, one that reflected much more favorably on England. England did not lead in the formation of each coalition, nor did it always put its empire first. In this respect, a balance of power was genuine, and only Napoleon ensured the conflict persisted and for as long as it did. He irrationally forced war when he did not need to, leading to the rupture of the Peace of Amiens, war against the Russian homeland, and when he stood at bay but did not make peace, this in 1813, 1814, and his foolish gamble in 1815. He perpetuated conflict long enough to lose everything, meaning that a state system may have germinated the outbreak of war for Napoleon even into 1800, but not after. The period from 1803 to 1815 reflected the man's determination to go to war, and while the rationale may have been the intractable foe of England, a closer look suggests that the simplification in this respect was all Napoleon's.[66]

Rationale is one thing, results another. The true test of Napoleon's benevolence offered under the law, and his desire to spread this to all of Europe, lies in the results. Like so much of the Napoleonic era, the outcome is mixed. After returning to Italy in 1800, Napoleon created the Kingdom of Italy in the north. Liberties were granted by governmental bodies that ruled under the auspices of French control and, from the French point of view, in a fashion dispensing religious toleration, fairness before the law, and under a Catholic church judiciously kept in check by a temperate state authority. By this measure, Italy was a great success that could be grouped with other pacified states in the "inner core" of the empire such as Switzerland, Belgium, and Holland.[67] But recent scholarship attests to the fact that many throughout the Italian peninsula objected to this boon and believed that Napoleon's rule did not successfully change Italy simply by remaking it in the image of the Code.[68] Undeniably, the results of Napoleonic liberation were uneven in all parts of the empire, so in this respect, Italy was typical.

Poland exemplified the uneven results in another way. As in Italy, reforms were allowed, and they followed the French lead. But this change did not amount to much, as an entrenched elite blunted most if not all of the radical reforms offered by France. Yet Poland paid great service to the empire in providing troops in large numbers and supplying them, therefore establishing that kingdom as a staunch ally, which was its primary value as far as Napoleon was concerned.[69] Certainly Napoleon created the Duchy of Warsaw to check Russian power in the region, and given the presumed threat Russia posed to the French empire, it was hard to see how Poland could escape from the subservient relationship of a pawn in the greater struggle between France and Russia. This entity was never allowed to be considered a state, its title a clear indication of its dependence on the empire. So in this case, Poland illustrated the use of the Code as a tool of foreign policy more than an expression of the desire for genuine reform. The image of a presidential Napoleon legislating on behalf of Europe suffers as a result.

The majesty of Napoleon liberating Europe from feudal backwardness suffers again when other parts of Europe are considered, but an accurate accounting is difficult in light of the threat of war and the wars that remained ongoing. There could be few advances in such a state of siege. In fact, the converse won out. Spain remained a war zone, and no final tally could be taken of the Civil Code there. While Spanish resistance speaks to a rejection of French liberation, only one motive was a defense of the ancien régime in the face of sweeping change imposed by outsiders. In fact, a call to defend the homeland seldom translated into more than a defense of a local town or province, and many guerrillas were in fact thugs who merely sought to capitalize on the chaos of war to enrich themselves, an end served at the expense of Spaniards and Frenchmen alike. The idea of survival stirred the good people of Spain more than nationalism in the name of god or country.[70] War was indeed a scourge in Spain and blunted any official decrees sanctifying the fighting perpetrated by all of the combatants, a development there no doubt repeated throughout the war-torn empire.

Germany was complex in the extreme. The many principalities in Napoleon's creation of the Confederation of the Rhine did allow for sweeping implementation of French freedoms. Their acceptance was harder to gauge. Bavaria and Württemberg appeared to relish French modernity, and the elite in these states took the lead in reforms such as ending feudalism. But the model French states of Westphalia and Berg never achieved the ideal of displaying the superiority of the French system. Certainly this outcome detracted from Napoleon's legacy of success in terms of advancing civil liberties in Germany, but, at the same time, the war that came in 1813 was different in character than the war Napoleon fought in 1806 and 1807. German society had changed, the feudal grip of the aristocracy shaken if not destroyed in Prussia, and the French presence there was the main reason why Germans wished to avenge their humiliating military defeat. Nationalism came later. Consequently, Germany, when given the chance, struggled to unite against Napoleon in the War of Liberation in 1813.[71] Still, by creating a limited German unity, Napoleon had made a great impact and had done so far beyond the armies he had sent to the region.

At first glance, Napoleon enjoyed only limited success in integrating Europe, the supposed hallmark of the empire. The problems inherent in Napoleon's inability to be served well by his family members ruling satellite kingdoms have been noted. His "allies" were no great benefactor either. Austria came into the French camp only after defeat in four wars, hardly a strong endorsement of French leadership on the continent. Prussia, crushed by Napoleon in 1806, also was forced into allegiance, deploying a corps in the French army when Napoleon attacked Russia in 1812. The Austrians were compelled to do this as well. Once the French defeat in Russia became apparent, however, the defections set in, Prussia being the first ally to break with French hegemony and Austria following in mid-1813. The resistance and resentment surprised no one, least of all Napoleon. Keeping Prussia and Austria weak was certain to arouse resentment against French rule, but it was a precaution inflicted on suspect allies. Talleyrand attempted to convince Napoleon to act in a contrary fashion, strongly advocating a generous peace with Austria after that nation's defeat in 1805, but Napoleon chose a different path.[72] The emperor believed that both Prussia and Austria had ceased to be powers influencing German affairs once reduced in size—

Prussia to a rump state and Austria stripped of its possessions in Bavaria and the Tyrol, not to mention its expulsion from Italy. Here there seems no escaping a conclusion that Napoleon's vision was limited, but one more factor mitigates this criticism to some extent— compelling enemies to become allies. After all, shifting alliances were common throughout Europe, and Napoleon could expect that powerful France could dictate such changes and have them obeyed.

At times, his worldview appeared to compromise this European outlook, that the ogre would be satisfied with only world conquest. In this respect, such an assessment is again too narrow, since his global aspirations complemented his vision of a unified Europe in an important way. He told the Russian czar Alexander to divide the world with him, France earning the western world and Russia dominating the east. Here was a bold endorsement of Europe—not simply France—on two accounts. First, the many wars he waged for control of Europe spoke less to an aggrandizement of French power than it did to a rising European identity destined to shape the world. Second, his idea of unity among European nations clearly did not smack of strictly French dominion; he would share the burden with Russia. This view dispels some of the grandiosity ascribed to the Napoleonic vision that critics often use to demean the man: he was a world conqueror, his wars a paean to his clearly misguided ego. On the contrary, he was a man understanding Europe's destiny all too well. That host of nations would act collectively, if not always in unison, to exert power throughout the world, as indeed did occur a century later. But under Napoleon, the bounty of such an accomplishment was to benefit all of Europe, not simply the trading empire of England.[15]

In this respect, Napoleon the statesman fully understood the implications of his local wars in Europe, the stakes involved, and the unlikelihood of completing the task at hand, at least in his lifetime. Yet undertaking the end with a modest initial goal in mind—forging a France that would rule on behalf of some of Europe and not simply itself—could be done during his reign. For this reason, the wars of the consul and emperor appear the selfless enterprise of a benevolent statesman. No matter the starts and stops, this larger picture redeems Napoleon. As one scholar described the scene, the source of Napoleon's optimism of that unity was not his armies but his Code, those laws serving as the "real constitution" of France and surviving perpetually, even if requiring changes with the passage of time.[74] That Napoleon looked to encompass all of Europe with such a "constitution," one that hoped to guarantee personal liberties, was presidential in act and thinking and represents a great accomplishment even if the head of state were defeated in battle and the aim put on hold because of that result.

Despite the litany of successes, mixed or not, the great criticism remains and returns Napoleon to his box of oppressor: his constant wars that expanded French borders and his resultant rule of much of Western Europe by force of arms. Ostensibly he defended the Revolution at home by advancing and defeating its enemies abroad. This line of argument became harder to justify as Napoleonic successes mounted on the battlefield. Could not France be defended well enough by meeting its enemies at or near its borders? Napoleon had certainly proved himself to be a good enough general to do this. Why wage war as far away as Poland and Russia? What compelled a French military presence in Spain? Napoleon could answer that he was a symbol of fear to all other monarchs, a rallying point for those wishing to end royal rule as an archaic model of barbaric, unenlightened thought. At the same time, he drew the ire of those resisting this new Europe caught up in an age espousing modernity. Here was the Napoleon standard in foreign affairs, an ambiguity forced upon him that compelled him to act. He carried this standard well by engaging in a preemptive foreign policy that bore the onus of the French Revolution, all the while serving the interests of France in terms of security, hence the exploitation in terms of requisitions of troops and supplies and a demand for uniformity throughout the empire with the Continental system. So the confused realities of the European landscape that he traversed forced Napoleon to compromise his own ideal of defending the Revolution by at times acting as if he had ended it.

STATESMEN AND REVOLUTION

It would be difficult, if not impossible, to deny that Washington was an able statesman. As president, he showed skill as a manager and leader of men by helping cement the ties between the states and establishing centralized authority in a way that had not been thought possible in the allegedly "united" United States. Under his guidance, the nation negotiated a longer-lasting peace with Britain and avoided war with France. He proffered a doctrine of neutrality that would last in principle well into the twentieth century. This pseudo-isolationism undoubtedly benefited the United States. Other issues were more muddled. The new government clashed with native tribes on the undefined border of the United States, and while Washington authorized a brutal military campaign in the Ohio territory, the conflict between the Euro-American and the Native American was hardly of his creation and spoke more to other challenges facing the new nation, as well as how to avoid European entanglement. In the final measure, the tally is mixed, but the boon of a Washington presidency is that he did set the nation on a course of long-lasting republican government, a notable success.

The key issue remains: how much of the virtue of American republicanism was Washington's own? It is difficult to say what Washington's true political convictions were, or if he ever had any to begin with other than protecting and serving his reputation. He had little reason to deviate from this end, since it placed him at the top of the new nation. He favored the centralization of government, but he accomplished it to the detriment of the stated principles of the U.S. Constitution and the recent Revolution. When citizens of Pennsylvania complained about being taxed without proper representation, Washington marched against them at the head of an army. But when Washington needed to avoid a war with European powers, he proved he could do so, as he showed by charting an unpopular foreign policy that also avoided the important constitutional consideration of senatorial consultation. Centralization and order trumped adherence to revolutionary principles more than once. Such was Washington's conviction; to him, the Revolution was over. It is difficult to accept his less-than-republican decisions, but they are plain to see. Political expediency and practicality, however, are poor guardians of life, liberty, and the pursuit of happiness.

In France Napoleon assumed the difficult burden of restoring law and order in a nation clearly in disarray. His task became choosing between allowing further chaos or adopting measures seemingly transgressing on the ideals of the Revolution. He proved at least as capable as Washington at melding two realities together, that of centralized authority and the preservation of revolutionary ideals. France enjoyed a body of laws espousing revolutionary dogma in the Code Napoléon, an accomplishment that sits alongside that of the American Constitution. For this, France rewarded him first with the consulship for life and then with a promotion to emperor. Leading an empire would appear too much a departure from the American experiment of limited government in terms of the territory and peoples now ruled by France, and this was so to a point. But Napoleon soon exported French revolutionary ideals abroad and did so with some success. Some states in Italy, for example, boasted a government enjoying much autonomy and enforcing a number of revolutionary principles. Other parts of Europe under his control also enacted reforms even as the blight of war curbed all such developments. Napoleon's convictions stand out as an endorsement of good government, and although this may have come with a restriction of political liberty, the gains from law and order spoke for themselves. For this reason, he was just as much a republican ruler as Washington, dispensing civil liberties from an exalted office that allowed power to disseminate from one man and checked not by France but by the continental enemies plotting with England.

The difference then between Washington and Napoleon, between republicanism and dictatorship, is that ambition in Washington's case did not lead to authoritarianism. The American colonies created a system whereby Washington struggled to wield effective political authority at times. At least on paper, the opposite was the case in France. Still, the systems through which both men governed allowed them to achieve the apex of their ambitions but within the varying degrees of the Enlightenment. No man in the newly minted United States was more respected than George Washington, and his reputation was such as to gratify his social ambition by filling the key role in the emerging nation of the United States, the office of the president. This respect, however, did not translate into unfettered power. Washington accepted the resistance, though he was gratified that he remained the chief icon of the American experience and that the American compromise with revolution and good government rested on his well-earned and staunchly defended reputation. In like fashion, Napoleon could boast of his rise to prominence, but his acclaim rested fully with the French people. Even if he realized that he could move to unprecedented heights given this dynamic, he still had to honor the Revolution, which he did through his statesmanship. Beyond this larger "good" loomed the fact that the French

Revolution had so unsettled this nation and all of Europe that Napoleon appeared a moderate to many. When tied to the familiar trappings of royalty, the Revolution appeared caged by his person, a combination of revolution and royalty, and he became palatable to most European monarchs, so long as he remained confined to France. In this context, his title of emperor meant everything and nothing at the same time. The result was that both of these men became the Enlightenment incarnate as served differently by two great statesmen separated by an ocean but tied together by an age.

5

GOOD INTENTIONS
Leading in the Age of the Enlightenment

A martially successful George Washington did much to arouse fears among his peers in the now-victorious colonies. Abigail Adams wrote to her sister that "if he was not really one of the best intentioned men in the world he might be a very dangerous one."[1] Adams made this foreboding observation as Washington assumed the presidency. He had played the gentleman too well and now stood poised to hold the fate of the country in his hands. Tyranny was but a person away. Yet his previous actions suggested the country was safe: he had refused to lead a military coup at Newburgh, and he had surrendered his sword after the Revolutionary War. Even more compelling were his constant reassurances that he had no interest in power. In fact, he had been forced out of retirement in order to be president. But his deference marked ambition at every turn. As Joseph Ellis writes in his book *His Excellency*, Washington's "disciplined denials" point to a man trying to control his great passions and emotions—his ambition.[2] Adams could calm her fears with assurances of his "good intentions," but what was the limit on this man? The answer was that, in the end, Washington did not succeed in containing himself as much as he learned to operate within an American society that rejected authoritarianism as leading to despotism. It was a constraint that the greatest of the founding fathers learned to accept and overcome as best he could by personifying republicanism.

173

An equally famous woman across the Atlantic made a similar observation about Napoleon Bonaparte. Germaine de Staël confided in a letter to her father that "the terror he inspires is inconceivable."[3] Napoleon had just seized power in the coup of Brumaire, and the implications frightened this politically astute woman. At least in her estimation, there were no consoling thoughts of good intentions. The record appeared to justify her fears, since the usurper did not stop accumulating power until he ruled France with an iron fist. Yet her damnation of Napoleon for this sin obscured the more complicated reality that he did not wield power simply to satisfy his own ambitions. The benefits to France were real, and many a Frenchman supported the Corsican in recognition of these deeds. In this respect, his tyranny was shared by millions of French citizens, his hold on power an endorsement by the French people of his strongman rule. In the end, one of Napoleon's greatest accomplishments was recognizing that by operating as an enlightened leader dedicated to the public good, he could gratify the needs of France as well as his own.

Like Napoleon's, Washington's foremost passion was ambition, yet good intentions are what most Americans remember about Washington. Presumably, these virtues would be magnified when Washington is compared to Napoleon. But the opposite is the case. So strong are the parallels between the two men that Washington's virtues can be questioned, as can Napoleon's supposed depravity. Either Washington was not the saint we like to think him to be, or Napoleon was not the devil that we would like him to be. Clearly, Americans need to undergo a more thoughtful historical introspection, and this bold step invites the comparison of the one man to the other undertaken here. At stake is a fearful possibility that Washington looked to attain power for its own sake, as did the depraved Napoleon, or that Napoleon considered wielding power as sacred a duty as Washington did. For Americans, a trip down this road calls forth a reconsideration of the notion that the morality of an age might rest on a single person. It was always too much weight for Washington to carry. He was at once virtuous on behalf of his nation, on behalf of mankind, and on behalf of providence. Revered as almost God's messenger on earth, he has often been viewed as too much a saint and not enough man. Now Washington is contrasted with Napoleon, a man who could not reach a saintly status in the eyes of Americans no matter how much the Enlightenment redeemed his reputation or excused his actions. Americans can at last see the way clearly enough to include in their founding generation not just the handful of notable individuals—of which Washington's name is paramount—but also the people who constituted colonial society.

A fall from grace is never as sudden or complete as one might think it to be, and this is the case here. Letting go of an icon as large as Washington is admittedly difficult, but citizens of the United States can try and find some solace in recognizing the differing outcomes of the respective revolutions: the Americans gave birth to a republic, the French to an autocracy. For many, here is proof of the innate goodness of Washington and further proof of Napoleon's venality. But ambition drove Washington as much as it did Napoleon. The most flattering validation of this ambition lay in wielding power, and Washington, like Napoleon, sought it out to the best of his abilities. The contrasting outcome in revolutionary governments highlights a key difference not between the two men but between the two societies. The Enlightenment shaped American and French political culture in two very contrary ways. Here is the key point of separation between them. Americans refused to countenance any authoritarian form of government, while the French did not share this apprehension. Working within this context, Washington adjusted his steps to power accordingly, ultimately accepting the role of president in a government that limited executive power but still stood at the apex of American society. Napoleon slowly came to understand that no such inhibitions were present in France, where a benevolent despot could win the day. This recognition on the part of each man translated to a win-win for America and France, for Washington and Napoleon. Both nations got the government it most desired, and each man won for himself the power he coveted.

A familiar motive such as ambition is not hard to track. It is present in the earliest stages of each man's career, in their rise to power, and in their use of that power. Ambition never left either man; it merely adapted itself to circumstance. If not for revolution, both of these famous historical figures were destined for at best a modest existence with little recognition at the time and certainly registering little for posterity. They understood this limitation in its most practical ramification—a future with limited horizons—

and they fumed at their lot in life. Their unease came from ambition, and they were afraid they could not satiate it. The goal was to reach the pinnacle of success in society: Washington's choice of the gentleman farmer was no accident, just as Napoleon finding success through military conflict was typically European. Before revolution and war, the paths to success lay in exploiting what connections they could to elevate their social standing. Washington relied on his brother's association with the Fairfax family. Napoleon relied on his father's ties to the French crown. The result was a surprisingly close career track: at the end of their formative years, each man found himself commissioned in the army and relying on that institution to advance his career. True, Washington did not enjoy a formal military education as Napoleon had, but an army career catapulted each man from local success to national greatness. It enabled them to achieve the principal goal of their ambition: social standing.

In viewing their military careers, one finds even more compelling parallels. Both men were able to turn stunning reverses into extreme popularity while turning mediocre successes into greater popularity still. In his first commands, Washington fumbled a series of diplomatic missions on behalf of the governor of Virginia, helping provoke war between France and England. He then lost the first battle he fought in this war, presided over another disaster, and finally participated in the anticlimactic campaign that saw the end of French power in the Ohio Valley. Nevertheless, he was known at the time for his brave stand against French aggression. He is remembered today for undergoing a needed period of military self-education, a view that hides an ugly fact. Washington certainly learned a lot at this time, but there was no more important lesson than realizing that fame could eclipse failure, and his ambition could stand above any blemish if the people willed it to be so. He was a quick study of the assertive power of the American public where substance seemed irrelevant. In this early episode, the French had been rebuffed then beaten, and he had played a key role. That this outcome came after much trial and error and near-comical mistakes mattered little. He contributed so much to this dismal means to a desired end but still enjoyed public acclaim—this revelation was a valuable lesson in itself.

Napoleon's early career was marked by similar failures and youthful indiscretions. Initially, he was seemingly disgruntled with army service, at least while in the employ of France. He spent a number of years trying to free Corsica from what he perceived as French "oppression." Each scheme failed on a scale larger than the next, and each action moved him closer to treason. When he eventually returned to France, he was charged with desertion. Napoleon capitalized on the chaos of the Revolution to use political ties to get the charges against him dropped. Reintegrated into the French army, he then expelled state enemies from the port of Toulon and defended the revolutionary government in Paris. The irony of the once-deserter as national hero did not escape him. Military failure could be overcome in such a climate with a subsequent brave showing on the battlefield. Napoleon's ambition could be served by pleasing a fickle population inclined to dismiss military failure as a national blight but elevate martial success as a personal accomplishment. The way forward was clear. Military prowess meant social advancement.

Actual success netted a favorable result for both men, a catapult to societal recognition and prominence. The necessary prerequisite was an interim role as a general. Washington's record clearly shows he struggled in this role but persevered. Napoleon's achievements uphold his generalship even as his lack of success was monumental and resulted in the loss of his throne. To advance by military success, each man adopted a similar strategy. Enemy armies were to be met on the field of battle, the contest decided in one glorious day, and the winner would enjoy much acclaim. This ideal of decisive battle characterized both Washington and Napoleon. They pursued this high-risk strategy confident of victory due to a belief in the revolutionary zeal of their men. Each man tested this strategy repeatedly, but lack of success made it necessary to carry on the fight. Indeed, the similarities between Washington and Napoleon are so strong in this aspect that it quickly becomes apparent that Napoleonic warfare had an antecedent in Washington's leadership of the Continental Army.

Difference again clouds our judgment. Washington's military record cannot compare to that of Napoleon. The American general fought too few battles and nothing on the scale of Napoleon, who stood at the head of armies numbering in the hundreds of thousands. Washington's inability to field an army capable of standing on the field with British regulars meant that his dream of decisive battle was a fiction. His efforts to enact such a strategy nearly ended the Revolution on several occasions, most notably in New York in 1776, but his opening and closing victories, Boston and Yorktown, were decisive battles indeed. They sandwiched a strategic success, the ability to utilize irregular warfare to his advantage both in the middle colonies and in the South. One way or the other, the strategic advantage he held during the American Revolution was something he came to value, and he did so by trial and error once again in that he listened to advice, adhered to the wishes of Congress, and remained focused on winning a conventional battle. The Enlightenment had subsumed this warrior and his battlefield, and once he discovered the prescription for success, ultimate victory greeted Washington's efforts. His was an impressive achievement.

Napoleon's reputation as a capable general is well earned. In 1797 he took a depleted French force in Italy and defeated the Austrians time after time in a whirlwind campaign. As his next campaign in Egypt showed, he was not without his military flaws, and the loss of his army during this operation largely rested on his shoulders. But his strategic follies to this point hardly mattered. France remembered his Italian triumph and installed him as their leader. Napoleon fought and won decisive battles at Austerlitz, Jena, Friedland, Wagram, Borodino, and Dresden. He also had Waterloo. The recurring wars testified to the limited utility of his decisive battles. His strategic limitations remained his Achilles' heel, and the weakness cannot be corrected now by an appeal to the larger view supposedly underpinning his overall record—that he was a military genius. If he strove to correct his strategically perilous role in Europe with the Continental System, he failed to understand how warfare was evolving beneath his feet. He paid little regard to the guerrilla resistance that surfaced in many parts of Europe, which eroded his military might. The Enlightenment had both created him and robbed him of his strength, a dilemma easier to ignore than to face.

The track record of the two men does indicate some separation between them even as it underscores that they were the same kind of general, for whom military successes fueled political ambition (and thus generated more similarities). Each man was a military leader who used his popularity to gain the highest political office in his nation. Washington clearly held the love and adoration of his fellow countrymen when he was elected president for having distinguished himself as the most adept military officer in the colonies. His squelching of the Newburgh Conspiracy, his retirement from military duty, his forced return from private life to become president—all these measures stripped the military from the man and prepared him for public office as a servant of republicanism. But the military and civilian goals he espoused were the same, a quest to satisfy ambition requiring social advancement through recognition. Therefore, the separation was never entirely complete. Reputation mattered most to him, not the preservation of an ideal of republicanism that reflected a new Enlightenment era. The same base goal persisted as he sat atop the American experience: social achievement. From the colonial world to revolution to the emerging new nation, Washington remained the same man, a beneficiary of the new age but also its tool and pawn, even if he was grateful for the ride on the changing tide.

In Napoleon France received both a general and an enlightened despot. The French people supported this Corsican who crowned himself emperor regardless of the record of violence at home and abroad that accompanied his important civil reforms, or the strongman rule that undermined the many civil liberties he bestowed on them. It cannot be denied that the wars he fought made France great in a manner craved by the French. To dominate the European scene and challenge hated England were as much French byproducts of enlightened thinking as any other intellectual outgrowth of the movement. The French would stick with the Corsican until they realized that perhaps they could do better. But by that point Napoleon had enshrined in French law the best ideals of the French Revolution with his Civil Code. That much of Europe faced this transformation as well, as a result of the expansion of French power under Napoleon, meant that, like Washington, he was as much an agent of the Enlightenment as he was its tool. To gain power and then lose it under the guise of the Enlightenment era largely affected Napoleon alone, the long-lasting impact of the age set in motion and sure to continue without him. But the Napoleon years were more than a time of tyranny. They were also a time of melding absolutism and liberty to produce the Napoleonic legend imparted onto European culture that still lurks there today.

The political comparisons end there and face a significant difference. Washington settled for something far less than absolute power. Napoleon grasped total control of the state and held on as long as he could. To suggest that a certain justice lay in the different outcomes of their careers misses the point. The difference between republicanism and absolutism did not rest on the shoulders of these two men. Rather, one must understand that the United States was a nation founded in war but wary of an army. It was a nation that loved liberty and personal destiny, so much so that Washington may have been "first in the hearts of his countrymen," but he was only so because the American public in 1790 would have found a political strongman unacceptable. It was an American citizenry cherishing representative government that prevented a Napoleon in the wake of the American Revolution. In contrast, the French public, enraptured with the concept of an enlightened despot and equally fond of French military success, allowed the creation of Emperor Napoleon—in fact, Frenchmen sought him out even as Napoleon seized every opportunity. Success surpassed his more conservative goal of social advancement to a prominent place assuring comfort and security, and the avenue to a greater destiny was open: controlling his adopted country. That he struggled to hold on to his exalted position should surprise no one. That the Enlightenment had made him possible and soon looked to discard him was a bitter pill for anyone to swallow.

A tamed Washington but a validated Napoleon is not a surprising outcome, since each man was ambitious and sought the laurels of his society very proactively. The gains were different, but ambition was equally served. That at times Washington appeared far more deferential to power than did Napoleon points to Washington's success as the great political actor. It is not a leap to question whether Washington's deference to power represented his true feelings. Each and every time he secured a post in civilian government, he earned for himself further praise from the nation, and public praise was a lifelong Washington ambition. Thus, Washington willingly served in a civilian government that he knew limited his authority so long as he gained the laudatory ovations that flattered his vanity. When the ovations slowed, Washington looked to discard the office but always with an eye on attaining a new one. This he did until reaching the presidency. Napoleon did not see a need to act, and he never apologized for his hunger for power. Nor did France expect him to. Rather, he flattered France with military success, and he strove to deliver these successes in tandem with preserving civil liberties at home and abroad. For ten years, the means—his many wars—

were in fact justified by the albeit frequently uneven end of bestowing the fruits of the Enlightenment upon a not always grateful Europe.

These parallels serve to humanize both figures, drawing down the acclaim paid to Washington while at the same time offering a reprieve to Napoleon. The totality of the comparison reminds us that this investigation has been a lengthy process and the results are clear only at the end of the analysis. In between comes a reexamination of the character, impact, and legacy that means so much to the current reputations of both men. A role reversal is not a product of this study, however. Washington did not become Napoleon; Napoleon did not become Washington. Instead, the insight is subtler. Americans could not have a general who rose to the level of Napoleon but somehow remained aloof from the consequences of such success. In turn, Napoleon could not be just a general, deprived of his successes as a statesman on par with Washington. Military prowess could not be both exalted and damned; government service could not be both a fortuitous end and a frivolous afterthought.

When using Napoleon to ensure that Americans undertake a more realistic and critical view of Washington's role in early America, the temptation to cling to excuses to exonerate the great patriot is overwhelming. Washington's youth is a tale of trial and error, not one of folly imperiling himself and his fledging colony. His generalship during the Revolutionary War contributes to a folklore that sanctifies his mistakes and poor decisions at the time, rather than serving as a testimonial to his lack of qualifications to wage war. His service as president augments his legacy because it underscores his circumspection regarding the use of power, rather than casting light upon his wariness to risk his reputation, something that created self-imposed limits on his service, save for the urge of desiring power. The fact is that Napoleon could be so redeemed as well. He was more a disadvantaged young man than he was an opportune youth ruthlessly exploiting the Revolution for personal gain. It was fortunate for France that so talented a general rose to high command at a time when the nation faced numerous and intractable enemies, not a curse that one soldier used France as a personal proving ground of his martial abilities. Napoleon centralized state power to stabilize France at a time of great unrest, not to establish a tyranny seeking power for its own sake. When set alongside each other, the need for criticism and praise of both men becomes apparent. When Washington is considered individually, American critical analysis lapses in favor of paying homage to one man's great accomplishments on behalf of America, a merciful development considering the doomed path taken by France.

Determining how these two men help to define each other is a timely step to take for many reasons, most importantly to force Americans to recognize their desire for historical simplicity when it comes to violent change stemming from cataclysmic events—war and revolution. Clearly as an instrument of war, Washington's exalted morality is in need of redress. Stressing his similarities to Napoleon certainly makes this step possible. A study of Washington is complete by comparing him to Napoleon, and if diminishing the American's stature somewhat, the converse is also true. Some of Washington's "goodness" rubs off on Napoleon. The altered picture of both men may serve as an affront to some Americans, but it is still a good exchange to make. It calls into question a disturbing conclusion. The foremost founding father stands as a product of war, and therefore he breathes goodness into the moral vacuum that is war. To think this is a uniquely American accomplishment is as absurd as believing that it is a good accomplishment. The morality attached to America's leading general and statesman by its citizens was never more than a vindication of war as a means to an end. What could be more Napoleonic than this?

The fact is that a comparison of these two lives does not offer much separation between them. A further look at their personal makeup promises to establish some profound differences. After all, Washington appears to have maintained a rational disposition in reaction to holding power, more so than Napoleon. Many scholars assert that Napoleon's need to always seek out more power came from "Napoleon being Napoleon."[4] What this means is open to wide conjecture, but certainly the man is seldom defended as a victim of circumstance. In fact, personal flaws appear the best explanation for his refusal to make peace when fortune had turned against him, his insistence on carrying on the war after 1813 an irrational response and one that cost him his throne. Washington appears to have lacked any such character defect or irrationality until one points out that standing at the center of contradiction was the Washington path to power. So in this sense, "Washington was Washington," a man who felt compelled to live decrying power and shunning the limelight only to the point of ensuring that both of these proceeds came to him. He could not help being himself any more than Napoleon could stop being Napoleon and make peace with Europe. Ambition carried both men to a finale that simply was more favorable to Washington than Napoleon because of circumstance, not because of a personality flaw in Napoleon and a blessing inherent in Washington's disposition.

Another facet influencing both men makes this clear. In July 1799 Washington crafted his last will and testament, in which he attempted to address the chief moral ambiguity that had plagued him throughout his life: slavery. His decision to free his slaves after his death and then the death of Martha was a powerful statement at the time, one intended to distance himself from that distasteful practice. In a larger sense, however, one has to agree with Ellis that this last document was to ensure that Washington had his characteristic departure from the scene, a chance to practice the dramatic exit that had served him so well before, in this case serving as a symbol of freedom to all Americans.[5] Alas, his symbolism is remembered more than the limited reach of the act, since he only freed the slaves he owned. Of the 317 enslaved persons living on the estate at the time of his death, he owned 124, less than half, leaving some 193 still in bondage because they belonged to Martha or the Custis estate. How successful he was as an emancipator thus remains in the eye of the beholder. Napoleon shares this fate, since he looked to serve as a banner of enlightened thought even as he acted to return slavery to Haiti in 1803. A combination of disease and effective native resistance meant failure, and military defeat again left his plans unfulfilled. This situation spared him from taking a less-than-flattering step for mankind, one that would have transgressed upon his pending role as emancipator of Europe, a probably too generous description of his military conquests after 1804. However, given that circumstances could either redeem or condemn each man with regard to slavery, the issue is unlikely to yield a definitive understanding of the morality to be found within them.

The differences between these two individuals continue to fade upon further examination. For example, Washington also remains a majestic figure in historical memory due to his personal bravery on the battlefield. His courage as a young man served him well in the field and later during the Revolutionary

War, when he often exposed himself to enemy fire. That he survived unscathed, never even slightly wounded, speaks to his destiny as something great and ordained by a higher power. Napoleon is not so lucky in the eyes of posterity. But he too exhibited extraordinary courage on the battlefield, receiving slight wounds on two occasions. Still, scholars diminish his accomplishments when viewing his supposed exploits more the product of a skilled public relations campaign than reflecting a true measure of the man. It seems "being Napoleon" has tarnished even his esteemed military reputation, an irony Washington is shielded from despite the obvious similarities he shares with Napoleon when in command of soldiers. Both men were revered for their leadership—often their mere presence steadying the troops—and both men earned this distinction. In fact, they sought it out, if in contrasting fashion, Napoleon clad in a corporal's uniform, a symbol of his common touch, and Washington donning a splendid general's uniform of his own design, his effort to lend legitimacy to the cause. Alas, the disrespect shown to Napoleon by those wishing to discredit him continues, his attire considered no more than a mere act of identifying with the foot soldier. Washington, conversely, remains a striking figure, a genuine actor playing the difficult part of personifying a seemingly hopeless cause. Sincerity, much like morality, remains something open to interpretation, and for this reason, so too does an estimation of each man's courage.

A further look at them again stresses more strands for comparison, such as emphasizing that each man was aloof from those they led. Washington embraced Lafayette and Hamilton, but it was father to sons in tone and effect. A distance thus remained between them. Washington also shed friendships when need be, with Jefferson most famously, but also James Madison and Edmund Randolph, after thirty years of friendship with the latter. After serving in the public eye for so long, he soon found himself isolated and alone, very much a retired figure at Mount Vernon after 1796. His isolation was not as acute as what Napoleon endured after imprisonment on St. Helena, of course, but the parallel impresses itself on those wishing to look closely at this point. Napoleon's comrades in arms such as Desaix, Lannes, Ney, and many more were dead. Marshals Murat, Marmount, and Bernadotte had turned against him, and his sense of betrayal or at least cynicism was as keen as what Washington felt toward Madison and Jefferson. Napoleon's estrangement due to death or choice was as pronounced as what weighed down Washington in his later years, as both lived on bereft of companionship from men in arms or those with whom they had shared governmental service. Perhaps Napoleon's isolation was even more so. Having given up so much to produce a male heir, he was stunned and hurt to discover that his wife, Marie-Louise, chose not to join him on the island. Nor would he see his son again, the King of Rome. Other confidants were unavailable. Josephine had died in May 1814. After 1815 the authorities kept his brother Joseph away from St. Helena, fearing the truth of the fantastic rumors that he planned to free his brother with a bold raid on the island.

For both men, isolation, either by choice or circumstance, increased due to a failure to find meaningful companionship with the opposite sex. Washington's infatuation with Sally Fairfax apparently produced his lone bout of passion, which went unfulfilled. His wife, Martha Custis, represented the appropriate marriage for a gentleman, an arrangement that primarily secured his place in Virginian society. His later involvement with Elizabeth Powel was more an intellectual infatuation. A man accustomed to saying little to his peers because he feared exposing his knowledge as inadequate, he would take this chance with this woman. The safety he found with Martha also served as a release, but it was not love. One could argue that he developed strong affection for her over time, but this attachment signified that Washington had jettisoned any carnal feelings in service to his ambition of social advancement. Far more fortunate was Napoleon, since early on he developed a great infatuation with Josephine. However, her initial disdain for him and her many affairs while married to him meant Napoleon suffered a rebuke that Washington was spared. The tyrannical temperament that many observed in Napoleon surfaced when he finally accepted the unfaithfulness of his wife while he campaigned in Egypt. Here was a profound moment for him, more so given its larger significance. Napoleon had been an odd exception to French and European social norms, since he sought sexual gratification within the bounds of marriage rather than in numerous mistresses and affairs. These indiscretions did occur, particularly after he established himself in control of France. But in this later context, Napoleon's interaction with women was typical and as "arranged" as was Washington's, since he did the expected, albeit in a way that American society simply did not openly condone. Ultimately, the emperor settled for a match as appropriate as Washington's with Martha when he married Marie-Louise in a bid to solidify his hold on power by advancing his social status among European monarchs. Even while learning to enjoy the company of his new wife, he pined for Josephine, an acknowledgment of his lost chance at partnering with this woman and achieving a companionship that would have stood out as rare in his social world. In feeling this loss he was still more fortunate than Washington, who apparently never had this opportunity at all.

Posterity again awards Washington higher marks than Napoleon for his clear ability to command in the civilian arena. But to argue that Washington was more than a general and achieved a civilian acclaim that escaped Napoleon is not just in error—it fails to take a measure of the courage of each man beyond the battlefield. The simple reason why is that each man was pushing his nation in the same direction, so the ramifications of their rule are at issue. In the post-Washington era, the United States stood poised for greater expansion. Just as Americans eyed Europe as a competitor to be treated with much caution, so too did these rival nations understand the latent potential of the United States. European states feared a future America just as they did a continuance of the Napoleon regime in France, which meant a clear threat of French hegemony on the continent. Now, across the ocean in another hemisphere, lay a new power with the same potential. The overt call for neutrality fooled no one, particularly since Americans persisted in a self-righteous rationalization of their existence as God's chosen people in a new land. Europeans were on their guard, even as Americans embraced the feigned reality of American exceptionalism, a budding ideology that worked to portray American interests as benevolent and therefore palatable to all. But this American vision of itself also allowed American citizens to shrink from acknowledging part of the Washington legacy, from the implications of his success; Americans came to represent the very thing the Europeans hated in Napoleon—the call to champion a radicalism shaped by ideals used to justify the actions of only an elite few. The United States lacked the military means at the time to impose its form of republican zeal beyond its continental borders, but its push westward offered a sample to all those paying attention to what this nation intended. The Enlightenment in the Americas became a scourge in this respect, leaving Washington and Napoleon indeed two giants of an age who overtly linked the Atlantic and European worlds.

Given the immediate consequence of greatness in this age, words such as honor, character, and virtue fail to adequately define either man. Defining a "good" is at stake here, and it hinges on understanding power. Honoring a republic meant acting as a responsible citizen and judiciously treating power by guarding against its abuse. A person's character either possessed this virtue or did not, meaning that honor escaped that individual as well if he lacked the virtue of responsibly wielding power. In surrendering power, Washington proved that his character possessed ample virtue, thereby bestowing honor upon him. But a person had to proceed in voluntary compliance to these traits, and once transgressed upon, they were forfeited. Such was the fate of Napoleon, the Jacobin turned tyrant. His formative republican years did not take hold, his transformation becoming the symbol of a corruption of power and therefore a loss of virtue in the man. His honor so blemished, Napoleon could not and did not redeem his character. Rather, he became the example of a failure of virtue, since power consumed him and led to his ruin. Here is the thin line between republicanism and authoritarianism.

Such character assessment backs away from a consideration of the intellect of each man. Washington defenders generally focus on his supposed stellar character, a focus made necessary because of Washington's repeated doubts as to his own intellectual ability, particularly when compared to his peers.[6] Some argue that a lack of education explains this paucity and that ultimately Washington overcame this handicap, since he possessed an innate intelligence that served him well. This second view is an accurate judgment. However, Washington's reserve was certainly a great character trait too, a mannerism couched in an assumed honor that testified to virtue. Austere, morose, even withdrawn, Washington assumed a "sobriety that stopped short of sadness," left many in doubt as to his thinking, and therefore masked his intellectual self-consciousness as well.[7] His demeanor was an effective approach to accumulating and holding power, and it complemented the cultivation of his reputation as the virtuous republican. Beneath this façade, however, he remained a calculating and cunning politician, an indication of his shrewd intellect. In this respect, retirement meant much to the man who in fact withdrew from public life three times. The first came in the wake of his inability to win recognition of his service to the Crown with a promotion to a high-ranking regular officer in the king's army. The next two were closely related to each other. Indeed, while some scholars stress how the circular letter Washington issued in 1783 announcing his retirement mirrored his Farewell Address in 1796, few point to the gambit in both. Retiring in 1783 meant a possible return.[8] Retiring from the presidency in 1796 ostensibly meant a return to civilian life and living as any other American. But this step was impossible because of his stature. He was the giant of his age and so important as a symbol that he elevated the entire country to greatness, a final act of service, as Matthew Spalding and Patrick Garrity put it in *A Sacred Union of Citizens*.[9] Maybe so, but if this logic is sound, then this relationship meant the acknowledgment of his power source—his reputation among the public—something he had defended successfully all his life and capitalized on throughout. The act of honoring republicanism is not the same thing as honoring it, meaning that Washington's second and third retirements, and his other acting when it came to surrendering power, undid his virtue. In fact, since Washington always had acted the part, Napoleon was the better man. His transformation from republican to tyrant may have led Napoleon to forfeit his virtue when it came to power, but at least he had had this good quality at some point. The same cannot be said of Washington.

Napoleon reaps a healthy bounty as a man possessing superior intellect. Johann Wolfgang von Goethe is the most famous endorsement in this regard, supposedly declaring that Napoleon was "the greatest mind the world has ever seen."[10] While preferring the world of practicality, Napoleon could understand and thrive in more theoretical pursuits. In this sense, he greatly exceeded Washington, who did not even try to do this; Washington clearly shunned philosophical thought as a defining aspect of his worldview. He lived as a practical man, much like Napoleon chose to do. But ability in this respect led to some harmful implications for Napoleon, including an inability to service honor, character, and virtue, since he preferred practicality. These personal traits could not survive when it came to wielding power. With Napoleon's acceptance of this reality, he became a better practitioner of democracy than Washington. Ideals seldom withstand good governing, and Napoleon did not fool himself into thinking that he was an exception. In fact, the rumination over such sentiment he gradually dispensed with, and here defined the difference between Napoleon and Washington as practitioners of republicanism. The people entrusted power into the hands of both men, but results counted for much more in European society than in America. Put another way, a plodding and refractory public debate counted as good government in the United States. In contrast, results counted most in France as the primary measure of having moved beyond the philosophical debates endemic to the too-often alarming period of the Revolution. On the whole, only a small minority of the inhabitants of Napoleon's France and his European empire cared for the ideals that the Enlightenment espoused, most preferring results. This is something Napoleon delivered. Honoring republicanism in this way meant a tenfold return on Napoleon's intellect, so his character possessed a great deal of virtue indeed, and in a similar vein as Washington.

One last bogeyman remains, one that grows out of the consideration of intellect, and that is the topic of religion. Here again, in contemporary assessment, Washington is able to exude a goodness that escapes Napoleon. Washington's church attendance, his assumed morality resting on a Christian outlook—these personal qualities dominate that man, while their absence diminishes the personal standing of Napoleon, a man seldom endorsing any religious sensibilities save for those that bolstered his political control, such as those existing in the Concordat. However, both men largely kept religion in the background, passing through life aware of only an all-powerful creator that spoke to the limits of man's knowledge. This outlook led to a fatalism that was pronounced and best surfaced in Washington when he neared death but refused any final prayers and demanded that he not be buried for two days in case he repeated the fate of Christ and be buried alive.[11] That such doubt is hard to see earlier in his life merely adds to the evidentiary trail that Washington was the consummate actor, a man filling religious shoes because it was good politics. In fact, Napoleon appears the more devoted to providence, living a life that required him to believe in his "star" as a guiding prophecy leading to his domination of Europe. That his hold on Europe ended in precipitous fashion explains his absolute dejection in 1815 and his early death six years later. His defeats represented a final break with providence, and so he ended his days similar to Washington, as something of an unbeliever. But before this, Napoleon's fatalism was as immediate as the belief in "providence" that guided Washington, and both men strove to take a more activist role on behalf of the masses in the name of destiny. Washington assigned those he led to the care of a divine creator who had initiated a reality and appeared indifferent to its consequences, leaving men to act.[12] He cast his errors to the heavens that he saw as indeterminable and beyond his mortal sensibilities, allowing him to safeguard the public good with a clean conscience. If Napoleon can be faulted for seeing religion as facilitating his political hold, he also can be complimented for trying to shape the temporal world as an active agent of the creator. So too can Washington be admired for his efforts to guarantee the "pursuit of happiness." As in other respects, offering happiness as a right would force each man to interpret what their respective societies desired in this regard. It was an imperfect effort with imperfect results, but it was a shared endeavor.

Considering how very similar their careers were and the lack of separation when defining each man's character, it hardly seems fair that only Washington's legacy is without controversy. But this is largely the case. In fact, Washington did more than secure a legacy for himself as a military commander and republican proponent. He secured a place in the "hearts of his countrymen," as was pointed out immediately upon his death by Henry Lee, congressman from Virginia and former major general in the Continental Army.[13] Lee's eulogy expressed the sentiment of a saddened nation that owed a great debt to the former leader. While Washington's place in the pantheon of American civil culture is secure, the question remains as to the value of what can now only be classified as a myth. Americans are still brought up on the idea of a Washington who could not tell a lie and who was practically a god. For the purposes of teaching morality to American youths, Washington is imbued with these fictional attributes.[14] If giving the Virginian such a reputation is perhaps patriotic, what if Washington is not what he seemed? The evaluation of the origins of the great American republic requires sober assessment, and none is provided by portraying Washington as a divine hero without failings. If Washington was special, without vice and without ambition, then the government he helped found is in great trouble, since it was not designed to rely on such divinity. Given the expected absence of Washingtonian virtue, this republic relies on the checks and balances of American civic involvement. Therefore, one should know the limits of Washington, because the vitality of the American republic does not rest in the virtue of great men. That virtue, or vice, is found in the whole population. One cannot wait for heroes to rise from Virginia to save the republic; it never happened, nor will it ever happen. The safety of the nation's representative institutions is the responsibility of every citizen. Such was the measure of Washington's America, and such is its measure today.

For Napoleon, much of the adulation heaped on the man came from those exiled with him on St. Helena who offered their own account of his last years on the island, including his physician, Barry Edward O'Meara, and a close confidant, Emmanuel, comte de Las Cases. These admirers and others faced the difficult task of how to compel even a sympathetic audience to identify with Napoleon despite his record in the aftermath of revolution—his shift to absolutism. The French answered by undergoing a metamorphosis in terms of the Napoleon legacy, and as one might guess, the journey is very different from the American experience with Washington: from vilification to adulation in the case of Napoleon, and from adulation to glorification in the case of Washington. The French embrace of the man did not come early. For a long time, Napoleon's grave remained on St. Helena. Only in 1840 did the French public demand the return of their hero, and when his corpse was brought to France, it was enshrined in a tomb in Les Invalides. It is there still. The adulation attributed to the man at that time reflected the call to a nostalgic memory of the Napoleonic era and the attempt to forge another that came under his nephew, Louis-Napoleon Bonaparte (Napoleon III). Bonapartism became a formal movement, certainly political but also cultural, and France experienced a renewal of prestige born of empire building once again. It was short-lived and not as brilliant as what had come before, but the first Napoleon could be proud of the reach of his legacy. His adoptive country had immortalized him after all.

Napoleon remained a reviled figure in the United States for the obvious reason that Americans viewed him as no more than a petty tyrant, the antithesis of democracy and the American ability to turn along a new path toward republicanism. The negative American view of Napoleon has its place. Laudatory remembrance of the emperor too often glosses over the carnage and loss of life left in the man's path. The tally of more than five million killed in the Napoleonic Wars justifies the label of warmonger to a great extent, and just as plain is the need to put war at the center of the Napoleon experience and therefore legacy.[15]

It seems Napoleon will always pale in comparison to Washington, since the former embraced absolutism, while the latter put a nation on the path to democracy. The contrast appears to signify the gap between debasement and virtue. But this superficial conjecture means that to focus on the apparent gulf between these two giants born of revolution is to miss the larger movement that engulfed both men, and that was the Enlightenment. As this book has made clear, this European reality made a virtue of absolutism, especially as practiced by Napoleon, and deemed the democratic experiment just that— an uncertain political adventure that was not for the weak of heart. When Napoleon's career in France is seen as one that included the Revolution, it is clear that he only carried out the French will of gravitating to absolutism and shunning the chaos born of the democracy glimpsed during the Revolution. The French comfort level with absolutism could not have contrasted more sharply with the American abhorrence of such an end, something Gertrude Himmelfarb in *The Roads to Modernity* has labeled the French willingness to serve under an "enlightened despot" and the American obsession with a "politics of liberty," a push toward a trust in the institutions of self-government and not the rule of one man.[16] The contrasting ends appear defined in these two leaders emerging from revolution, but this is not the case. Stendhal described this best because he believed that Washington would have struggled in Napoleon's seat: "Washington himself would have found it difficult to judge the amount of liberty to be granted safely to a supremely childish people, for whom experience meant nothing and who at heart still cherished all the stupid prejudices to which ancient monarchy gives rise."[17] In other words, the new polity that defined the American public held Washington in check by offering him no temptation. He may well have succumbed to a body politic in love with old traditions favoring absolutism. Ambition ensured that Washington and Napoleon were the same man. Rather it was the times that defined their leadership; each man merely played their accepted role. This conclusion speaks to the enlightened legacy of each man that brings them together, even as popular conception wishes to keep them apart.

6

EPILOGUE
A Similar End

T hroughout his retirement until his death in December 1799, George Washington remained a player on the American stage, but the nature of his role shifted dramatically. While in office, he had felt duty-bound to consider all sides of any particular issue. Now, released from official obligations, Washington showed his clear preference for the Federalists. His open support of John Adams's administration and of the Federalist Party grew, and the sentiment was returned. When war again loomed with France in July 1798, Adams appointed Washington, without consulting him, to once again head the American army, with the rank of lieutenant general. After some confusion helped along by Washington's misunderstanding of the tacit and explicit agreements between himself and President Adams, Alexander Hamilton became the second in command of the armed forces, although de facto commander under the close eye of Washington, who served as "provisional" commander. Retirement had been seemingly brief.

The war with France did not come outside of the naval quasi-war Adams waged in the Atlantic Ocean, and Washington did not take the field one final time. This fortunate development thwarted Hamilton's plans to use his military position to intimidate all Republican political rivals, a ploy unwittingly supported by Washington because of his staunch backing of Hamilton

as active commander of the army.[1] Once the emergency passed, he again retired his commission, but not before he validated those who now directed
scorn and ridicule at the retired president, accusing him of being senile and
a dupe for monarchists. Washington had grown tired of what he viewed as
near-treasonous attacks on his character and his motivations. Now free of
the restraints of public office, he broke with many of his Virginian friends
in the name of honor and defending his reputation. By this late stage, he
had become a partisan, though not necessarily a vocal one, since he vowed
to remain publicly silent on the decisions of the executive. He could do little
else. Americans, especially Federalists, still wrote to the great man to seek
advice and to have his name lent to projects, but his refusal or assent was
no longer the deciding factor. The next generation of American politicians
had already taken the reigns, leaving the great Washington more a make-
weight than a decision maker. In that sense, the system he had helped create
had worked. The system was more important than the man.

With the political chasm between Federalists and Republicans, it appeared a trying time for the new country to function without the "father of
the nation." And with Washington's final retirement in 1798 came the first
period in the history of the young country where Washington, the fail-safe,
was not an option. After his brief stint as a provisional commander, it was
clear to all that there could be no recourse to calling Washington back from
retirement to defend the nation against a possible invasion. Washington
could not be asked to rise above politics, take the helm of government, and
rally the nation. The elder statesman had sequestered himself at Mount
Vernon, leaving the country to fend for itself.

James Flexner's volume *George Washington: Anguish and Farewell* paints a
vivid picture of Washington's retirement, the former president alone in a
crowd of visitors.[2] People came and went from Mount Vernon, but rarely
those he wished to see. The guests were mostly strangers who vied with one
another to get a glimpse of the great hero. His friends were gone. Instead, he
looked to manage his estate, perhaps the greatest love of his life. This task
became increasingly important to him, since his property was in a dreadful
way. To pay for repairs and renovations, he was reduced to trying to sell the
western tracts acquired in his youth. Unable to find reliable buyers and a
source of liquid capital, he eventually borrowed from a bank to keep Mount

Vernon afloat. Cincinnatus had come home, but his immediate reality was toil and worry. Still he took much comfort in having fulfilled the calling of providence to deliver a nation into the hands of his worthy countrymen, earning a veneration that would extend long after his was gone.

The only thing left was playing the part of the stoic as death approached. Washington prepared himself for this role as he again fell into the pattern of seeing his end at every turn. His death did come just a few years after retirement and, as he put it, came "hard." On December 12, 1799, Washington rode across his land, ignoring the snow on the ground. The next day, Washington again rode out in the snow to supervise the removal of some brush. When the general returned home, he felt poorly and thought he had caught a cold while riding. The ailment was to prove much more serious. Later that same evening, Dr. Craik arrived at his bedside and diagnosed what today would be quickly recognized as a bacterial infection. Lacking an understanding of the malady, Washington's doctors did what medical science of the day instructed that they do. They bled him and inflicted blisters on the severely infected throat that was giving him trouble. After a time, Washington called off his doctors. He then mustered his last strength to instruct Tobias Lear, his personal secretary, on how to place his body in the family tomb. With this last order given, he muttered his final words, "'Tis well," and shuffled off this mortal coil to the long expected rest with his ancestors.[3] To the end, Washington remained in command of his situation. He was placed in the family vault after four days, age sixty-seven, survived by his wife, Martha.

■ ■ ■ ■

After defeat at Waterloo, Napoleon Bonaparte soon found himself on his second island exile in less than fifteen months, this time at St. Helena in the south Atlantic. But circumstances were distinctly different in July 1815 than in April 1814, when he had "ruled" the island of Elba while in exile in the Mediterranean. This time around, he was more prisoner than ex-monarch. There would be no great escape and return to France, as there had been in 1814, although the main reason for this was that Napoleon did not wish it. As James Lawford wrote in *Napoleon: The Last Campaigns, 1813–1815*, he was still the same man after Waterloo, only his "mainspring" was broken.[4] Catastrophic defeat twice in such a short period of time had weakened even

Napoleon's iron constitution. Once on St. Helena, he accepted his lot despite the perceived insults, such as the constant supervision he endured by a British escort detached from the garrison on the island and his protests against the brutish behavior of the island's governor, Lord Hudson Lowe. His reaction no doubt reflected a large element of genuine loss; he now commanded little. In this respect, Lowe's refusal to call Napoleon "emperor" speaks volumes. It was a grudge match, and Napoleon lost the outward exchange. Of course, the British government had never recognized him as emperor. Still, he brooded, drew back, limited his forays outdoors, and refused any visits from English official personnel, achieving a small measure of defiance.

For Napoleon, the legacy he strove to create for himself while at St. Helena became his new battlefield, and he full well understood both the importance and the magnitude of the task of rehabilitating his reputation. It was a Herculean undertaking, since Napoleon's legacy confronted an almost insurmountable obstacle: his military defeat. It is far more difficult to create legend from defeat than it is from victory, such as was Washington's task. In Napoleon's case the starting point of his legacy had to be defeat on the battlefield. He admitted as much when he said, "The great glory of my reign is not in having won forty battles. . . . That which can never be denied, and that [which] will live on forever, is my Civil Code."[5] The desire to emphasize the civil accomplishments more than the military exploits also would seem a difficult task given the preponderance of the latter. This realization may explain the limited memoir he did produce. A recounting of his youth and campaigns till Marengo occupies some two-thirds of this official record, leaving less than a third of the text to examine Waterloo and its consequences. There is nothing in between. The large omission—an effort to gloss over this period of militarism and absolutism—reflects badly on Napoleon. But it is also surprising. The gap excluded some fine moments, particularly on the battlefield. Still, the oversights in his memoir, purposeful or otherwise, did not prevent some rather sweeping statements for posterity recorded by his followers that now appear almost prophetic. Chief among them is his claim that in having so challenged England, he had helped paved the way for the rise of Russia to world domination—unless England, France, and the United States acted in unison.[6] A sweeping look at the twentieth century suggests that he had an aptitude for long-range historical analysis.

Napoleon had protested the decision to send him to St. Helena, arguing instead for retirement in England, the land of his steadfast enemy. His plea failed, and his journey to the island found him quiet and resigned to his fate. Just over six years later, he was dead. The causes of his death have received much attention since his early demise, coming at the age of fifty-one while in excellent health and at the beginning of his exile. Conditions on the island can hardly be blamed for his death. He was sheltered in a modest home, Longwood House—not a palace certainly but not a prison either, as was the fate preferred by many in Europe for the ogre.

Officially, he died of stomach cancer, an ailment that had prematurely killed his father. Others whispered about assassination at the hand of his British overseer. Lowe had come to his new post as the jailor of the most famous prisoner in Europe after having spent time at the Prussian court where he absorbed an inordinate disdain for Napoleon. Other accounts state that Lowe admired Napoleon's military exploits and that he was not unfavorably disposed toward the man. In any case, Lowe refused to offer the ex-emperor the dignity he deserved, most notoriously insisting on two-hour checks to ensure his continued presence on the island. Napoleon protested but was ignored, a keen offense to his now embedded royal disposition. His response was to refuse to leave his home. Such self-confinement impaired his health due to lack of exercise and may have contributed to his death in just a matter of years. The reports that Lowe had the doctor assigned to Napoleon poison him are mere speculation. Others believe that one of his fellow French exiles poisoned him to end that man's internment on the island with his master.[7] More likely the cause was the debilitating impact of routine. No longer was every minute of every day needed to run an empire. Rather, the tedium and boredom was acute and no doubt helped explain his exhaustion. Napoleon's fate was a curious one in that he had spent his body in attempting prodigious tasks, and it now faced exhaustion, but the mind refused the reprieve that exile offered the body. A steady decline from this circumstance stared the great man in the face. Whatever the cause, he died painfully, a slow suffocation that left him languishing in pain for a number of days. In this respect, at least, his death mirrored that of Washington, who had expired over two days as his breathing failed him and he slowly suffocated. Such was the torment and physical end of two great men.

A NOTE ON SOURCES

D espite the voluminous literature on each man, there is almost no scholarship or writing directly comparing George Washington to Napoleon Bonaparte. The lone text offering this comparison is but a twelve-page "fragment" of an article written by Francis Lieber in 1864, titled "Washington and Napoleon," and printed two hundred times for distribution at the metropolitan fair in New York held in April of that year. This oversight is most likely due to prejudice on both sides of the Atlantic: the Americans label Napoleon a petty tyrant; the French dismiss Washington as a military lightweight.

While this book presents the first lengthy comparison of Washington to Napoleon, others have compared these figures to a number of individuals. In the literature focused on Washington, the approach is typically one of utmost respect, as writers portray him as setting a standard other U.S. citizens must meet in order to be considered great Americans. A collection of essays in a book edited by Ethan Fishman and titled *George Washington: Foundation of Presidential Leadership and Character* (2001) is a paramount example of this laudatory treatment. In one essay, "Duty, Honor, Country: Parallels in the Leadership of George Washington and Dwight David Eisenhower," written by Philip G. Henderson, Washington leads the way for another of America's generals who became president. The most daring comparison in this book is one that does move in the direction of looking at Washington alongside Napoleon, and that is Jim Piecuch's essay, "Washington and the Specter of Cromwell." However, Piecuch's assessment of Washington in relation to Oliver Cromwell, the Puritan who ruled England as dictator from 1653 to 1658, reassures the reader that Washington was no Cromwell and that this difference is a good thing. More recently, Washington has been compared to Benedict Arnold in Dave R. Palmer's *George Washington and Benedict Arnold: A Tale of Two Patriots* (2006), with predictable results. The point made here and elsewhere is that Washington was a statesman first who acted the role of the general out of necessity. In this way, the American system of government owes its beginnings to a man who embraced the rule of law rather than to a conqueror who established his own laws.

Napoleon has fared less well than Washington has in comparisons to historical figures. Most damning and for obvious reasons is Desmond Seward's *Napoleon and Hitler* (1988). Much more frequently, Napoleon is cast alongside famous conquerors in Western history, such as Alexander the Great or other great military captains. J. F. C. Fuller did this in his *Decisive Battles of the Western World* (1954), as did Russell F. Weigley in *The Age of Battles* (1991). The evaluation is generally favorable but tends to ignore Napoleon's achievements as a statesman while ruling France and a good portion of Europe. The military man is foremost in the mind of these writers, and the rigid portrayal is intentional, designed to keep the view of this historical figure as that of a soldier so that his contribution to warfare is paramount and his threat to representative government assumed.

In the case of Washington, in recent years authors have done a fine job of detailing Washington's exploits in life in a more critical fashion. For example, Washington's foremost biographer, Joseph Ellis, in *His Excellency* (2004), stresses the ambitions Washington held and how his feigned deference to power was just that—feigned. In so doing, Ellis follows the lead of Paul K. Longmore and his book *The Invention of George Washington* (1988), where Longmore depicts Washington often acting as a self-serving man in an analysis that traced Washington's career from its origins up to the time he accepted command of the Continental Army. That same year, 1988, John E. Ferling offered *The First of Men: A Life of George Washington*, again presenting two

Washingtons, the private and the public, and seeking to better understand aspects of his character and personality as Peter R. Henriques tries to do in *Realistic Visionary: A Portrait of George Washington* (2006). Of course, Marcus Cunliffe, in *George Washington: Man and Monument* (1958), had attempted something like this years before, as did Noemie Emery in *Washington: A Biography* (1976). In short, more contemporary writing has had to try and reconcile the ambitious Washington with the ideal he cultivated of the gentleman serving revolutionary virtue. In fact, Ferling has resumed the attack, publishing a very critical view of Washington titled *The Ascent of George Washington: The Hidden Political Genius of an American Icon* (2009). The recurrent theme in all this literature is that Washington used circumstance to advance his ambition.

To be clear, the tone of all this literature is favorable to Washington. The more current analysis is held up by its authors as more complete—that is, now things are not left out that reflect poorly on the man such as slavery, the wars against Native Americans, his vast land wealth, and his at times poor generalship. To this list should be added his occasional heavy-handedness while serving as president. Ferling's two books are the most critical of the titles offered above. Still, all these authors should be applauded because they have had to emerge from a burdensome historiography, since the defenders of Washington are formidable. Those writers painting a uniformly favorable picture of Washington and his circumspection when it came to wielding power include Ron Chernow's award-winning *Washington: A Life*. He offers a defense of the man by continuing the trend of "humanizing" Washington through excusing his ambitious traits and questionable decisions, something previous biographers had done such as Douglas Southall Freeman in *George Washington: A Biography* (1948–1957), and James Thomas Flexner's four volumes *George Washington* (1965–1972). Biographies dating back further still are similarly laudatory in tone and content and include Mason Weems's pamphlet and then book *The Life of George Washington* (ninth edition, 1809), John Marshall's five volumes also titled *The Life of George Washington* (1804–1807), Washington Irving's five volumes of *The Life of George Washington* (1856–1859), and Woodrow Wilson's *George Washington* (1896). Edward Lengel recently went through the various incarnations Americans have made of Washington in *Inventing George Washington: America's Founder, in Myth and Memory* (2011), from the B movies to reputable biographies.

Literature on Napoleon has not been so inspired. Polarization characterized depictions of Napoleon to the point where in 1949, Pieter Geyl could
write a lengthy text tracking the discrepancies titled *Napoleon: For and
Against*. Until the early 1990s, a good portion of the writing remained biography marked by a hostile or laudatory tone. For instance, Emil Ludwig's
Napoleon (1926) used the metaphor of a river to define the Napoleon tide,
but even as this river crested and receded, little was lost in his wake. More
recently, in the last fifteen years or so, biographers again have taken aim at
the man and found his record wanting. Alan Schom did this well in his
1995 book *Napoleon*, one that joins a host of others by that same name. In
this mix there are some fine studies, the best being J. Christopher Herold's
The Age of Napoleon (1963). Scholars continue to use biography to dissect
his career, as Steven Englund did in *Napoleon: A Political Life* (2004), an effort to again discover two Napoleons: the general and the statesman.

Following the lead of some of this literature, *Washington & Napoleon* looks
to bring equal weight to both aspects of each man's life. The first four chapters focus on specific facets of their formative years, careers as military men,
and as statesmen. Chapter 5 evaluates the comparison offered and comments on their character as well. An epilogue describes the final years of
both men. Throughout the text the differences that separate each man fade
from view as these towering figures are held in comparison to one another.

In chapter 1, "Humble Beginnings: The Makings of a Gentleman," the
issue is how each man used a military career to serve their ambition to elevate themselves socially. A number of books sketch Washington's youth,
such as the first two volumes of Freeman's *George Washington* and Flexner's
first volume, *George Washington and the Forge of Experience (1732–1775)*.
Owing to the brevity of sources on Washington's early years, studies of his
life prior to 1760 quickly shift focus to his career as a rising colonial officer,
as is the topic of Thomas A. Lewis in *For King and Country: The Maturing of
George Washington, 1748–1760* (1993). Also of interest for their studies of
Washington's early military career are Paul E. Kopperman's *Braddock at the
Monongahela* (1977), and recently, Alan Axelrod's *Blooding at Great Meadows:
Young George Washington and the Battle That Shaped the Man* (2007). Peter
Russell's "Redcoats in the Wilderness: British Officers and Irregular Warfare
in Europe and America, 1740–1760," in *The William and Mary Quarterly*

(October 1978), defends Braddock for having properly adjusted to irregular war in the Americas. The significance of Washington's battles in Ohio beyond merely shaping that man's future is best covered in two recent studies, Fred Anderson's *Crucible of War: The Seven Years' War and the Fate of Empire in British North America, 1754–1766* (2000) and *The French and Indian War: Deciding the Fate of North America* by Walter Borneman (2006).

Aside from tracing Napoleon's youth in a number of biographies that do so in greater or lesser detail depending on the book, there are a number of other facets to consider. These again reflect more recent scholarship. The role of his parents is considered in Dorothy Carrington's *Napoleon and His Parents* (1988). In English the best recent study of Napoleon's beginnings is Philip Dwyer's *Napoleon: The Path to Power, 1769–1799* (2007), an attempt to put Napoleon's developmental years in the broader context of the Revolution and separate myth from reality. In this way, some Napoleon staples are thrown into disarray, including his relationship with his parents; his interactions with the leader of the Corsican independence movement, Pascal Paoli; his contemplation of suicide; his determination to seize the moment created by revolution; his flirtations with republicanism; his bravery under fire; and his ascension to power as First Consul.

In chapter 2, "A Tried and Tested Formula: In Search of Decisive Victory," the military careers of each man are addressed to better understand how the role of commander served their ambition. Washington's generalship is critically appraised by Flexner in the second volume of his biography, *George Washington in the American Revolution*. More favorable to Washington's generalship is David Lengel's *General George Washington: A Military Life* (2005), and Don Higginbotham's *George Washington and the American Military Tradition* (1985), though neither dismiss Washington's faults. Thomas G. Frothingham, in *Washington Commander in Chief* (1930), and Curtis P. Nettels, in *George Washington and American Independence* (1951), offer two older accounts. The Revolutionary War is of course extensively covered, and some of the best analysis of the military campaigns is done by Howard Henry Peckham in *The War for Independence: A Military History* (1958), and John Ferling in *Almost a Miracle: The American Victory in the War of Independence* (2007). Higginbotham also contributes with *The War of American Independence: Military Attitudes, Policies, and Practice, 1763–1789*

(1983). The various key battles have drawn extensive attention in the literature. The New York campaign is placed in proper perspective by Barnet Schecter in *The Battle for New York: The City at the Heart of the American Revolution* (2002) and more sympathetically in David McCullough's *1776* (2005). An extensive treatment of the Yorktown campaign is provided by Burke Davis in *The Campaign That Won America: The Story of Yorktown* (1970) and Richard Ketchum in *Victory at Yorktown: The Campaign That Won the Revolution* (2004).

More specialized literature delves into some crucial aspects of the war, a complex event. Most relevant to our work in chapter 2 is Washington's use of militia and his development of a professional army, a topic of an extensive literature, including *A Respectable Army: The Military Origins of the Republic, 1763–1789* (1982) by James K. Martin and Mark Edward Lender, and James Whisker's *The Rise and Decline of the American Militia System*, (1999). Bruce Chadwick, in *The First American Army: The Untold Story of George Washington and the Men Behind America's First Fight for Freedom* (2005), and Caroline Cox, in *A Proper Sense of Honor: Service and Sacrifice in George Washington's Army* (2004), downplay the leadership role of Washington. Mark Kwasny's *Washington's Partisan War, 1775–1783* (1996) extends the discussion of militia to include the role of guerrilla warfare and how this helped Washington prolong the war in the Middle Colonies. Before this book, the guerrilla campaign in the South dominated the discussion in books such as *Partisans and Redcoats: The Southern Conflict that Turned the Tide of the American Revolution* (2001), by Walter Edgar, and two edited volumes, *An Uncivil War: The Southern Backcountry During the American Revolution* (1985), edited by Ronald Hoffman, and *The Revolutionary War in the South: Power, Conflict, and Leadership* (1979), edited by W. Robert Higgins. John Buchanan's *The Road to Guilford Courthouse: The American Revolution in the Carolinas* (1997) is a more recent treatment.

There is no shortage of books when it comes to Napoleon's military career. The definitive study of all Napoleon's military campaigns is David Chandler's *The Campaigns of Napoleon* (1966). More recent scholars try to connect the military theme to broader issues, such as in David Gates's *The Napoleonic Wars, 1803–1815* (1997), Gunther E. Rothenberg's *The Napoleonic Wars* (1999), and Charles Esdaile's *The French Wars, 1792–1815* (2001). The changing nature of Napoleon's art of war is best examined in Harold T. Parker's *Three Napoleonic Battles* (1983). *Washington & Napoleon* looks to diminish Napoleon's accolades as a general, something Jonathon Riley also did in *Napoleon as a General: Commanding from the Battlefield to Grand Strategy* (2007). We, like Riley, find Napoleon's strategic vision lacking, particularly in comparison to Washington's. Yet we agree, at least to some extent, with authors Michel Franceschi and Ben Weider in *The Wars against Napoleon: Debunking the Myth of the Napoleonic Wars* (2008) that there was a measure of self-defense in Napoleon's actions, almost amounting to preemptive war, as one of us, Matthew Flynn, argues in a chapter of his *First Strike: Preemptive War in Modern History* (2008). Napoleon had the series of wars that bear his name thrust upon him by England to some extent, regardless of his character defects that might have welcomed the challenge. The evolution of the French army from revolution to empire receives attention in a number of books addressing tactics and motives, including John Lynn's *The Bayonets of the Republic: Motivation and Tactics in the Army of Revolutionary France, 1791–94* (1984) and *Napoleon's Men: The Soldiers of the Revolution and Empire* (2002) by Alan Forrest.

Washington & Napoleon has had to come to terms with much of Esdaile's writing in important ways, including that regarding the military career of Napoleon. Esdaile commands the study of guerrilla warfare during the Napoleonic era with books such as *Fighting Napoleon: Guerrillas, Bandits, and Adventurers in Spain, 1808–1814* (2004) and the book he edited, *Popular Resistance in the French Wars: Patriots, Partisans, and Land Pirates* (2005). More significantly, Esdaile, with his *Napoleon's Wars: An International History, 1803–1815* (2007), expands the range of the Napoleonic Wars to produce a pan-European account of the time by featuring regions such as Scandinavia and countries such as Turkey. With this expanded scope, Esdaile stresses the international scene and strives to render Napoleon but a symptom of the French Revolution and the French Revolution but a symptom of the larger changes affecting Europe at this time. In so doing, he is responding to Paul Schroeder's impressive study, *The Transformation of European Politics, 1763–1848* (1994). In our own way, and in introductory fashion, our study responds to Esdaile's *Napoleon's Wars* by defending the importance of Napoleon to the age and offering a different orientation, one of the Atlantic world united in revolution emerging under the auspices of the Age of Enlightenment. After all, Washington and Napoleon opposed England, although for complex reasons that both separate them and also tie them together. So Atlantic world history can offer a broad understanding of the Napoleonic empire, a "comprehensive portrait of the whole damned dappled, divided, endlessly shifting tableau vivant that was Napoleonic Europe." See Steven Englund, "*Monstre Sacré*: The Question of Cultural Imperialism and the Napoleonic Empire," *The Historical Journal* 51, no. 1 (2008): 249.

Our third chapter, "Leading by Default: The Chance to Wield Power," covers the greatest topic of divergence between the two men—attaining power—although, as is made clear in this book, the divergence is not as great as believed. In Washington's case, the uncertainty of the aftermath of the Revolutionary War is the focus of a voluminous literature. Some scholars put him at the center of that experience, such as Don Higginbotham in *George Washington: Uniting a Nation* (2002), while others look to the domestic political system he helped establish as being the most important factor, something Scott A. Silverstone did in *Divided Union: The Politics of War in the Early American Republic* (2004). In this case, Washington is but a tangential figure. Some famous names have addressed this period of the Washington career, and they do so in laudatory terms. A good portion of James Thomas Flexner's third volume, *George Washington and the New Nation*, does this, as does the middle portion of John Ferling's *A Leap in the Dark: The Struggle to Create the American Republic* (2003). In *The Perils of Peace: America's Struggle for Survival after Yorktown* (2007), Thomas Fleming shortens this analysis to Washington's stewardship over the army from Yorktown until the peace treaty was signed with England in 1783, revealing the general's prominent role at this time. The best treatment is probably that of Richard B. Morris, who devotes his entire text to this period in *The Forging of the Union, 1781–1789* (1987). Finally, we agree with Peter Henriques's assertion in his "Notes on Sources" in *Realistic Visionary* that Ellis's *His Excellency* is a very important work, and we relied on it to a great extent throughout the book, especially in chapter 3.

Of course, Washington's "second" retirement (1783) and activities during that retirement receive close attention in other respects. In *The Forging of the*

Union, Morris offers the best breakdown of Newburgh. Washington's role at the Constitutional Convention is looked at by a number of writers and scholars, including Christopher Collier in *Decision in Philadelphia: The Constitutional Convention of 1787* (1986) and Carol Berkin in *A Brilliant Solution: Inventing the American Constitution* (2002). Edward J. Larson and Michael P. Winship offer a recent presentation of James Madison's notes taken during the Convention in *Constitutional Convention: A Narrative History from the Notes of James Madison* (2005). James Sharp's *American Politics in the Early Republic: The New Nation in Crisis* (1993) and Glenn A. Phelps's *George Washington and American Constitutionalism* (1993) address the long-term implications of Washington's role in birthing republican government and are generally favorable to him. The debate as to whether an elite looked to protect its economic privileges, as Charles Beard famously argued in *An Economic Interpretation of the Constitution of the United States* (1913), or whether the founders exerted control in order to curb democratic excesses, as Gordon Wood asserted in *The Creation of the American Republic* (1969), matters less here than does the foremost contrast in results: the Constitution allowing Washington to successfully wield a government apparatus that bound dissimilar states together, something Napoleon could not do. This uniquely American success is emphasized in Peter S. Onuf's *The Origins of the Federal Republic* (1983).

Biography again dominates the discussion of Napoleon's ability to jump from obscurity to emperor of France, but some authors tackle only a portion of this sweeping and hard-to-delineate period of his life. Malcolm Crook offers a solid examination of the coup of Brumaire and the consummation of this act with the inauguration of the Empire in *Napoleon Comes to Power: Democracy and Dictatorship in Revolutionary France, 1795–1804* (1998). Dwyer's *Napoleon* ends with Napoleon seizing control of the government in 1799. The first volume of Robert Asprey's two-volume *The Rise and Fall of Napoleon Bonaparte* (2000) concludes with the emperor safely in power given his triumph at Austerlitz. More often the shift from consul to tyrant is the focus of Napoleon's rise to power and depicted as a determination to satisfy a consuming ambition with absolute power in his hands. The leading French historian of the Napoleonic era, Jean Tulard, titles his book *Napoleon: Savior or Despot* (1984) and captures this view perfectly. *Washington & Napoleon* diverges from Tulard's take in that we see Napoleon as a product of the times, and when assessing his rise to power, it is important to remember how he was carried on the tide of history in this respect as well. He was not a man consumed by power, but even if he was, he still needed a fortuitous moment with which to act. As we have stated, he was slow to grasp that this moment had arrived—or at the very least he was slow to realize the moment's full potential—and this moment came from the Enlightenment and resultant revolution. France welcomed authoritarianism because it reflected enlightened despotism, which promised to quell revolutionary excess.

Chapter 4, "Enlightened Statesmanship: Winning the People's Favor," emphasizes the context of the Enlightenment and its impact on the statesmanship of both men. For Washington, biography offers insightful accounts of complicated topics including the Federalist and Republican cabinet rivalries and Washington's decision for a second term. Hamilton's response to the nation's financial troubles is best understood in Ellis's *His Excellency* and Flexner's *George Washington and the New Nation*. Washington's determination to lean in favor of England as the bulk of the nation favored France is commented on by his biographers, Ferling in particular in *The First of Men*. The complications in foreign policy because of this Federalist outlook is a much covered topic, perhaps best done by Frank T. Reuter's *Trials and Triumphs: George Washington's Foreign Policy* (1983) and the older *To the Farewell Address: Ideas of Early American Foreign Policy* (1961), by Felix Gilbert. See Louis Sears for Washington's reactions to the French Revolution, in *George Washington and the French Revolution* (1960). Two good studies of Washington's presidency are Richard Norton Smith's *Patriarch: George Washington and the New American Nation* (1993), and more recently *George Washington: President of the United States, 1789-1797* (2004), by James MacGregor Burns and Susan Dunn. More useful are those scholars asking questions about Washington's understanding and use of power. Edmund Morgan in a brief analysis, *The Genius of George Washington* (1981), complemented this ability as a key to his success. Our study is less complementary for the same reason: by understanding power, Washington could bend it to his will once he realized he could hold on to power best by relinquishing it. Some of this reflection also appears in Noemie Emery's *George Washington: A Biography* (1976). Finally, the spectacle of the Whiskey Rebellion is covered by Thomas P. Slaughter's *The Whiskey Rebellion: Frontier Epilogue to the*

American Revolution (1986) and *The Whiskey Rebellion: Past and Present Perspectives* (1985), edited by Steven R. Boyd.

Any look at Napoleon as a statesman confronts an imposing trend in the historiography. While there is no agreed-upon tally of how many persons died in the course of the Napoleonic Wars, the carnage and great loss of life left in his path too much diminish any benefit of what can be termed the Napoleon Revolution. Still, authors have tried, and naturally the debate devolves into attempting to understand Napoleon's role in ending or advancing the French Revolution. An early attempt is Charles Downer Hazen's *The French Revolution and Napoleon* (1917), one that is laudatory of the man but at the same time reduces his importance by examining the French Revolution largely independent of Napoleon for more than half the book. In *The Napoleonic Revolution* (1967), Robert B. Holtman affirms the importance of the man for the era of revolution and therefore contrasts with Martyn Lyons's *Napoleon Bonaparte and the Legacy of the French Revolution* (1994), where Napoleon is not bigger than the age. In fact, Lyons argues that his best results came when he acted in stride with the Revolution. For Lyons, Napoleon's greatest accomplishment is that he founded a modern state that outlasted him, so in this respect, Napoleon, in tandem with the French Revolution, had a monumental impact on the times and thereafter. This is true even as his key role as statesman is diminished to some extent by realizing that the apparatus he initiated throughout his empire carried on the import of the Revolution more than the man himself. Consequently, Napoleon's role is diminished, as is our point in chapter 4. He could never be the despot envisioned by his critics given the limited reach of the man. Instead, as Michael Rowe writes in *From Reich to State: The Rhineland in the Revolutionary Age, 1780–1830* (2003)—and is stressed by Steven Englund in his review article "*Monstre Sacré*: The Question of Cultural Imperialism and the Napoleonic Empire" in *The Historical Journal* (2008) —Napoleon's ability to create a culture that was "'imperial,' 'European' or 'Bonapartist,'"—something not really even "French"—was his chief impact, the means of his tyranny, as far as his administration of the empire was concerned. Napoleon's despotism was achieved at least in part in the functioning of the bureaucracy of empire, a keen limit on the man indeed. Stuart Wolf initiated this approach in his *Napoleon's Integration of Europe* (1991), followed by a series of titles by

Michael Broers, his most important being *Europe Under Napoleon, 1799–1815* (1996). Philip Dwyer's edited book, *Napoleon and Europe* (2001), kept this line of inquiry going, as did Alexander Grab's *Napoleon and the Transformation of Europe* (2003). The Napoleonic Empire, interrupted as it was in midstream with the military defeat of Napoleon's armies, leaves the literature incomplete and uncertain as to what the long-term impact would have been and scholars reduced to making assessments based on a short window.

Chapter 5 reflects our effort to better understand the Enlightenment's relation to the Atlantic world. Gertrude Himmelfarb's *The Roads to Modernity: The British, French, and American Enlightenments* (2004) influenced our thinking the most in that the American experience in forming government in the wake of revolution offered a historical break from the European experience that, as we say often, welcomed authoritarianism because it reflected enlightened despotism. The American conservatism that rejected centralized rule because it threatened to advance to despotism had to be defended as radical in its own right, as did Bernard Bailyn in *The Ideological Origins of the American Revolution* (1967) and Gordon S. Wood in *The Radicalism of the American Revolution* (1992). In so arguing, the emphasis is constantly taken off Washington. This is true even when examining the Founding Fathers in books such as *The Founding Fathers and the Politics of Character* (2004), by Andrew S. Trees, and *Hamilton, Adams, Jefferson: The Politics of Enlightenment and the American Founding* (2005), by Darren Staloff. But the key, as is so often the case in this early period of American history, is Washington, and an analysis of him is attempted in a number of ways. For instance, an examination of artistic renderings of Washington as portrayed by his contemporaries is discussed at length in Gary Wills's *Cincinnatus: George Washington and the Enlightenment* (1984). Wills's belief in enlightened thinking as informing such imagery of Washington is countered in Barry Schwartz's *George Washington: The Making of an American Symbol* (1987), where the monarchial aspirations of the American public are confirmed in the person of Washington until that audience shifted its veneration to the Constitution. Either way, Washington is the glue that informs the Enlightenment experiment in this part of the Atlantic World, as has been John Ferling's point in his writings, specifically in *Setting the World Ablaze: Washington, Adams, and the American Revolution* (2000).

The landscape is more mixed than Himmelfarb presents; all of France did not welcome despotism nor did all colonials defend self-rule. At the same time, her Atlantic world comparison is crucial to adjusting the perspective to revolution by acknowledging that this aspect of the Enlightenment started in the Americas, not in France, and the source of this revolution was the Enlightenment, despite the tendency to see this movement as confined to the elite and therefore limited in scope. Ideology may have been the reserve of a select few in America as well as in Europe, although much writing says otherwise, that the elite found a responsive body politic in the colonies. See, for instance, Richard Buel's *Securing the Revolution: Ideology in American Politics, 1789–1815* (1972). But the military and political dimensions of this conflict soon engulfed millions living in the Atlantic world in both Europe and the American colonies. In this respect, a more base issue comes to the fore, and that is the American challenge to England's mantra of "balance of power," twenty-five years before France initiated such a movement under Napoleon. So this Atlantic world struggle has multiple fronts and victors, England successfully thwarting the challenge of France but not that of its thirteen colonies in North America. This means that Washington and Napoleon assume very important roles in leading this struggle against England in different parts of the world, and over a sustained period of time, as their careers unfolded one after the other. It was a good time to be a leader in the age of revolution.

NOTES

Introduction

1   "A Leader Like No Other," exhibit in the Donald W. Reynolds Education Center, Mount Vernon Estate and Gardens, Alexandria, VA.

2   "Ordre du Jour" pour La Garde des Consuls et pour Toutes les Troupes de la Républic, *Correspondance de Napoléon I*, vol. 6 (February 7, 1800), 183.

3   Emmanuel Auguste-Dieudonné, comte de Las Cases, *The Life, Exile and Conversations of the Emperor Napoleon*, vol. 1, bk. 1 (London, 1835), 381–82.

1. Humble Beginnings: The Makings of a Gentleman

1   Paul K. Longmore, *The Invention of George Washington* (Berkeley: University of California Press, 1988), 7, 32. Joseph Ellis, perhaps the foremost biographer of Washington, writes in *His Excellency* that biographers such as Longmore overstate the case and that the *Rules of Civility* served only "as a mere exercise in penmanship." See Ellis, *His Excellency: George Washington* (New York: Knopf, 2004), 9.

2   James Thomas Flexner, *George Washington: The Indispensable Man* (Boston: Little, Brown, 1974), 5. Flexner wrote the most extensive biography of Washington. He also wrote a condensed version, and that is cited here. There is very little difference between the presentation of Washington's youth in that book and what is offered in the first of his four volumes, *George Washington: The Forge of Experience, 1732–1775* (Boston: Little, Brown, 1965). In *Inventing George Washington: America's Founder, in Myth and Memory*, Edward Lengel criticizes

Flexner's work for being overly literary and for making use of "imaginative writing." See *Inventing George Washington,* (New York: Harper, 2011), 144.

3   Flexner, *George Washington: The Indispensable Man*, 11. This quote is in the condensed version only.

4   Longmore, *The Invention of George Washington*, 18.

5   Edward G. Lengel, *General George Washington: A Military Life* (New York: Random House, 2005), 20.

6   John Ferling, *The Ascent of George Washington: The Hidden Political Genius of an American Icon* (New York: Bloomsbury, 2009), 19. A letter from Dinwiddie to Washington dated June 4, 1754, makes it clear that Dinwiddie placed great hope in the ability of a reinforced Washington and an independent company of royal soldiers to expel the French force, even after the death of Colonel Fry. See Letter, Robert Dinwiddie to George Washington, June 4, 1754, *The Papers of George Washington*, digital edition (accessed February 23, 2010), http://rotunda.upress .virginia.edu:8080/pgwde/dflt.xqy?keys=print-Col01d56.

7   Ferling states that the root cause of the debacle with the French party was that "Washington was mad for glory." Ferling, *The Ascent of George Washington*, 21. Lengel says "Washington *wanted* a fight" (emphasis Lengel's). Lengel, *General George Washington*, 36. Ron Chernow places the blame more on extenuating circumstances than on Washington. See Chernow, *Washington: A Life* (New York: Penguin, 2010), 69.

8   Ellis, *His Excellency*, 17. Chernow places the blame squarely on the poor translation. Chernow, *Washington: A Life*, 79.

9   Ellis, *His Excellency*, 18.

10   Ellis claims that deference did not come naturally to Washington. At this point, all he was being asked to do was play the part of hero, with no deference required even if a fair amount of acting was. See Ellis, *His Excellency*, 38. Chernow suggests Washington's manner was "studied." Chernow, *Washington: A Life*, 172.

11   The first quote is from Gen. James Wolfe. See Michael P. Gabriel, *Major General Richard Montgomery: The Making of an American Hero* (Madison, NJ: Fairleigh Dickinson University Press, 2002), 36. Wolfe achieved fame during the French and Indian War when he died leading the successful British assault on Quebec. Braddock's comment is in Robert Leckie, *The Wars of America*, vol. 1, *Quebec to Appomattox* (New York: Harper & Row, 1968), 45. Abercromby's assessment is in Allan R. Millett and Peter Maslowski, *For the Common Defense: A Military History of the United States of America* (New York: Free Press, 1994), 9.

12   For Washington's disappointment over not being promoted, see Flexner, *George Washington: The Forge of Experience, 1732–1775*, 112–13; and Noemie Emery, *Washington: A Biography* (New York: Putnam, 1976), 92. Dinwiddie himself noted

that part of Virginia's problems stemmed from "the want of proper command." See Ferling, *The Ascent of George Washington*, 26.

13   Flexner, *George Washington: The Indispensable Man*, 22.

14   According to one Washington biographer, Braddock "bent backwords" to get Washington to join his expedition in order to benefit from his backwoods experience. See Emery, *Washington*, 77. A letter from Col. Robert Napier, aide-de-camp to the Duke of Rochester, to Gen. Edward Braddock recommends the use of colonial troops as pathfinders, as they are "best acquainted with the country." See Winthrop Sargent, *The History of an Expedition Against Fort Du Quesne, in 1755 under Major-General Edward Braddock* (Philadelphia: Lippincott, Grambo, 1856), 399.

15   Peter Russell, "Redcoats in the Wilderness: British Officers and Irregular Warfare in Europe and America, 1740-1760," *William and Mary Quarterly* 35, no. 4 (October 1978): 642–44. Alan Axelrod asserts that Washington did not believe Braddock failed because he did not adopt Indian tactics, but because his men lacked discipline. See Axelrod, *Blooding at Great Meadows: Young George Washington and the Battle that Shaped the Man* (Philadelphia: Running Press, 2007), 258.

16   Ferling, *The Ascent of George Washington*, 42.

17   Biographers suggest that Washington's feelings for Martha grew over time into a deep, lasting friendship. They stress that his more passionate love likely remained his youthful memory of Sally Fairfax. As examples see Chernow, *Washington*, 118; Ferling, *The First of Men*, 78; and Lengel, *General George Washington: A Military Life*, xxxv.

18   Steven Englund, *Napoleon: A Political Life* (New York: Scribner, 2004), 6.

19   Emil Ludwig, *Napoleon* (New York: Boni & Liveright, 1926), 19. Napoleon's full name in Italian was Napolione Buonaparte.

20   Robert B. Asprey, *The Rise of Napoleon Bonaparte* (New York: Basic Books, 2000), 15.

21   Philip G. Dwyer takes issue with this aspect (and others) of the Napoleonic legend, doubting it occurred at all. See Dwyer, *Napoleon: The Path to Power, 1769–1799* (London: Bloomsbury, 2007), 29, 30. Napoleon's use of rocks in the snowball fight is described by Napoleon's classmate and future secretary Louis Antoine Fauvelet de Bourrienne. See Bourrienne, *Memoirs of Napoleon Bonaparte*, trans. John S. Memes, vol. 1 (New York: P. F. Collier, 1892), 35.

22   Dwyer, *Napoleon*, 34.

23   See Englund, *Napoleon*, 22; and Asprey, *The Rise of Napoleon Bonaparte*, 19.

24   Dorothy Carrington, *Napoleon and His Parents: On the Threshold of History* (London: Viking, 1988), 92.

25 Alan Schom, *Napoleon Bonaparte* (New York: HarperCollins, 1997), 9.

26 Gunther E. Rothenberg, *The Napoleonic Wars* (London: Cassell, 1999), 24–32.
    Charles Esdaile adjusts this view of the transformation of war and objects to a
    number of these changes, arguing the French Revolutionary armies did not
    represent a nation-in-arms in many respects. See Esdaile, *The Wars of Napoleon*
    (New York: Longman, 1995), 49–65.

27 Englund, *Napoleon*, 39.

28 Englund, *Napoleon*, 50–51; Charles Esdaile, *Napoleon's Wars: An International
    History, 1803–1815* (New York: Viking, 2007), 34.

29 Asprey, *The Rise of Napoleon Bonaparte*, 65–66.

30 Englund, *Napoleon*, 62.

31 Several scholars dispute Napoleon's contribution to the plan to end the siege,
    arguing that he merely helped execute an existing and obvious plan of attack. See
    Dwyer, *Napoleon*, 144; and J. Christopher Herold, *The Age of Napoleon* (New York:
    American Heritage, 1963), 45. Englund argues that the "scores of letters" he wrote
    and the "plans he submitted to the authorities" meant he imposed his plan on the
    battle. See Englund, *Napoleon*, 65. Napoleon's missives to the revolutionary
    government are readily available in his correspondence. For this report, see
    Napoleon to the Committee of Public Safety, October 25, 1793, *Correspondance de
    Napoléon I*, vol. 1, no. 1, 11.

32 Dwyer, *Napoleon*, 137–38.

33 Most accounts acknowledge Napoleon's bravery while fighting at Toulon. See
    David G. Chandler, *The Campaigns of Napoleon* (New York: Macmillan, 1966), 24–
    27; and Schom, *Napoleon Bonaparte*, 21–22.

34 Martyn Lyons, *Napoleon Bonaparte and the Legacy of the French Revolution* (New
    York: St. Martin's, 1994), 14. The more recent scholarship stresses that Napoleon's
    artillery did not single-handedly end the affair as was conveyed in earlier accounts
    such as Chandler, *The Campaigns of Napoleon*, 39.

2. A Tried and Tested Formula: In Search of Decisive Victory

1   James Thomas Flexner, *George Washington: Anguish and Farewell (1793–1799)*
    (Boston: Little, Brown, 1972), 397.

2   Ferling, *The Ascent of George Washington*, 69, 76.

3   Flexner states that Washington did not want the command, suggesting that he
    even had others campaign against him. Flexner, *George Washington: The Forge of
    Experience, 1732–1775* (Boston: Little, Brown, 1964), 334. Ferling, however,
    argues that Washington must have known that he was the natural choice. See
    Ferling, *The Ascent of George Washington*, 85–86. Joseph Ellis also supports the

idea of Washington seeking the command by using deference as a "pattern of postured reticence." See Ellis, *His Excellency*, 70.

4   Don Higginbotham, *George Washington and the American Military Tradition* (Athens: University of Georgia Press, 1985), 51.

5   John Ferling, *Almost a Miracle: The American Victory in the War for Independence* (New York: Oxford University Press, 2007), 76–78.

6   Ellis, *His Excellency*, 78.

7   Ferling, *Almost a Miracle*, 104.

8   Lengel, *General George Washington: A Military Life*, 119.

9   Ferling suggests that Howe had decided to abandon Boston three months before Washington garrisoned Dorchester Heights. See Ferling, *The Ascent of George Washington*, 101.

10 Ferling has Lee attempting only to "disrupt" the British should they attack. Ferling, *Almost a Miracle*, 123. David Fischer has Lee understanding the difficulty of mounting a defense but having few good options. Fischer, *Washington's Crossing* (New York: Oxford University Press, 2004), 81.

11 Lengel, *General George Washington*, 137. Ferling presents Washington as "more circumspect," hedging his bets about defending New York but believing that it could be defended. Ferling, *The Ascent of George Washington*, 108.

12 David McCullough, *1776* (New York: Simon & Schuster, 2005), 191.

13 Lengel, *General George Washington*, 180.

14 Fischer, *Washington's Crossing*, 372.

15 John E. Ferling, *The First of Men: A Life of George Washington* (Knoxville: University of Tennessee Press, 1988), 277.

16 Ellis, *His Excellency*, 101.

17 Lengel, *General George Washington*, 180.

18 Ferling states that Washington felt no pressure from Congress to defend Philadelphia but did so in order to save his reputation as a commander. He also maintains that Washington fought because of his temperament; he always preferred to give battle. Ferling notes that while Washington took no blame for the loss of Philadelphia, this "brush" with disaster prompted him to focus on the Fabian tactics he would employ for much of the rest of the conflict. Ferling, *The Ascent of George Washington*, 128–29, 132–33.

19 Best on this is Thomas J. Fleming, *Washington's Secret War: The Hidden History of Valley Forge* (New York: Smithsonian Books/Collins, 2005). See also Ferling, *The Ascent of George Washington*, 139–81; and James Thomas Flexner, *George Washington in the American Revolution, 1775–1783* (Boston: Little, Brown, 1968), 253–77.

20 See Ferling, *The First of Men*, 232. A good recent treatment focused on von Steuben's role in the war and giving him much more credit for revitalizing the Continental army while it camped at Valley Forge is Paul Lockhart, *The Drillmaster of Valley Forge: The Baron de Steuben and the Making of the American Army* (New York: HarperCollins, 2008), 113.

21 Higginbotham stresses that the Howes did not voluntarily resign. See Don Higginbotham, *The War of American Independence: Military Attitudes, Policies, and Practice, 1763–1789* (Boston: Northeastern University Press, 1983), 197–98.

22 Ferling, *The Ascent of George Washington*, 176.

23 The best treatment of this topic is Mark V. Kwasny, *Washington's Partisan War, 1775–1783* (Kent, OH: Kent State University Press, 1996).

24 Gregory Urwin, "When Freedom Wore a Red Coat," *Army History* (Summer 2008), 8–9.

25 John S. Pancake, *This Destructive War: The British Campaign in the Carolinas, 1780–1782* (Tuscaloosa: University of Alabama Press, 2003), 106.

26 For labeling the war a partisan war, see Terry Golway, *Washington's General: Nathanael Greene and the Triumph of the American Revolution* (New York: Henry Holt, 2005), 241. Washington's orders admitted his lack of understanding of the war in the South, and therefore he offered "no particular instructions," leaving Greene to do as he saw fit when he arrived. See Letter, George Washington to Nathanael Greene, October 22, 1780, *The Papers of General Nathanael Greene,* ed. Richard K. Showman (Chapel Hill: University of North Carolina Press, 1976), 424.

27 Barbara Alice Mann, *George Washington's War on Native Americans* (Westport, CT: Praeger, 2005), 2.

28 Ferling calls Washington's focus on New York "intransigent" and gives credit for the march on Yorktown to Jean-Baptiste Donatien de Vimeur, comte de Rochambeau, commander in chief of the French expeditionary force in the colonies. Ferling, *The Ascent of George Washington*, 210.

29 Lengel, *General George Washington*, 337–38.

30 Compendiums of his military accomplishments are plentiful. See a recent critical assessment by Jonathon Riley both assessing his generalship and acknowledging its long reach to today. See Riley, *Napoleon as a General* (London: Hambledon Continuum, 2007), 203–4.

31 For Napoleon's belief in his "star," see Philip G. Dwyer, "Napoleon and the Drive for Glory: Reflections on the Making of French Foreign Policy," in *Napoleon and Europe*, ed. Philip G. Dwyer (London: Longman, 2001), 130.

32 Chandler, *The Campaigns of Napoleon*, 54.

33 Dwyer, *Napoleon: The Path to Power, 1769–1799*, 4.

34 For Talleyrand's reasoning on the Egyptian expedition, see Esdaile, *Napoleon's Wars*, 65; and Englund, *Napoleon*, 191. Englund goes further and agues that "Egypt had many fathers besides the general who led the expeditionary force." Englund, *Napoleon*, 269.

35 See John Naylor, *Waterloo* (London: B.T. Batsford, 1963), 38.

36 Alan Schom, *One Hundred Days: Napoleon's Road to Waterloo* (New York: Maxwell Macmillan International, 1992), 256.

37 Naylor, *Waterloo*, 109.

38 James Lawford, *Napoleon: The Last Campaigns, 1813–1815* (New York: Crown, 1977), 156.

39 Naylor, *Waterloo*, 173.

40 Owen Connelly, *Blundering to Glory: Napoleon's Military Campaigns*, 3rd ed. (New York: Rowman & Littlefield, 2006), 194.

41 Alan Forrest, *Napoleon's Men: The Soldiers of the Revolution and Empire* (London: Hambledon and London, 2002), 100–101.

42 An often-quoted estimate. See one instance in Esdaile, *Napoleon's Wars*, 221.

43 Robert M. Epstein, *Napoleon's Last Victory and the Emergence of Modern War* (Lawrence: University Press of Kansas, 1994).

44 Connelly, *Blundering to Glory*, 65.

45 Rothenberg, *The Napoleonic Wars*, 166.

46 Raymond Horricks, *Marshal Ney: The Romance and the Real* (New York: Hippocrene Books, 1982), 128.

47 Esdaile complicates this view by stressing that such promotion was exceedingly rare in the French army, although more common than any other. See Esdaile, *The Wars of Napoleon*, 56.

48 Esdaile downplays the impact of guerrilla war on the defeat of Napoleon. In Spain, for instance, Esdaile says Napoleon would have won but for attacking Russia, which prevented a concentration of French forces in Iberia. Allowing for the counterfactual, the error was strategic, not one of facing an unwinnable guerrilla war. See Esdaile, *The Wars of Napoleon*, 141–42. He advances this view again in a review essay, "Recent Writing on Napoleon and his Wars," *Journal of Military History* 73, no. 1 (January 2009), 219. The same mixed record is present in Russia, according to Esdaile. Guerrillas arose in large numbers but did not represent a movement of the people. See Esdaile, *Napoleon's Wars*, 10, 472. In our view, while a national crusade may have been lacking in the guerrilla fighting, the military impact of that guerrilla fighting was still significant.

49 Jonathon P. Riley, *Napoleon and the World War of 1813: Lessons in Coalition Warfighting* (London: Frank Cass, 2000), 87.

50 Esdaile, *Napoleon's Wars*, 499; and Esdaile, *The Wars of Napoleon*, 267. In both cases, Esdaile stresses that even with the call to arms, changes in the structure of Prussian society were limited, reducing the impact of the movement and calling into question Prussia's "national crusade." Guerrilla warfare at best was to be an adjunct to conventional military operations.

51 Michael Broers argues that Napoleon "resurrected" the gendarmerie "wherever the Napoleonic regime held sway." Even if effective, and Broers says it was, this police force was Napoleon's lone contribution to French counterinsurgency efforts. Nor did this step constitute a move toward countering guerrilla warfare, but instead focused on crushing "brigandage" that fostered "rural disorder." See Broers, *Napoleon's Other War: Bandits, Rebels and Their Pursuers in the Age of Revolution* (London: Peter Land, 2010), 85–87.

3. Leading by Default: The Chance to Wield Power

1 Flexner, *George Washington in the American Revolution, 1775–1783*, 491. For Nicola's entire letter, see *Writings of Washington*, 1931, vol. 24, 272–73.

2 Lengel, *General George Washington*, 346; for the Hamilton letter, see Flexner, *George Washington: The Indispensable Man*, 171–72.

3 Flexner, *George Washington in the American Revolution, 1775–1783*, 506–7.

4 Congress officially assumed the title conferred upon it by the Articles of Confederation of the "United States in Congress Assembled" on March 2, 1781. See Richard B. Morris, *The Forging of the Union, 1781–1789* (New York: Harper & Row, 1987), 56.

5 Richard Norton Smith, *Patriarch: George Washington and the New American Nation* (Boston: Houghton Mifflin, 1993), 19.

6 Flexner, *George Washington in the American Revolution, 1775–1783*, 493. He offers another comment on fascism in James Thomas Flexner, *George Washington and the New Nation, 1783–1793* (Boston: Little, Brown, 1969), 86.

7 Ellis, *His Excellency*, 143.

8 For King George III's comment, see Garry Wills, *Cincinnatus: George Washington and the Enlightenment* (New York: Doubleday, 1984), 13; for Samuel Adams's, see John P. Kaminski and Jill Adair McCaughan, eds., *A Great and Good Man: George Washington in the Eyes of His Contemporaries* (Madison, WI: Madison House, 1989), 23.

9 Flexner, *George Washington and the New Nation, 1783–1793*, 8.

10 Ellis, *His Excellency*, 151.

11 Flexner, *George Washington and the New Nation, 1783–1793*, 6.

12 Ibid., 13, 23.

13 Ibid., 25.

14 Wills, *Cincinnatus*, 118.

15 Ellis, *His Excellency*, 152.

16 Ibid., 152. On August 31, 1785, Washington sent Gordon his own account and recollections of the war, noting that Gordon would "desire to receive every information which will enable you to do justice to the principal Actors therein; it cannot be unpleasing to you to receive a narrative of unadorned facts which serve to bring forward circumstances which, in some measure, may be unknown to you." See *Washington Papers, Confederation Series*, vol. 3, 211.

17 Ellis, *His Excellency*, 153.

18 Flexner, *George Washington and the New Nation, 1783–1793*, 66.

19 Ellis, *His Excellency*, 146, 168.

20 Don Higginbotham, *George Washington: Uniting a Nation* (Lanham, MD: Rowman & Littlefield, 2002), 37–38.

21 Flexner, *George Washington and the New Nation, 1783–1793*, 91.

22 Ron Chernow, *Alexander Hamilton* (New York: Penguin, 2004), 232.

23 Flexner, *George Washington and the New Nation, 1783–1793*, 96.

24 Ellis, *His Excellency*, 171, 173.

25 Chernow, *Alexander Hamilton*, 225.

26 John Ferling argues that Washington attending a convention that would likely produce an executive office—one that he would likely occupy—would be seen as "grasping for power," which would be abhorrent to his reputation. Ferling, *The Ascent of George Washington*, 266.

27 James Madison's notes taken during the convention remain the authoritative source on Washington's limited involvement in the debates of the convention. See Edward J. Larson and Michael P. Winship, *Constitutional Convention: A Narrative History from the Notes of James Madison* (New York: Modern Library, 2005).

28 Ellis, *His Excellency*, 179.

29 Flexner, *George Washington and the New Nation, 1783–1793*, 139.

30 Herold, *The Age of Napoleon*, 19.

31 Will Durant and Ariel Durant, *The Story of Civilization: Part XI, The Age of Napoleon* (New York: Simon and Schuster, 1975), 237; and Herold, *The Age of Napoleon*, 59.

32 Chandler, *The Campaigns of Napoleon*, 53. Charles Esdaile calls the famous proclamation a "fabrication." The loyalty of soldiers was gained by appealing to their self-interest more than to service to the state. See Esdaile, *Napoleon's Wars*, 53.

33 Schom, *Napoleon Bonaparte*, 64–65.

34 Esdaile, *Napoleon's Wars*, 56.

35 Ludwig, *Napoleon*, 120.

36 Esdaile stresses this point, Napoleon posing as a "patron of the arts" when attacking Egypt. See Esdaile, *Napoleon's Wars*, 63. Some acting was involved certainly, but Napoleon maintained an interest in science throughout his life and often fostered its development while in power. For instance, in 1808, even while France was at war with England, Napoleon awarded a British subject a medal for achievement in the sciences. That man, Humphry Davy, came to France in 1813—a low point for the fortunes of Napoleon—to collect the award. See "Sea Search for Napoleon's Medal," BBC, March 16, 2008 (accessed September 16, 2010), http://news.bbc.co.uk/2/hi/uk_news/england/cornwall/7299656.stm.

37 Schom, *Napoleon Bonaparte*, 35.

38 Both cited in Guy Breton, *Napoleon and His Ladies*, trans. Frederick Holt (New York: Coward-McCann, 1965), 115–16, 131.

39 Englund, *Napoleon*, 359; Englund believes that divorce even strengthened Napoleon and Josephine's friendship. See Englund, *Napoleon*, 418.

40 Schom, *Napoleon Bonaparte*, 67, 194.

41 Englund, *Napoleon*, 158.

42 Ibid., 164–65.

43 Schom, *Napoleon Bonaparte*, 237.

44 Louis Bergeron makes this point in *France Under Napoleon*, trans. R. R. Palmer (Princeton, NJ: Princeton University Press, 1981), 5.

45 For the quote of finding a middle way and this action taken in the Vendée, see Philip G. Dwyer, *Napoleon and Europe*, 7.

46 Esdaile, *Napoleon's Wars*, 68.

47 Chandler, *The Campaigns of Napoleon*, 268; Gunther Rothenberg, *The Napoleonic Wars* (New York: Smithsonian Books, 2006), 58; and James R. Arnold, *Marengo and Hohenlinden: Napoleon's Rise to Power* (Barnsley, South Yorkshire, UK: Pen & Sword Military, 2005), 35.

48 Lyons, *Napoleon Bonaparte and the Legacy of the French Revolution*, 131.

49 Englund, *Napoleon*, 225, 234–35.

50 Herold, *The Age of Napoleon*, 123.

51 Lyons, *Napoleon Bonaparte and the Legacy of the French Revolution*, 61, 65.

52 Bergeron, *France Under Napoleon*, 12.

53 Englund, *Napoleon*, 170–71.

54 Ludwig, *Napoleon*, 166.

55 Esdaile stresses the popularity of the Napoleon regime in 1802. Esdaile, *Napoleon's Wars*, 126. For Schom see *Napoleon Bonaparte*, 305.

56 Lyons, *Napoleon Bonaparte and the Legacy of the French Revolution*, 111, 163.

57 Durant and Durant, *The Age of Napoleon*, 184.

58 Stendhal, *A Life of Napoleon* (New York: Howard Fertig, 1977), 51.

59 Bergeron, *France Under Napoleon*, 14.

4. Enlightened Statesmanship: Winning the People's Favor

1 James Roger Sharp, *American Politics in the Early Republic: The New Nation in Crisis* (New Haven, CT: Yale University Press, 1993), 27.

2 For instance, Joseph Ellis has noted Washington did not "share the deep aversion to executive power, or for that matter centralized political power of any kind." Ellis, *His Excellency*, 140.

3 Ibid., 185.

4 Paul E. Johnson, *The Early American Republic* (New York: Oxford University Press, 2007), 3. The verse reads in part:

> "God save the thirteen states,
> Thirteen united States,
> God save them all"

Joseph Johnson, *Traditions and Reminiscences, Chiefly of the American Revolution in the South: Including Biographical Sketches, Incidents and Anecdotes, Few of Which Have Been Published, Particularly of Residents in the Upper Country* (Charleston, SC: Walker & James, 1851), 320.

5 Congress overruled the new president, granting an annual salary of $25,000 to ensure that the presidency was not held only by the extremely wealthy. Ferling, *The Ascent of George Washington*, 281.

6 Flexner, *George Washington and the New Nation, 1783–1793*, 212.

7 Ibid., 242–43.

8 Ellis, *His Excellency*, 204–5.

9 Hamilton's key role is covered well in Ferling, *The Ascent of George Washington*, 289–95.

10 David Brion Davis, "American Equality and Foreign Revolutions," *The Journal of American History* 76, no. 3 (December 1989): 731.

11 Flexner, *Washington: The Indispensable Man*, 275. Other examples of how republican papers viewed the Washington style as too full of pomp and ceremony can be found in Flexner, *George Washington and the New Nation, 1783–1793)*, 201. The role of Adams and Hamilton in creating this ceremonial and presidential style

can be found in Ferling, *The Ascent of George Washington*, 278–81. Also see Ellis regarding the debate over the title of the executive as too formal and eventually adopting "president." Ellis, *His Excellency*, 193.

12 See Felix Gilbert, *To the Farewell Address: Ideas of Early American Foreign Policy* (Princeton, NJ: Princeton University Press, 1961), 84, 116. He addresses the commercial treaty on the former page, the military treaty on the latter. For the Treaty of Alliance, See Flexner, *George Washington: Anguish and Farewell (1793–1799)*, 24–45.

13 Flexner, *Washington: The Indispensable Man*, 283. The French issue is further covered in Ferling, *The Ascent of George Washington*, 308–12.

14 Flexner, *Washington: The Indispensable Man*, 284. See "The Proclamation of Neutrality of 1793," The Avalon Project: Documents in Law, History, Diplomacy, Yale Law School, http://avalon.law.yale.edu/18th_century/neutra93.asp.

15 Flexner, *Washington: The Indispensable Man*, 277.

16 Peter R. Henriques, *Realistic Visionary: A Portrait of George Washington* (Charlottesville: University of Virginia Press, 2006), 116–19, 123.

17 Smith, *Patriarch*, 164.

18 Flexner, *George Washington and the New Nation, 1783–1793*, 361.

19 Ibid., 365, 377.

20 Ibid., 379; Smith, *Patriarch*, 151. See also Hamilton's comment to Washington in the same vein as Powel's in Flexner, *George Washington and the New Nation, 1783–1793*, 366. Lisa Wilson Waciega demonstrates how shrewd Powel was as a correspondent with many of the important figures at the Constitutional Convention. See Waciega, "'A Man of Business': The Woman of Means in Southeastern Pennsylvania 1750–1850," *William and Mary Quarterly* 44, no. 1 (January 1987): 53.

21 Richard Brookhiser, *Alexander Hamilton, American* (New York: Free Press, 1999), 67.

22 Flexner, *Washington: The Indispensable Man*, 261.

23 Henriques, *Realistic Visionary*, 55–56.

24 Sharp, *American Politics in the Early Republic*, 124–26; Thomas P. Slaughter, *The Whiskey Rebellion: Frontier Epilogue to the American Revolution* (New York: Oxford University Press, 1986), 133. Some biographers dismiss the underlying representative issues associated with the rebellion, focusing only on Washington's involvement and emphasizing his restraint. For example, Chernow, *Washington: A Life*, 931, 937.

25 Henriques, *Realistic Visionary*, 110.

26 Smith, *Patriarch*, 232. Ellis agrees on the equitable nature of the exchange but notes the deep rancor the debate caused not only in America but in France as well. Ellis, *His Excellency*, 231.

27 Ferling, *The Ascent of George Washington*, 307.

28 Slaughter, *The Whiskey Rebellion*, 109–11; and Ferling, *The Ascent of George Washington*, 329.

29 Slaughter, *The Whiskey Rebellion*, 119; James Roger Sharp, "The Question of Representation," in *The Whiskey Rebellion: Past and Present Perspectives*, ed. Steven R. Boyd (Westport, CT: Greenwood, 1985), 122–23.

30 Sharp, "The Question of Representation," 123; Ellis, *His Excellency*, 224.

31 Number arrived at by taking the seats added because of the 1790 Census (36) and multiplying by the 33,000 citizens represented in theory when the tax was passed. Numbers are available at www.census.gov statistics.

32 Sharp, "The Question of Representation," 126. Sharp here addresses Washington's linking of Democratic-Republican societies to the "insurrection." Ellis stresses the similar spirit to 1776. Ellis, *His Excellency*, 225.

33 Schom, *Napoleon Bonaparte*, 339.

34 Armand-Augustin-Louis de Caulaincourt, *With Napoleon in Russia: The Memoirs of General de Caulaincourt, Duke of Vicenza*, ed. Jean Hanoteau (New York: William Morrow, 1935), 25. According to Caulaincourt, Napoleon "tweaked my ear, with weak protest that it was not so."

35 Englund, *Napoleon*, 204. Schom says Napoleon wrongfully treated Bourrienne for "speculating on margin at the stock market." Schom, *Napoleon Bonaparte*, 383.

36 Schom, *Napoleon Bonaparte*, 249.

37 Bergeron, *France Under Napoleon*, 11–12. Englund echoes this point, arguing that the "Life Consul's power is not well described as despotic. . . . His power, both consular and imperial, pointed to something new: a form of democratic authoritarianism." Englund, *Napoleon*, 222.

38 J. F. Bernard, *Talleyrand: A Biography* (New York: Putnam, 1973), 53, 93; for Fouché, see Hubert Cole, *Fouché: The Unprincipled Patriot* (New York: McCall Pub., 1971), 14–15. When Napoleon removed both men from office in 1809 for plotting against him, he castigated each with the comment that they would be the first crushed by any new revolution. See Bernard, *Talleyrand*, 301.

39 Robert B. Holtman, *Napoleonic Propaganda* (Philadelphia: Lippincott, 1967), 173.

40 Durant and Durant, *The Age of Napoleon*, 287. Metternich put the number much higher, writing, "The newspapers alone are worth an army of 300,000 to Napoleon." Englund, *Napoleon*, 317.

41 Angelica Goodden, *Madame de Staël: The Dangerous Exile* (New York: Oxford University Press, 2008).

42 Englund, *Napoleon: A Political Life* (New York: Scribner, 2004), 388.

43 Schom, *Napoleon Bonaparte*, 415–16.

44 Chandler, *The Campaigns of Napoleon*, 319.

45 Henry Lachouque, *The Anatomy of Glory: Napoleon and His Guard*, trans. Anne S. K. Brown (New York: Hippocrene, 1978), 256.

46 David Chandler, *On the Napoleonic Wars: Collected Essays* (Mechanicsburg, PA: Stackpole, 1994), 103.

47 Epstein, *Napoleon's Last Victory and the Emergence of Modern War*, 170.

48 Durant and Durant, *The Age of Napoleon*, 243. For a list of Napoleon rants about diplomats, see Dwyer, "Napoleon and the Drive for Glory: Reflections on the Making of French Foreign Policy," 133.

49 Herold, *The Age of Napoleon*, 291.

50 For this colorful exchange, see Ludwig, *Napoleon*, 342–43.

51 Esdaile, *Napoleon's Wars*, 528.

52 Harold T. Parker famously makes this case in *Three Napoleonic Battles* (Durham, NC: Duke University Press, 1983), xix. Epstein disputes this view. See Epstein, *Napoleon's Last Victory and the Emergence of Modern War*, 7, 182.

53 Stuart Woolf tracks Napoleon's absenteeism in *Napoleon's Integration of Europe* (New York: Routledge, 1991), 38–39. Michael Broers emphasizes the administration supplanting Napoleon in *Europe Under Napoleon 1799–1815* (London: Hodder Arnold, 1996), 271.

54 Broers leads the charge of the "Enlightenment project" amounting to a cultural imperialism, perhaps even within France, and its crowning achievement of 1815 France. See Broers, *Europe Under Napoleon 1799–1815*, 5, 259, 270. Steven Englund cautions against fully accepting Broers's cultural imperialism thesis in "*Monstre Sacré*: The Question of Cultural Imperialism and the Napoleonic Empire," *The Historical Journal* 51, no. 1 (2008): 248–49.

55 Bergeron, *France Under Napoleon*, 14; Englund, *Napoleon*, 205.

56 Lyons contests the view that the Revolution had dramatically improved the political rights of women, so Napoleon's restrictions expressed continuity rather than a retreat. See Lyons, *Napoleon Bonaparte and the Legacy of the French Revolution*, 99, 102. An older treatment draws a clear distinction between Revolutionary advances and Napoleon's retrograde movement of civil liberties for women. See Robert B. Holtman, *The Napoleon Revolution* (Philadelphia: J. B. Lippincott, 1967), 91.

57 See chapter 2 in Alexander Grab, *Napoleon and the Transformation of Europe* (New York: Palgrave Macmillan, 2003); see also Englund, *Napoleon*, 335.

58 Lyons, *Napoleon Bonaparte and the Legacy of the French Revolution*, 44. Steven Englund disputes that Napoleon said this. See Englund, *Napoleon*, 470.

59 Herold, *The Age of Napoleon*, 25.

60 Geoffrey Ellis, *The Napoleonic Empire* (Houndmills, UK: Palgrave Macmillan, 2003), 44.

61 Ludwig, *Napoleon*, 162. Englund says Napoleon attended half the meetings in the Council of State when it addressed the code and "weighed in frequently with opinions." Englund, *Napoleon*, 189. Schom says Napoleon had discussed every article of the proposed code with the Judicial Commission of the Council. Schom, *Napoleon Bonaparte*, 293.

62 A point Charles Esdaile repeatedly stresses in *Napoleon's Wars*, 46, 77.

63 Schom, *Napoleon Bonaparte*, 698.

64 Paul W. Schroeder, *The Transformation of European Politics 1763–1848* (Oxford: Clarendon Press, 1994), 116–17.

65 Peter Jupp, "The British State and the Napoleonic Wars, 1799–1815," in *Collaboration and Resistance in Napoleonic Europe: State-Formation in an Age of Upheaval, 1800–1815*, ed. Michael Rowe (New York: Palgrave Macmillan, 2003), 222; Linda Colley, *Britons: Forging the Nation, 1707–1837* (London: Pimlico, 2003), 5; and J. E. Cookson, *The British Armed Nation, 1793–1815* (New York: Oxford University Press, 1997), 9.

66 Paul Schroeder blames both England and France, but then condemns Napoleon. See Schroeder, *The Transformation of European Politics 1763–1848*, 176, 230. Charles Esdaile maintains this view in, *Napoleon's Wars*, 13. Englund is conflicted, both condemning the famed Napoleon ambition but arguing that the emperor's actions in 1814 (his refusal to make peace) went far beyond a personal ambition to that of seeking a more honorable peace. Englund, *Napoleon*, 269, 409.

67 Michael Broers defines inner and outer parts of the Napoleonic Empire. See Broers, *Europe Under Napoleon 1799–1815*, 69. Alexander Grab gives different names to similar groupings: annexed lands, conquered countries, and allied countries. See Grab, *Napoleon and the Transformation of Europe*, 2. Both authors present a mixed view of French rule inside and outside its borders in that the French administration featured some useful law and order, albeit with the price of exploitation. Grab was more explicit in an earlier essay, saying Napoleon mixed great reforms with harsh repression. See Grab, "State, Society, and Tax Policy in Napoleonic Europe," in Dwyer, ed., *Napoleon and Europe*, 186.

68 See Michael Broers's evolving critique denouncing French cultural imperialism in Italy in *The Politics of Religion in Napoleonic Italy: The War Against God, 1801–1814* (London: Routledge, 2002), and *The Napoleonic Empire in Italy, 1796–1814:*

Cultural Imperialism in a European Context? (New York: Palgrave Macmillan, 2005). On the other hand, John A. Davis offers a positive evaluation of French rule in Naples. See Davis, *Naples and Napoleon: Southern Italy and the European Revolutions, 1780–1860* (New York: Oxford University Press, 2006).

69 For blunted reform efforts, see Broers, *Europe Under Napoleon*, 93. For the elite allying with Napoleon, see Jarostaw Czubaty, "The Attitudes of the Polish Elite Towards the State in the Period of the Duchy of Warsaw, 1807–1815," in *Collaboration and Resistance in Napoleonic Europe: State-Formation in an Age of Upheaval, 1800–1815*, ed. Michael Rowe (New York: Palgrave Macmillan, 2003), 181–82.

70 Charles Esdaile, *Fighting Napoleon: Guerrillas, Bandits, and Adventurers in Spain, 1808–1814* (New Haven, CT: Yale University Press, 2004), 193–94, 204.

71 For those disputing a "people's war" in Prussia, see Michael Rowe, "Napoleon and State Formation in Central Europe, in Napoleon and Europe," in Dwyer, ed., *Napoleon and Europe*, 222; and John Breuilly, "Napoleonic Germany and State-Formation," in Rowe, *Collaboration and Resistance in Napoleonic Europe*, 122–23.

72 Esdaile, *Napoleon's Wars*, 229. Teaming with Austria remained a long-term objective of Talleyrand's even after Austerlitz. See David Lawday, *Napoleon's Master: A Life of Prince Talleyrand* (New York: Thomas Dunne Books, 2006), 186.

73 A long-standing fear among European states. Esdaile, *The Wars of Napoleon*, 155.

74 Lyons, *Napoleon Bonaparte and the Legacy of the French Revolution*, 103. Schroeder rejects this view and labels Napoleon a "scourge of God" rather than a "potential unifier of Europe." See Schroeder, *The Transformation of European Politics 1763–1848*, 395.

5. Good Intentions: Leading in the Age of the Enlightenment

1 Phyllis Lee Levin, *Abigail Adams: A Biography* (New York: St. Martin's, 1987), 261.

2 Ellis, *His Excellency*, 274.

3 Herold, *The Age of Napoleon*, 123.

4 Englund, *Napoleon*, 282.

5 Ellis, *His Excellency*, 265.

6 Jefferson, for instance, questioned Washington's intellectual capabilities. See Lengel, *General George Washington*, 10.

7 Smith, *Patriarch*, 26.

8 Higginbotham, *George Washington: Uniting a Nation*, 37–38.

9 Matthew Spalding and Patrick J. Garrity, *A Sacred Union of Citizens: George Washington's Farewell Address and the American Character* (Lanham, MD: Rowman & Littlefield, 1996), 88.

10   Durant and Durant, *The Age of Napoleon*, 226.

11   Ellis, *His Excellency*, 269.

12   Henriques, *Realistic Visionary: A Portrait of George Washington*, 173.

13   Ellis, *His Excellency*, 270.

14   Mason Locke Weems, *The Life of George Washington*, ed. Marcus Cunliffe (Cambridge, MA: Belknap Press of Harvard University Press, 1962). Weems propagated the first popular biography of George Washington and was largely responsible for creating some of the most long-lived fallacies about Washington's life. It was Weems who outright invented the story about young Washington zealously chopping down his father's cherry tree and not being able to lie about it later due to his personal sense of truth and honor. This one story has survived into the stories Americans continue to tell about Washington until this very day. By the time of Weems's death in 1825, his pamphlet had undergone twenty-nine various iterations. Cunliffe edited the 1809 version, or ninth edition.

15   Esdaile estimates five to seven million dead in the "French wars." See Esdaile, *Napoleon's Wars*, 561. Schom puts the number at three million. See Schom, epilogue to *Napoleon Bonaparte*. Lyons wrote that French dead alone totaled nearly one million. See Lyons, *Napoleon Bonaparte and the Legacy of the French Revolution*, 46.

16   Gertrude Himmelfarb, *The Roads to Modernity: The British, French and American Enlightenments* (New York: Knopf, 2004), 163, 167, 193, 198.

17   Stendhal, *A Life of Napoleon*, 36–37.

6. Epilogue: A Similar End

1   Ellis, *His Excellency*, 251.

2   Flexner, *George Washington: Anguish and Farewell, 1793–1799*, 332–56.

3   Ellis, *His Excellency*, 269.

4   Lawford, *Napoleon: The Last Campaigns, 1813–1815*, 150.

5   Schom, *Napoleon Bonaparte*, 293.

6   Durant and Durant, *The Age of Napoleon*, 765.

7   Schom convincingly argues that Lowe hoped to appease Napoleon and worked hard to that end. Also, Schom concludes that Napoleon's companion Charles Tristan, marquis de Montholon, poisoned him so Montholon could leave St. Helena. See Schom, *Napoleon Bonaparte*, 770–72, 783.

SELECTED BIBLIOGRAPHY

GEORGE WASHINGTON

Anderson, Fred. *Crucible of War: The Seven Years' War and the Fate of Empire in British North America, 1754–1766.* New York: Knopf, 2000.

Axelrod, Alan. *Blooding at Great Meadows: Young George Washington and the Battle That Shaped the Man.* London: Running Press, 2007.

Bailyn, Bernard. *The Ideological Origins of the American Revolution.* Cambridge, MA: Belknap Press of Harvard University Press, 1967.

Berkin, Carol. *A Brilliant Solution: Inventing the American Constitution.* New York: Harcourt, 2002.

Boyd, Steven R., ed. *The Whiskey Rebellion: Past and Present Perspectives.* Westport, CT: Greenwood, 1985.

Brookhiser, Richard. *Alexander Hamilton, American.* New York: Free Press, 1999.

Buel, Richard. *Securing the Revolution: Ideology in American Politics, 1789–1815.* Ithaca, NY: Cornell University Press, 1972.

Burns, James MacGregor, and Susan Dunn. *George Washington: President of the United States, 1789–1797*. New York: Times Books, 2004.

Chadwick, Bruce. *The First American Army: The Untold Story of George Washington and the Men Behind America's First Fight for Freedom*. Naperville, IL: Sourcebooks, 2005.

Chernow, Ron. *Alexander Hamilton*. New York: Penguin, 2004.

———. *Washington: A Life*. New York: The Penguin Press, 2010.

Collier, Christopher. *Decision in Philadelphia: The Constitutional Convention of 1787*. New York: Random House, 1986.

Cox, Caroline. *A Proper Sense of Honor: Service and Sacrifice in George Washington's Army*. Chapel Hill: University of North Carolina Press, 2004.

Cunliffe, Marcus. *George Washington: Man and Monument*. New York: New American Library, 1958.

Davis, Burke. *The Campaign That Won America: The Story of Yorktown*. New York: Dial Press, 1970.

Davis, David Brion. "American Equality and Foreign Revolutions." *Journal of American History* 76, no. 3 (December 1989): 729–52.

Edgar, Walter. *Partisans and Redcoats: The Southern Conflict that Turned the Tide of the American Revolution*. New York: Morrow, 2001.

Ellis, Joseph J. *His Excellency: George Washington*. New York: Knopf, 2004.

Emery, Noemie. *Washington: A Biography*. New York: Putnam, 1976.

Ferling, John E. *A Leap in the Dark: The Struggle to Create the American Republic*. Oxford: Oxford University Press, 2003.

———. *Almost a Miracle: The American Victory in the War of Independence*. Oxford: Oxford University Press, 2007.

———. *The Ascent of George Washington*. New York: Bloomsbury, 2009.

————. *The First Of Men: A Life Of George Washington*. Knoxville: University of Tennessee Press, 1988.

————. *Setting the World Ablaze: Washington, Adams, Jefferson, and the American Revolution*. Oxford: Oxford University Press, 2000.

Fishman, Ethan. *George Washington: Foundation of Presidential Leadership and Character*. Westport, CT: Praeger, 2001.

Fleming, Thomas J. *The Perils of Peace: America's Struggle for Survival after Yorktown*. New York: Smithsonian Books, 2007.

————. *Washington's Secret War: The Hidden History of Valley Forge*. New York: Smithsonian Books, 2005.

Flexner, James Thomas. *George Washington and the New Nation: 1783–1793*. Boston: Little, Brown, 1970.

————. *George Washington: Anguish and Farewell (1793–1799)*. Boston: Little, Brown, 1972.

————. *George Washington in the American Revolution, 1775–1783*. Boston: Little, Brown, 1968.

————. *George Washington: The Forge of Experience, 1732–1775*. Boston: Little, Brown, 1965.

————. *Washington: The Indispensable Man*. Boston: Little, Brown, 1974.

Freeman, Douglas Southall. *George Washington: A Biography*. 6 vols. New York: Scribner, 1948–57.

Frothingham, Thomas Goddard. *Washington, Commander in Chief*. Boston: Houghton Mifflin, 1930.

Gabriel, Michael P. *Major General Richard Montgomery: The Making of an American Hero*. Madison, NJ: Fairleigh Dickinson University Press, 2002.

Gilbert, Felix. *To the Farewell Address: Ideas of Early American Foreign Policy*. Princeton, NJ: Princeton University Press, 1961.

Golway, Terry. *Washington's General: Nathanael Greene and the Triumph of the American Revolution*. New York: Henry Holt, 2005.

Gregg, Gary L., II and Matthew Spalding. *Patriot Sage: George Washington and the American Political Tradition*. Wilmington, DE: ISI Books, 1999.

Henriques, Peter R. *Realistic Visionary: A Portrait of George Washington*. Charlottesville: University of Virginia Press, 2006.

Higginbotham, Don. *George Washington and the American Military Tradition*. Athens: University of Georgia Press, 1985.

————, ed. *George Washington Reconsidered*. Charlottesville: University Press of Virginia, 2001.

————. *George Washington: Uniting a Nation*. Lanham, MD: Rowman & Littlefield, 2002.

————. *The War of American Independence: Military Attitudes, Policies, and Practice, 1763–1789*. Boston: Northeastern University Press, 1983.

Higgins, W. Robert, ed. *The Revolutionary War in the South: Power, Conflict, and Leadership*. Durham, NC: Duke University Press, 1979.

Himmelfarb, Gertrude. *The Roads to Modernity: the British, French and American Enlightenments*. New York: Random House, 2004.

Hoffman, Robert, ed. *An Uncivil War: The Southern Backcountry During the American Revolution*. Charlottesville: University Press of Virginia, 1985.

Johnson, Joseph. *Traditions and Reminiscences, Chiefly of the American Revolution in the South: Including Biographical Sketches, Incidents and Anecdotes, Few of Which Have Been Published, Particularly of Residents in the Upper Country*. Charleston, SC: Walker & James, 1851.

Johnson, Paul E. *The Early American Republic*. New York: Oxford University Press, 2007.

Kaminski, John P. and Jill Adair McCaughan, eds. *A Great and Good Man: George Washington in the Eyes of His Contemporaries*. Madison, WI: Madison House, 1989.

Ketcham, Ralph Louis. *Presidents Above Party: The First American Presidency, 1789–1829*. Chapel Hill: University of North Carolina Press, 1984.

Ketchum, Richard. *Victory at Yorktown: The Campaign That Won the Revolution*. New York: Henry Holt, 2004.

Kopperman, Paul E. *Braddock at the Monongahela*. Pittsburgh, PA: University of Pittsburgh Press, 1977.

Kwasny, Mark V. *Washington's Partisan War, 1775–1783*. Kent, OH: Kent State University Press, 1996.

Larson, Edward J. and Michael P. Winship. *Constitutional Convention: A Narrative History from the Notes of James Madison*. New York: Modern Library, 2005.

Leckie, Robert. *The Wars of America*. Vol. 1, *Quebec to Appomattox*. New York: Harper & Row, 1968.

Lengel, Edward G. *General George Washington: A Military Life*. New York: Random House, 2005.

———. *Inventing George Washington: America's Founder in Myth and Memory*. New York: Harper, 2011.

Levin, Phyllis Lee. *Abigail Adams: A Biography*. New York: St. Martin's, 1987.

Lewis, Thomas A. *For King and Country: The Maturing of George Washington, 1748–1760*. New York: HarperCollins, 1993.

Lockhart, Paul. *The Drillmaster of Valley Forge: The Baron de Steuben and the Making of the American Army*. New York: HarperCollins, 2008.

Longmore, Paul K. *The Invention of George Washington*. Berkeley: University of California Press, 1998.

Mann, Barbara Alice. *George Washington's War on Native Americans*. Westport, CT: Praeger, 2005.

Martin, James Kirby and Mark Edward Lender. *A Respectable Army: The Military Origins of the Republic, 1763–1789*. The American History Series, edited by John Hope Franklin and Abraham S. Eisenstadt. Arlington Heights, IL: Harlan Davidson, 1982.

McCullough, David. *1776*. New York: Simon & Schuster, 2005.

———. *John Adams*. New York: Simon & Schuster, 2001.

Millet, Allan R., and Peter Maslowski. *For the Common Defense: A Military History of the United States of America*. New York: Free Press, 1994.

Morgan, Edmund Sears.*The Birth of the Republic, 1763–89*. Chicago: University of Chicago Press, 1992.

———. *The Genius of George Washington*. New York: Norton, 1981.

Morris, Richard Brandon. *The Forging of the Union, 1781–1789*. New York: Harper & Row, 1987.

Nettels, Curtis P. *George Washington and American Independence*. Boston, MA: Little, Brown, 1951.

Pancake, John S. *This Destructive War: The British Campaign in the Carolinas, 1780–1782*. Tuscaloosa: University of Alabama Press, 2003.

Peckham, Howard Henry. *The War for Independence: A Military History*. Chicago: University of Chicago Press, 1958.

Phelps, Glenn A. *George Washington and American Constitutionalism*. Lawrence: University Press of Kansas, 1993.

Reuter, Frank T. *Trials and Triumphs: George Washington's Foreign Policy*. Fort Worth: Texas Christian University Press, 1983.

Russell, Peter. "Redcoats in the Wilderness: British Officers and Irregular Warfare in Europe and America, 1740–1760." *William and Mary Quarterly* 35, no. 4 (October 1978): 629–52.

Sargent, Winthrop. *The History of an Expedition Against Fort Du Quesne, in 1755 under Major-General Edward Braddock*. Philadelphia: Lippincott, Grambo, 1856.

Schecter, Barnet. *The Battle for New York: The City at the Heart of the American Revolution*. New York: Walker, 2002.

Schwartz, Barry. *George Washington: The Making of an American Symbol*. New York: Free Press, 1987.

Sears, Louis. *George Washington and the French Revolution*. Detroit: Wayne State University Press, 1960.

Sharp, James Roger. *American Politics in the Early Republic: The New Nation in Crisis*. New Haven, CT: Yale University Press, 1993.

Silverstone, Scott A. *Divided Union: The Politics of War in the Early American Republic*. Ithaca, NY: Cornell University Press, 2004.

Slaughter, Thomas P. *The Whiskey Rebellion: Frontier Epilogue to the American Revolution*. New York: Oxford University Press, 1986.

Smith, Richard Norton. *Patriarch: George Washington and the New American Nation*. Boston: Houghton Mifflin, 1993.

Spalding, Matthew and Patrick J. Garrity. *A Sacred Union of Citizens: George Washington's Farewell Address and the American Character*. Lanham, MD: Rowman & Littlefield, 1996.

Staloff, Darren. *Hamilton, Adams, Jefferson: The Politics of Enlightenment and the American Founding*. New York: Hill and Wang, 2005.

Trees, Andrew S. *The Founding Fathers and the Politics of Character*. Princeton, NJ: Princeton University Press, 2004.

Urwin, Gregory. "When Freedom Wore a Red Coat." *Army History* 20 (Summer 2008): 6–23.

Waciega, Lisa Wilson. "'A Man of Business': The Woman of Means in Southeastern Pennsylvania 1750–1850," *William and Mary Quarterly* 44, no. 1 (January 1987): 40–64.

Weems, Mason. "The Life of George Washington. 9th Edition, 1809. Edited by Marcus Cunliffe. Cambridge, MA: Belknap Press of Harvard University Press, 1962.

Whisker, James. *The Rise and Decline of the American Militia System*. London: Associated University Presses, 1999.

Wills, Garry. *Cincinnatus: George Washington and the Enlightenment*. Garden City, NY: Doubleday, 1984.

Wood, Gordon S. *The Radicalism of the American Revolution*. New York: Knopf, 1992.

NAPOLEON BONAPARTE

Arnold, James R. *Marengo and Hohenlinden: Napoleon's Rise to Power*. Barnsley, South Yorkshire, UK: Pen & Sword Military, 2005.

Asprey, Robert B. *The Rise of Napoleon Bonaparte*. New York: Basic Books, 2000.

Belaubre, Christophe, Jordana Dym, and John Savage. *Napoleon's Atlantic: The Impact of Napoleonic Empire in the Atlantic World*. Leiden: Brill, 2010.

Bell, David. *The Cult of the Nation in France: Inventing Nationalism, 1680–1800*. Cambridge, MA: Harvard University Press, 2001.

———. *The First Total War: Napoleon's Europe and the Birth of Warfare as We Know It*. Boston: Houghton Mifflin, 2007.

Bergeron, Louis. *France Under Napoleon*. Translated by R. R. Palmer. Princeton, NJ: Princeton University Press, 1981.

Bernard, J. F. *Talleyrand: A Biography*. New York: Putnam, 1973.

Blaufarb, Rafe. *The French Army, 1750–1820: Careers, Talent, Merit*. Manchester, UK: Manchester University Press, 2002.

Bourrienne, Louis Antoine Fauvelet de. *Memoirs of Napoleon Bonaparte*. Translated by John S. Memes. 3 vols. New York: P. F. Collier, 1892.

Breton, Guy. *Napoleon and His Ladies*. Translated by Frederick Holt. New York: Coward-McCann, 1965.

Broers, Michael. *Europe Under Napoleon 1799–1815*. London: Arnold, 1996.

———. *The Napoleonic Empire In Italy, 1796–1814: Cultural Imperialism in a European Context?* New York: Palgrave Macmillan, 2005.

———. *Napoleon's Other War: Bandits, Rebels and Their Pursuers in the Age of Revolution*. London: Peter Lang, 2010.

———. *The Politics of Religion in Napoleonic Italy: The War Against God, 1801–1814*. London: Routledge, 2002.

Carrington, Dorothy, *Napoleon and His Parents: On the Threshold of History*. London: Viking, 1988.

Caulaincourt, Armand-Augustin-Louis de. *With Napoleon in Russia: The Memoirs of General de Caulaincourt, Duke of Vicenza*. Edited by Jean Hanoteau. New York: W. Morrow, 1935.

Chandler, David G. *The Campaigns of Napoleon*. New York: Macmillan, 1966.

———. *On the Napoleonic Wars: Collected Essays*. London: Greenhill Books, 1994.

Cole, Hubert. *Fouché: The Unprincipled Patriot*. New York: McCall, 1971.

Colley, Linda. *Britons: Forging the Nation, 1707–1837*. London: Pimlico, 2003.

Cookson, J. E. *The British Armed Nation, 1793–1815.* New York: Oxford University Press, 1997.

Connelly, Owen. *Blundering to Glory: Napoleon's Military Campaigns.* Wilmington, DE: Scholarly Resources, 1987.

———. *Napoleon's Satellite Kingdoms.* New York: Free Press, 1965.

———. *The Wars of the French Revolution, 1792–1815.* London: Routledge, 2006.

Crook, Malcolm. *Napoleon Comes to Power: Democracy and Dictatorship in Revolutionary France, 1795–1804.* Cardiff: University of Wales Press, 1998.

Davis, John A. *Naples and Napoleon: Southern Italy and the European Revolutions, 1780–1860.* Oxford: Oxford University, 2006.

Duffy, Christopher. *Austerlitz 1805.* London: Seeley Service, 1977.

Durant, Will, and Ariel Durant. *The Story of Civilization, Part XI, The Age of Napoleon.* New York: Simon & Schuster, 1975.

Dwyer, Philip G., ed. *Napoleon and Europe.* New York: Longman, 2001.

———. *Napoleon: The Path to Power, 1769–1799.* London: Bloomsbury, 2007.

Dwyer, Philip G., and Alan Forrest, eds. *Napoleon and His Empire: Europe, 1804-1814.* New York: Palgrave Macmillan, 2007.

Ellis, Geoffery. *The Napoleonic Empire.* Houndmills, UK: Palgrave Macmillan, 2003.

Englund, Steven. "*Monstre Sacré*: The Question of Cultural Imperialism and the Napoleonic Empire." *Historical Journal* 51, no. 1 (2008): 215–50.

———. *Napoleon: A Political Life.* New York: Scribner, 2004.

Epstein, Robert M. *Napoleon's Last Victory and the Emergence of Modern War.* Lawrence: University Press of Kansas, 1994.

Esdaile, Charles. *Fighting Napoleon: Guerrillas, Bandits, and Adventurers in Spain, 1808–1814*. New Haven, CT: Yale University Press, 2004.

———. *The French Wars, 1792–1815*. London: Routledge, 2001.

———. *Napoleon's Wars: An International History, 1803–1815*. London: Allen Lane, 2007.

———, ed. *Popular Resistance in the French Wars: Patriots, Partisans, and Land Pirates*. Houndmills, UK: Palgrave Macmillan, 2005.

Forrest, Alan. *Napoleon's Men: The Soldiers of the Revolution and Empire*. London: Hambledon, 2002.

Gates, David. *The Napoleonic Wars, 1803–1815*. New York: St. Martin's, 1997.

——— *The Spanish Ulcer. A History of The Peninsular War*. New York: Norton, 1986.

Geyl, Pieter. *Napoleon: For and Against*. Translated by Olive Renier. New Haven, CT: Yale University Press, 1949.

Goetz, Robert. *1805, Austerlitz: Napoleon and the Destruction of the Third Coalition*. London: Greenhill, 2005.

Goodden, Angelica. *Madame de Staël: The Dangerous Exile*. New York: Oxford University Press, 2008.

Grab, Alexander. *Napoleon and the Transformation of Europe*. New York: Palgrave Macmillan, 2003.

Hazareesingh, Sudhir. *The Saint-Napoleon: Celebrations of Sovereignty in Nineteenth-Century France*. Cambridge, MA: Harvard University Press, 2004.

Hazen, Charles Downer. *The French Revolution and Napoleon*. New York: Henry Holt and Company, 1917.

Herold, J. Christopher. *The Age of Napoleon*. New York: American Heritage Publishing, 1963.

Holtman, Robert B. *Napoleonic Propaganda*. Baton Rouge: Louisiana State University, 1950.

———. *The Napoleonic Revolution*. Philadelphia: J.B. Lippincott Company, 1967.

Horne, Alistair. *How Far from Austerlitz? Napoleon 1805–1815*. New York: St. Martin's, 1998.

Horricks, Raymond. *Marshal Ney: The Romance and the Real*. New York: Hippocrene, 1982.

Kagan, Frederick. *Napoleon and Europe*. Vol. 1, *End of the Old Order, 1801–1805*. Cambridge, MA: Da Capo, 2006.

Lachouque, Henry. *The Anatomy of Glory: Napoleon and His Guard*. Translated by Anne S. K. Brown. New York: Hippocrene, 1978.

Las Cases, Emmanuel. *The Life, Exile and Conversations of the Emperor Napoleon*. 8 vols. London, 1835.

Lawday, David. *Napoleon's Master: A Life of Prince Talleyrand*. New York: Thomas Dunne, 2006.

Lawford, James. *Napoleon: The Last Campaigns, 1813–1815*. New York: Crown, 1977.

Lefebvre, Georges. *Napoleon*. 2 vols. New York: Columbia University Press, 1969.

Leggiere, Michael V. *The Fall of Napoleon*. Vol. 1, *The Allied Invasion of France, 1813–1814*. Cambridge, UK: Cambridge University Press, 2007.

———. *Napoleon and Berlin: The Franco-Prussian War in North Germany, 1813*. Norman: University of Oklahoma Press, 2002.

Ludwig, Emil. *Napoleon*. New York: Boni & Liveright, 1926.

Lynn, John. *The Bayonets of the Republic: Motivation and Tactics in the Army of Revolutionary France, 1791–94.* Urbana: University of Illinois Press, 1984.

Lyons, Martyn. *Napoleon Bonaparte and the Legacy of the French Revolution.* New York: St. Martin's Press, 1994.

Markham, J. David. *Napoleon's Road to Glory: Triumphs, Defeats, and Immortality.* London: Brassey's, 2003.

Naylor, John. *Waterloo.* London: B.T. Batsford, 1963.

Parker, Harold T. *Three Napoleonic Battles.* Durham, NC: Duke University Press, 1983.

Riley, Jonathon P. *Napoleon and the World War of 1813: Lessons in Coalition Warfighting.* London: Frank Cass, 2000.

———. *Napoleon as a General.* New York: Hambledon Continuum, 2007.

Rothenberg, Gunther E. *The Napoleonic Wars.* London: Cassell, 1999.

Rowe, Michael, ed. *Collaboration and Resistance in Napoleonic Europe: State-formation in an Age of Upheaval, 1800–1815.* New York: Palgrave Macmillan, 2003.

———. *From Reich to State: The Rhineland in the Revolutionary Age, 1780–1830.* New York: Cambridge University Press, 2003.

Schneid, Frederick C. *Napoleon's Conquest of Europe: The War of the Third Coalition.* Westport, CT: Praeger, 2005.

Schom, Alan. *Napoleon Bonaparte.* New York: HarperCollins, 1997.

———. *One Hundred Days: Napoleon's Road to Waterloo.* New York: Maxwell Macmillan International, 1992.

Schroeder, Paul W. *The Transformation of European Politics 1763–1848.* Oxford, UK: Clarendon Press, 1994.

Simms, Brendan. *The Impact of Napoleon: Prussian High Politics, Foreign Policy and the Crisis Of The Executive, 1797–1806*. New York: Cambridge University Press, 1997.

Stendhal [Marie-Henri Beyle]. *A Life of Napoleon*. New York: Howard Fertig, 1977.

Tone, John Lawrence. *The Fatal Knot: The Guerrilla War in Navarre and the Defeat of Napoleon in Spain*. Chapel Hill: University of North Carolina Press, 1994.

Tulard, Jean. *Napoleon: The Myth of the Saviour*. Translated by Teresa Waugh. London: Weidenfeld and Nicolson, 1984.

Woolf, S. J. *Napoleon's Integration of Europe*. London: Routledge, 1991.

INDEX

ABOUT THE AUTHORS

MATTHEW J. FLYNN, PHD, is a specialist in comparative warfare of the United States and the world. He has taught at a number of universities, most recently at the U.S. Military Academy, West Point, as an assistant professor of military and international history. Flynn is the author of a number of books, including *First Strike: Preemptive War in Modern History* and *Contesting History: The Bush Counterinsurgency Legacy in Iraq.*

STEPHEN E. GRIFFIN, MA, is a writer and scholar who teaches U.S. and world history at Palomar Community College in San Diego, California. He focuses on the study and writing of history for the general reader.